Pietas et Societas

New Trends in Reformation Social History
Essays in Memory of Harold J. Grimm

Edited by
Kyle C. Sessions and Phillip N. Bebb

Table of Contents

Illustrations

The permissions for the illustrations in the articles by Richard G. Cole and Bodo Nischan have been secured by the respective authors.

Acknowledgments

The editors are deeply grateful for the assistance and support of many people in making this volume possible. The authors and those who contributed financially are recognized elsewhere in these pages. For invaluable advice, assistance and support, we thank Robert V. Schnucker of Sixteenth Century Publishers, Inc. The photographs were contributed by Jane Grimm Minton and Capitol University. The index is the work of Miss Pamela Schell.

Kyle C. Sessions
Normal, Illinois

Phillip N. Bebb
Athens, Ohio

May 1985

Introduction

This volume is the outgrowth of a desire on the part of the editors to make a scholarly expression of appreciation toward their mentor, Harold J. Grimm. This goal took a specific form in October 1981 at the meetings of the Sixteenth Century Studies Conference. There it was announced that a conference celebrating the quincentennial of the birth of Martin Luther would take place in the Spring of 1983, sponsored by Concordia Seminary, St. Louis, and the Center for Reformation Research. A plan was initiated by one of the editors to offer at that conference a session entirely comprising Grimm students and dedicated to him. In the course of the next twenty months, this scheme was realized and a tape of the session was presented to Dr. Grimm in June 1983. Then arose a consequent idea, to bring together a group of essays made up of session papers and additional contributions from students of Dr. Grimm. These are further supplemented by works of other scholars willing to join in an expression of regard for his honored career as scholar, teacher, and statesman in Reformation studies.

This new project matured quickly in what proved to be a fertile environment. Harold Grimm's achievement already was the subject of substantial appreciation. Miriam U. Chrisman, at the Sixteenth Century Studies Conference in 1982, memorialized his accomplishment as a teacher in preparing some forty doctorates. At the American Historical Association meetings in December 1982, Phillip N. Bebb, one of those forty, reviewed the scholar's career-long pursuit of the enigmatic problem of how Luther's religious reforms were translated into political, social, economic and cultural phenomena. During the quincentennial year of 1983, unprecedented interest was generated in Luther and the Reformation, inspired by re-examination and re-exploration of the towering figure of the Reformer. Finally, the passing of Harold Grimm on November 10, 1983—five hundred years to the day after the birth of his enigma's inceptor—drew from all involved a renewed dedication to this project now honoring his memory.

The opening essay in this collection is appropriately Phillip Bebb's review, "Reformation History and Social History: The Contribution of Harold J. Grimm." He reveals sensitively how Grimm's personal concept of Reformation studies was imperishably rooted in his German-American Lutheran origins and never wavered from his conviction that the Reformation was fundamentally a religious phenomenon. But he also never relented in his effort to understand and explain the connection between religion and the other aspects of society during the Reformation. That search is manifested in his years of dedicated service to professional Reformation studies. It is expounded in his influential textbook, *The Reformation Era*, which clearly showed in its scope and coverage the importance Grimm acknowledged for cultural, intellectual and social factors, alongside the political events, that conferred

Luther's personal religious solution upon a receptive world. His concern is amplified in a generation of students stimulated by him to study problems of the social history of the Reformation; and in his late major work, *Lazarus Spengler*, a study of the patrician, humanist, civic leader, early Luther adherent, and hinge-figure in the swing of Nuremberg to Reformation.

Just how greatly the study of the Reformation by scholars today is framed by the study of social history is revealed in the second essay, by H. C. Erik Midelfort, "Toward a Social History of Ideas in the German Reformation." Midelfort surveys leading recent and current literature on the social history of the Reformation with the objective of laying groundwork for a necessary next step in Reformation studies. This should be to meld into a common understanding the two leading strains of modern Reformation research. The late-medieval sources of reform ideas and the social transmission of Reformation should conjoin in a social history of Reformation ideas embodying a methodology faithful to his assertion that "ideas, even Protestant ideas, were initiated, created and modified by . . . groups and individuals. . . ."

His point of departure is Bernd Moeller's groundbreaking *Imperial Cities and the Reformation* (1962). Scholars since have pursued Moeller's principal goals, to explain why so many towns, especially imperial cities, adopted or inclined toward the Reformation, and to understand why Upper German cities preferred the theology of Zwingli and Bucer to that of Luther. Researchers concentrating on the first issue have re-shaped Moeller's concept of popular motivation to mean that reform came when a city council reacted to popular agitation in order to retain control. Some studies so exaggerated Moeller's method as to show almost exactly the inverse of his popular-origin hypothesis.

On his second objective, Moeller concluded that the corporate theology of the South German reformers was more compatible with the guild-republican traditions of their cities than was Luther's theology of individual salvation. But Steven Ozment, in *The Reformation in the Cities* (1975), rounded on Moeller, arguing that early reformers all taught liberation from burdensome church oppressions even if later they re-instituted them as devices of control. Heiko Oberman, meanwhile, secured Reformation theology to late medieval theology, insisting that the Upper Germans were Thomists impressed with authority while the Lutherans were nominalists who understood the separation of spheres.

Midelfort's exegesis demonstrates that much current research has lost sight of Moeller's call to explore the real social history of the Reformation. He then analyzes several contemporary lines of study for their usefulness in building a social history of Reformation ideas. He notes an unexplained phenomenon, the enormous popularity in Germany of vernacular Bible translations. This puzzling social practice leads him to studies that probe local reformations in terms of their individual processes. Such studies have generated a theoretical "wave" system of three "phases," but have accomplished little toward a social history of ideas in the Reformation.

One possibly hopeful new direction is toward understanding what happened in social attitudes, expressions and practices following legal establishment of reform. In popular-culture media the evidence seems to reveal only crude and simplistic delineations of the faithful versus demons. The intrinsic dynamics of printing suggest that marketing factors shaped the packages containing Reformation ideas. New approaches to social class have recently examined the curious indifference of the free knights, the peasantry even when they were not in revolt, and the prominent fact of heterodoxy existing compatibly in many towns.

The author's final message is a call to use formulae and theories because historians must. But use them cautiously and critically, accepting the disparity, the discontinuity, the diversity and the irony of human ideas at work.

The three essays that follow in this volume are cautious and critical examples of the effort underway to understand events in the history of sixteenth-century society in relationship to the Reformation. The first concerns the multitude of popular uprisings in the momentous revolt-year of 1525. The Peasant War has magnetized for centuries the attention of scholars seeking to understand the revolts and their connection with Reformation. In the last generation, labors by ideologically inspired researchers in Marxist-oriented countries of Europe, paralleled by works of Western scholars, have revolutionized the entire conceptualization and methodology of studying the Peasant War. A major constituent of this redefinition is the cities, that is, the urban revolts of 1525. Lawrence P. Buck has made several contributions previously to our knowledge of popular unrest in Nuremberg and Frankfurt am Main. In the present installment, "The Reformation, Purgatory, and Perpetual Rents in the Revolt of 1525 at Frankfurt am Main," he ventures into the labyrinthine realm of tax reform. He narrates with grace and clarity the complex interrelation of rents and the institutional income of the church, correlating as well the integral role of that relationship in the history of the city and its inhabitants. Reformation issues are shown, when infused into this unstable urban distillation, to have intensified existing pressures for reform.

The next essay is by Thomas M. Safley. In "Protestantism, Divorce and the Breaking of the Modern Family," the author examines the family in early modern Europe. He establishes the values of kinship and community, as well as productivity, that society placed upon the family; then he posits against them the values of individuality, independence and self-sufficiency that are represented in the act of divorce. These highly regarded modern values are seen as genuine contradictions in the context of the early modern community.

Next, Safley introduces the Protestant Reformation into the issue of early modern divorce. He draws upon extensive archival research to establish a documentary base for his illuminating conclusions. Virtually every Protestant community endorsed divorce. The positive affirmation of personal freedom that so strongly was found in Protestant theology seems to show up in some increase in the rate of divorces petitioned and granted in the earlier years following the introduction of Protestantism in these communities. Over an extended period, however, the older values of kinship and community seem to have prevailed, at least as revealed in the laws and judgments issued by ruling magistrates.

Refined analysis of his evidence continues to demonstrate conclusively that, while legal divorce was possible on grounds usually limited to adultery, abandonment and abuse, the magisterial community continued to prefer to affirm fidelity, cohabitation and conjugality as evidences that the marriage still sustained its communal roles in the affective and productive needs of society.

The next author is Grethe Jacobsen, sometime Fellow in the Department of History of the University of Copenhagen. She has written "Women, Marriage, and Magisterial Reformation: The Case of Malmo, Denmark." Her essay combines an engaging narrative, based on minute analysis of judicial proceedings, with subtle analyses and conclusions concerning the status and conditions of women in the Danish city in the time of the Reformation. She documents carefully the introduction of magisterial reform and the consequent efforts by the city council to usurp jurisdiction over classes of litigation heretofore in the venue of Catholic church judicial processes. One such class, naturally, was marital issues. Against a backdrop of increasingly conservative and authoritarian—and uniformly male—magisterial governance, a drama was played out in the rights achieved by women to influence their legal status in marital concerns.

A study in social history at the time of the Reformation but without any reference to it is presented in the next essay. Merry E. Wiesner writes about a heretofore unnoticed group of people found in all cities of the time in "Making Ends Meet: The Working Poor in Early Modern Europe." These people were of all ages but disproportionately were old and young women. They were expelled or excluded from guild membership. They were virtually propertyless and survived precariously by occasional, seasonal or piecework labor; by low-level enterprise; by begging; and by religious and municipal charity.

The efforts of the working poor to survive met with various responses from elements of the community that were affected. Municipal governments, depending on the circumstances, viewed them as a burden on the relief rolls, as a source of tax revenue, as objects of official compassion, or as opportunities for Christian charity. Guilds and their members, especially journeymen, usually opposed the efforts of these people to exist, claiming that guild-protected tasks were being lost. In their subsistence-survival struggle, Wiesner concludes, the working poor displayed a tough and self-interested independence that suggests the vaunted Renaissance individualism was not limited to the educated elite.

Erik Midelfort's alertness toward expressions of the Reformation in popular culture and practices is amplified in three following essays. James M. Kittelson, in "Visitations and Popular Religious Culture: Further Reports from Strasbourg," returns to an established subject of scrutiny by him. He combines penetrating methodological critique with minute analysis of the records of parish visitations in Strasbourg late in the sixteenth century. His effort reveals some of the pitfalls that lurk in making generalizations about popular religion and popular culture. His study shows that reports on popular religious behaviors in Strasbourg's parishes must be interpreted through three ruling precepts: awareness of the human objectives involved, use of the exactly applicable data, and alertness to the immediate historical context.

Richard G. Cole, in "Pamphlet Woodcuts in the Communication Process of Reformation Germany," examines visual images imprinted in the voluminous pamphlet literature of the early stages of the Reformation. These pictures contained visual references to a vast storehouse of symbolic imagery in the high and the common mentality of pre-Reformation Europe. The effect of the reference was to reinforce the message of the pamphlet as the viewer connected a visual image with the symbolic meaning to which it referred. In addition to manipulation of the existing storehouse of meanings, new and specifically Reformation meanings were created. A mountain might be a symbolic play on Wittenberg. Barren trees and bushes on the left side of a picture and lush growth on the right traditionally contrasted Old Testament (Law) with New Testament (Grace); to this was added the contrast of the Church before Reformation and after.

Exploring a wide range of images—birds, animals, wild people, plants, trees and mountains—that are not specifically or exclusively Lutheran, the author expands our grasp of the role of pamphlet woodcuts in sixteenth-century communication processes. Through the use of visual symbols in the pamphlets, Cole provides additional information to help unlock the consciousness of the Reformation generation.

Kyle C. Sessions, writing on "Luther in Music and Verse," begins with Luther's own music, his hymns and liturgical writings, where profound and inspirational expressions of his central doctrines are found. A shift to verse expression leads to Hans Sachs and his composition, *The Wittenberg Nightingale*, in which Luther himself is featured and his principal teachings are broadly and copiously contrasted with existing doctrines and practices. Sessions concludes with an extended analysis of a 1527 verse drama. He shows it to move on several levels of mentality and culture. As a carnival play, it was in the mainstream of popular culture. As a dramatization of the parable of the Prodigal Son, it

Son, it employed a widely popular Reformation allegory. And as an exposition of Luther doctrine, it taught the Reformation to the popular mentality forcefully.

The concern of Harold Grimm for the history of the Reformation in German society has been reflected in the essays introduced so far. The remainder of the contributions focuses our attention on the teachings of Martin Luther himself. The person of the Reformer—who formed the axis upon which Harold Grimm's Reformation turned—is treated in a very special way by Jonathan W. Zophy in "We Must Have the Dear Ladies: Martin Luther and Women." From his own home and childhood, Luther unquestionably was aware of women and familiar with the female presence in the intimacy of the family. From the medieval church and traditions, he was thoroughly imbued with the disparagement and inferiority accorded women. He sustained both these characteristics throughout his life in his behavior toward women.

Luther's monastic life was, by his own profession, one that had almost nothing to do with women. But at least it did not encumber him with the burden of addressing the sinfulness and weakness assigned to them. Out of the monastery, he married and embraced sexuality enthusiastically and appreciatively. His home truly posed a model for the Protestant parish family. Yet he never substantially altered his acceptance of the traditional assignment of sex roles, in which the woman had distinct responsibilities and attendant honor, but was subordinate in every respect to her husband. Luther's life as a world figure brought him into awareness of and contact with important female persons but these experiences also did not substantially affect his conviction. Only in the strict confines of Scripture-based religion did Luther recognize female equality, and that was for religious reasons: there is only one faith for all.

Two of the scholars already introduced in this volume and the next author are women. Their scholarship affirms a basic precept of the historian's craft, always to be alert to new ways of viewing an established topic. Susan C. Karant-Nunn returns to a well-studied incident, the 1531 climax of disagreement between "Martin Luther and the City of Zwickau" over ecclesiastical authority. The city's civic structure was stressed by popular grievances. Yet commoners and council historically had an alliance in resisting outside incursions into Zwickau authority. Consequently, Luther alienated popular adherents through his stance toward the peasants and some ill will between Luther and the magistrates was generated as well. The mounting crisis of misunderstanding, misconception, misguided good will and misdirected vehemence found its catharsis in the climactic dismissal of preacher Lorenz Soranus in 1531.

The author's conclusions bring three new dimensions to modern understanding of the magisterial Reformation: 1) Luther in the case of Zwickau acted out of personal conviction regarding authority and without awareness of socio-governmental reality in the city; 2) Zwickau is a member of a presumedly hypothetical species, a city in which the council imposed its own Reformation preference on the citizenry;*   and 3) Zwickau's magistrates were determined to retain their hard-won authority and jurisdictions but were destined to lose out to the "higher authority" of their elector.

The social history of the Reformation, the social impact of Reformation ideas, the history of society in Reformation times, the reforming of popular culture, the Reformer's view of women—Harold Grimm would have understood and supported and gracefully critiqued all the efforts appearing thus far in this volume. Indeed, he inspired five of them and one yet to come. The remaining studies would gain his complete endorsement because they amplify the most clearly understood dimensions of Grimm's ceaseless quest for relating Reformation to society: Reformation politics and Lutheran theology.

William J. Wright, with "Philip of Hesse's Vision of Protestant Unity and the Marburg Colloquy," returns to a dramatic religious-political scene involving Luther personally. He makes an interpretation that perceives sociopolitical differences dividing North German nobles from South German burghers just as profoundly as did their religious differences. The author focus on Philip of Hesse and argues from Philip's unique unorthodoxy in politics and religion that the landgrave held firmly to an optimistic view about the colloquy's religious and political outcomes. He delineates in Philip's vision a hierarchy of four possible beneficent consequences: 1) general Protestant confessional concord, 2) general defensive Protestant political alliance, 3) improved relations founded in enhanced understanding between burghers and nobles, and 4) preservation of the empire federation, even though religiously bifurcated, as an alternative to division, which could only strengthen the emperor.

Robert Kolb, in "'Perilous Events and Troublesome Disturbances,' The Role of Controversy in the Tradition of Luther to Lutheran Orthodoxy," examines how the controversies of the late Reformation period shaped later understandings and interpretations of Luther's thought and career. Beyond the general influence of his teaching upon his students, Luther served as a model for the practice of theology in controversial form, as an authority figure whom controversial theologians could cite against each other, and as a source for well-expressed arguments in behalf of their causes. These controversies also helped determine the categories in which Luther's ideas were arranged and even influenced biographical treatment of certain elements of his life.

The appearance of Calvinism in Brandenburg in the seventeenth century is the subject of "Reformation or Deformation? Lutheran and Reformed Views of Martin Luther in Brandenburg's 'Second Reformation,'" by Bodo Nischan. In 1560, the Palatinate's Elector Frederick III had converted to Calvinism but insisted his action did not separate him from the Augsburg Confes-

*See Midelfort's discussion of Bernd Moeller, above p. x.

sion. Thus the stage was set for theological controversy in the next half-century. The dispute was framed by the issue of whether Luther's accomplishment was complete of itself and unalterable—as if he were a prophet of Scripture—or was a dynamic undertaking that must continue to reveal evangelical truth, especially in light shed by John Calvin. It was focused by the conversion in 1613 of another elector, John Sigismund of Brandenburg, to Calvinism. In form, it was a furious doctrinal debate between spokesmen of the Lutheran establishment on the one hand and representatives of Calvinist theology plus influential figures in the electoral court on the other.

The Reformed side argued that Luther's work was a reformation that needed to be continued and corrected. The Lutherans responded by condemning such a deformation of the very things Luther fought for. Taken together, the two claims reveal how widely divergent the Lutheran and the Swiss Reformations had become by the time of the Lutheran centennial.

The range and diversity of subjects in this volume make up a pattern that is completed and given coherence by the figure of Harold Grimm. Each scholar's work relates to an aspect of his interests and through him relates to each other. This statement is not hyperbole; rather, it affirms conclusively the breadth of his interests and awareness. To close this introduction where it was opened, Harold J. Grimm's distinguished career was anchored on the religious Reformation. From that anchorage, he navigated outward widely, seeking to understand in all ways how the religious event came into and affected the other events of the Reformation era. The voyage this volume takes was charted by Harold J. Grimm.

Acknowledgments

The editors are deeply grateful for the assistance and support of many people in making this volume possible. The authors and those who contributed financially are recognized elsewhere in these pages. For invaluable advice, assistance and support, we thank Robert V. Schnucker of Sixteenth Century Publishers, Inc. The photographs were contributed by Jane Grimm Minton and Capitol University. The index is the work of Miss Pamela Schell.

Kyle C. Sessions
Normal, Illinois

Phillip N. Bebb
Athens, Ohio

May 1985

Harold Grimm, June 3, 1975

Tabula Memorialis

Harry J. Ausmus, Louis E. Baer, Thomas Barnett-Robisheaux, Phillip N. Bebb, Warren A. Beck, Jerry H. Bentley, William J. Bouwsma, Lawrence P. Buck, Bartlett R. Butler, Carl C. Christensen, John R. Christianson, Miriam U. Chrisman, Richard G. Cole, Charles E. Daniel, Natalie Z. Davis, Allen W. Dirrim, John P. Donnelly, James M. Estes, Robert Fischer, George W. Forrell, Charles Garside, Jr., Jann W. Gates, Ray C. Gingerich, Elizabeth G. Gleason, Thelma Rickey Grimm for the Harold J. Grimm Essay Prize, Kurt K. Hendel, James Hinz, David M. Hockenbery, Elizabeth K. Hudson, De Lamar Jensen, Susan C. Karant-Nunn, Richard H. Kerbs, Robert M. Kingdon, Robert Kolb, Frank P. Lane, Robert D. Linder, Franklin Littell, William H. McNeill, The H. Henry Meeter Center for Calvin Studies of Calvin College, Jane Grimm Minton for the Harold J. Grimm Essay Prize, Otto M. Nelson, Donald G. Nugent, Heiko A. Oberman, R. Oxner, Jaroslav J. Pelikan, Edward L. Rice, Nancy L. Roelker, Robert V. Schnucker, Robert W. Scribner, Ernest G. Schwiebert, Kyle C. Sessions, Leo F. Solt, Wilfred J. Steiner, George H. Tavard, J. Alton Templin, Verein fu?r Reformationsgeschichte, Russell L. White, William J. Wright, Malcolm M. Wynn, Jonathan W. Zophy.

Reformation History and Social History:
The Contribution of Harold J. Grimm*

Phillip N. Bebb
Ohio University

IN TWO LESS WELL KNOWN ARTICLES ON AMERICAN HISTORY written in the 1940s, Harold J. Grimm dealt with concerns which occupied his entire career as a Reformation historian: man's faith in God and in the institutions man has created for his fellow man because of love based on faith. In a third article written during the same decade, Grimm cited a Renaissance biographer's words: "[He was an] extremely acute critic, a courageous preacher of truth, a profound thinker, the object of savage attacks, an untiring worker, a highly moral writer, and one of the most notable and brilliant spirits. . . ." The subject of such admiration was not Martin Luther but Lorenzo Valla.[1]

These statements by Harold Grimm, in such disparate historical areas as America and the Italian Renaissance, share in common not only his research and reflection but also his personal profession of faith. This profession must be recognized in the context of his childhood and early career because only by understanding his origins are we able to grasp the extent of his research and study of the Reformation and to appreciate why we honor him.

Grimm was a first generation German-American. His mother came from a Huguenot family which had fled to Mecklenburg from France following the revocation of the Edict of Nantes in 1685. In the aftermath of "the failure of the Revolution in 1848,"[2] the family migrated again, this time to America. His father, Henry Frederick, immigrated to the U. S. from the area of Hanover-Lüneburg. The elder Grimm became a Lutheran minister in this country, working at first in connection with the Michigan Lutheran Seminary at Saginaw. There Harold was born into a family that on both sides was directly related to the Reformation. This connection was a continuing influence on the young scholar.

Grimm persisted in the theological background of his father by taking two degrees at Capital University in Columbus, Ohio. The first was a B.A. at the university and the second was at the Evangelical Lutheran Seminar, "a graduate school of theology on the same campus."[3] Capital University was de-

*This paper was read at a joint meeting of the American Historical Association and the American Society for Reformation Research, Washington, D. C., December 1982.

[1]"The Genealogist as Historian," *The Ohio State Archaeological and Historical Quarterly* 49 (1940): 276-281; "The Founding of Franklinton: Its Significance Today," ibid., 56 (1947): 323-330; "Lorenzo Valla's Christianity," *Church History* 18 (1949): 75-88.

[2]"The Genealogist as Historian," 276. For the Huguenot relationship of Ella Emelie (Lepien) Grimm, I wish to thank Professor Hilmar Grimm.

[3]Harold L. Yochum, "Capital University, Columbus, Ohio," *The Encyclopedia of the Lutheran Church*, ed. Julius Bodensieck (Minneapolis: Augsburg Publishing House, 1965), 2: 1126.

voted to the "promotion of religion, morality, and learning." As the current bulletin maintains, it still "is rooted in the heritage of the Reformation, focusing on the freedom of all people to pursue truth."[4] Grimm did not become ordained but retained his interest in Luther and the Reformation by engaging in graduate work in history at The Ohio State University. Not surprisingly, both his master's and doctor's theses concerned Luther. The former is titled "Martin Luther as a Preacher" (1928); the latter is "Martin Luther: From Liberal Reformer to Conservative Church Father" (1932).[5]

To comprehend Grimm's convictions in the 1930s one need only cite from his dissertation:

> To the objective historian the Reformation is in its origin and nature fundamentally a religious movement, not primarily social, cultural, political, or economical. Naturally these factors soon found a prominent place in the development of the Reformation, but they occupied a position decidedly inferior to the religious factors.[6]

Here Grimm affirmed a principle he retained throughout his career: to study Luther correctly is to interpret the reformer in sixteenth century terms, not by the criteria of subsequent ages. To quote again, "[Luther] had absolutely no understanding of the economic, political or social problems of his day, but was forced to assume the role of leader in attempting to solve them."[7] This expression may be the enthusiasm of a young doctoral candidate; certainly, over time, Grimm modified his declaration that Luther had no understanding of non-theological problems. But in his conception that the Reformation was fundamentally religious he remained steadfast. He consistently acclaimed this position as recently, for example, as in his luncheon address to the Sixteenth Century Studies Conference in Terre Haute in October 1977. But there he also allowed that the study of religion alone does not go too far toward understanding the spread of the Reformation.

[4]*Capital University 1982-83 Bulletin*, 1.

[5]Grimm received one of the first Ph.D. degrees granted at The Ohio State University, following shortly the Department of History's initial award in 1925; see Francis P. Weisenburger, "A Brief History of the History Department at The Ohio State University," June, 1969, Private MS, Ohio State University Collection, Main Library. Interestingly, the director of both Grimm's master and doctoral theses was Wilbur H. Siebert who published in American history but taught in European history, probably because he had studied at Freiburg (Baden) and Berlin. The M.A. thesis was published under the same title, Columbus: The Lutheran Book Concern, 1929. For an abstract of the dissertation, see Ohio State University Abstracts of Dissertations, No. 10, 1932, 173 ff.

[6]"Martin Luther: From Liberal Reformer to Conservative Church Father," (Ph.D. diss., The Ohio State University, 1932), 9-10.

[7]Ibid., 153.

In 1935 Grimm wrote "Luther's Inner Conflict: A Psychological Interpretation"[8] in which he brought to the foreground the two historiographical interpretations of the reformer—medieval religious versus modern man of faith—that served to organize his later bibliographical articles.[9] Compressing the thoughts contained in his dissertation, he concluded that Luther, understood in the reformer's own terms, was both. Luther's residence at the Wartburg represented "the turning point in his career," for from that time he was forced to construct his church himself, on what he believed were divinely inspired principles.[10]

As for many German-Americans in the twentieth century, German involvement in the First and, especially, the Second World War constituted for Grimm epochal events that begged for interpretation. This was particularly so with regard to National Socialism and the propaganda use the party made of Luther's historical significance. Luther became a prophet of national unity led by the Führer and an opponent of social-economic disruption stemming from the lower orders.

In a series of writings through the 1940s, Grimm sought to clarify two points of contention.[11] First, he wished to exonerate Luther from the charge that he had given rise to totalitarianism. Such was the consequence claimed from Luther's support of the state in conflict with the peasants and from establishing what came to be the territorial church. Second, he reaffirmed the positive qualities in Western society that owed their origin to the Reformation, and which were under attack in World War II not only by Nazi Germany but by all forms of totalitarianism. For Grimm, the two points were simply two versions of the fundamental issue: the survival of Christianity and democracy.[12] He strongly asserted that one could find guidance to present problems through the study of Reformation sources. In "Luther's Conception of Territorial and National Loyalty," he wrote:

> That German scholars will again study Luther's writings for
> the purpose of finding hope and inspiration after the catastrophic
> consequences of the Second World War is already indicated by the

[8]*Church History* 4 (1935): 173-86.

[9]"Luther Research Since 1920," *The Journal of Modern History* 31 (1960): 105-18, and especially *The Reformation in Recent Historical Thought*, American Historical Association Service Center for Teachers of History, vol. 54 (New York: The Macmillan Co., 1964).

[10]"Luther's Inner Conflict," 177.

[11]See n. 1 above and the following: Harold J. Grimm, Francis J. Tschan, and J. Duane Squires, *Western Civilization: Decline of Rome to the Present*, 2 vols. (Philadelphia: Lippincott, 1942, 1947) and, significantly, a special wartime edition, *The First and Second World Wars*, War Backgrounds Edition of *Western Civilization* (c. 1943); "Luther, Luther's Critics, and the Peasant Revolt," *The Lutheran Church Quarterly* 19 (1946): 115-32; and "Luther's Conception of Territorial and National Loyalty," *Church History* 17 (1948): 79-94.

[12]"The Genealogist as Historian," 277.

frequent references to the importance of religion in Germany's historical evolution.[13]

If the Second World War served as the catalyst causing scholars to re-examine German history, its aftermath transformed the shape of Reformation research. The *Archiv für Reformationsgeschichte*, perhaps the leading journal in its field, had been founded in 1903, edited by Walter Friedensburg. Its chief purpose was to make available unpublished sources from the archives on German Reformation history. After Friedensburg's death in 1938 the journal took a new direction, as was indicated in its added subtitle: "Forschungen zur Geschichte des Protestantismus und seiner Weltwirkungen." Expanded coverage of the Protestant Reformation in other parts of Europe occurred, but the journal still concentrated heavily on Luther.[14] Toward the end of World War II however, the journal was suspended and the editor imprisoned.

Following 1945 the Verein für Reformationsgeschichte, publisher of the *Archiv*, was in a shambles and the German economy was shattered. In the summer of 1949, oral and written communication commenced between Gerhard Ritter on the one hand and Grimm, Roland Bainton, and Ernest Schwiebert on the other. The latter three were representatives of the new American Society for Reformation Research, founded in 1946.[15] The outcome was a decision to reactivate the *Archiv* under the joint editorship of the American Society and the German Verein. The journal would be truly international by countenancing no "national opposition" and would invite scholars from all areas of Reformation research to submit materials.[16] Grimm became the first American editor in 1949, a position he retained until 1962.[17]

New direction for the *Archiv* was apparent in its next volumes (1951-1952): few of the articles dealt with Luther and fewer concerned German politics. There occurred for Grimm a fortuitous coincidence at this juncture. He became the American editor of a journal that dealt with all aspects of the Reformation at the same time as he commenced work on what would become "the best survey of the Reformation" in English,[18] *The Reformation Era, 1500-*

---

[13]*Church History* 17 (1948): 79.

[14]See for example vol. 39 (1942); henceforth cited *ARG*.

[15]Harold J. Grimm, "Reformation Research," *The Lutheran Quarterly* 3 (1951): 313-14; he wrote that the ASRR was originally planned by Lutheran educators who met at Valparaiso University in August 1946 at the invitation of Ernest G. Schwiebert.

[16]See "Unser Program," *ARG* 42 (1951): 7-10.

[17]See *Who's Who in America*, 38th ed. (1974-1975), 1: 1239-40.

[18]Roland H. Bainton and Eric W. Gritsch, *Bibliography of the Continental Reformation: Materials Available in English*, 2d ed. (Hamden, CN: Archon Books, 1972), 18; cf. review by Robert Stupperich, *ARG* 48 (1957): 113-34. Stupperich writes that this kind of text dealing with the entire Reformation in all parts of Europe is at the present time entirely new to Germany.

1650.[19] This text reflected Grimm's role as editor in that the book was ecumenical, appreciating the wide and divergent strands within Protestant and Catholic Christianity. Although the "radicals" received little mention, they were not ignored; and Grimm, in irenic fashion, brought into his survey the interplay of theological and religious factors in their social, economic, political, cultural milieus. While adhering to the basic themes of his doctoral dissertation from twenty years before, he expanded his view to include the question: How can we understand the spread of the Reformation? It was this question that occupied him for most of the remainder of his scholarly career; and as he sought answers he broadened his focus to include social history in the study of the Reformation.

What Grimm meant by the social history of the Reformation was not especially clear at this point. He never doubted the fact that the Reformation began positively as a solution to Luther's theological question of how one might be saved. For Grimm this solution started the entire Reformation era. Religion was its base. Yet as he matured he began to ask: How did Luther make his solution known? What was in the content of Luther's messages that appealed to people? What motivated them to accept evangelical Christianity? Why did some accept, others reject, Luther? Implicitly, but not explicitly I hasten to add, Grimm began to acknowledge that mere religiosity in other people did not provide sufficient answers to the questions. In fact, he started to ask whether printed sources might ever provide such answers; after all, most printed sources had been around for some time.[20]

Toward the late 1950s Grimm expressed his concerns to a young German scholar who had been educated at Erlangen and had recently arrived in this country.[21] Gottfried Krodel mentioned that Grimm might try looking into the German archives, and provided some contacts. Not surprisingly, many of these were in Nuremberg, a city that maintained close relations with Erlangen. We can see Grimm making his way toward the archives by looking at his work in the late 1950s.

From 1957 to 1960 he edited and translated volume 31 of the American edition of *Luther's Works.*[22] He wrote "The Human Element in Luther's Sermons,"[23] in which he returned to themes in his first book in 1929; and

[19]New York: The Macmillan Co., 1954; revised and expanded bibliography, 1965.

[20]One of the first, and best, works in English—with which Grimm's text might profitably be compared—was Preserved Smith, *The Age of the Reformation* (New York: Henry Holt and Co., 1920). Smith wrote in a preface to his bibliography that while there remain unpublished documents on the Reformation, these are of less value and much smaller in number than published ones.

[21]Cf. Miriam U. Chrisman, "*Humanitas Pietas:* The Shoulders on Which We Stand," *The Sixteenth Century Journal* 13,1: 3-12.

[22]*Luther's Works: American Edition*, ed. Jaroslav Pelikan and Helmut T. Lehman, 55 vols. (St. Louis: Concordia Publishing House and Philadelphia: Muhlenberg Press, 1955-1977), vol. 31: *Career of the Reformer I* (Philadelphia: Muhlenberg Press, 1957).

[23]*ARG* 49 (1958): 50-60.

"Luther Research Since 1920."[24] In addition he presented three Martin Luther lectures at Luther College in Decorah, Iowa, on the reformer and education, published as *Luther and Culture*.[25] And he gave a paper at the Second International Congress for Luther Research at Münster, subsequently published as "The Relations of Luther and Melanchthon with the Townsmen."[26] As is apparent, Luther clearly remained the focus of Grimm's productivity, but the substance of what he wrote reflected his deepening concern with the spread of the Reformation. For example, he now maintained that the Protestant Reformation would never have succeeded without the vernacular sermon that Luther used to bring his doctrines to the immediate and practical needs of the people.[27] Among these needs was education, which Luther advocated should be universal and compulsory. In this area, Luther's theory coincided with governmental desires because governments needed educated people and establishing educational institutions helped consolidate control in their territories. As a preacher, teacher, and textbook author, Luther was directly responding to the social needs of his day, wrote Grimm.

Grimm's view became even more sharply focused toward the end of his bibliographical survey of Luther research and in his "Luther and Melanchthon." In the penultimate paragraph of the survey he listed six non-theological areas that still needed to be investigated, among which was "the support given him [Luther] and his movement by such social groups as townsmen, nobles, and peasants."[28] Grimm clarified his position orally in Münster in August 1960. He began his presentation by emphasizing once again the importance of religion for understanding the Reformation. Then he remarked:

> Nevertheless, other concerns were to a large degree responsible for the spread of the Reformation and often dictated the nature of the various religious settlements . . . . The papers and reports presented at the First International Research Congress at Aarhus in 1956 . . . as well as recent bibliographical surveys, indicate how little attention has been devoted to the influences of various social groups, particularly the townsmen, on the Reformation.[29]

In quick fashion he discussed the variety and differences among towns in Germany (there were approximately 3,000 of them) and many of the themes

[24]*The Journal of Modern History* 32 (1960): 105-18.

[25]George W. Forell, Harold J. Grimm, and Theodore Hoelty-Nickel, *Luther and Culture*, Martin Luther Lectures, vol. 4 (Decorah, IA: Luther College Press, 1960).

[26]In *Luther und Melanchthon: Referate und Berichte des zweiten internationalen Kongresses für Lutherforschung, Münster, 8.-13. August 1960*, ed. Vilmos Vajta (Göttingen: Vandenhoeck und Ruprecht, 1961), 32-48.

[27]*ARG* 49 (1958): 50 and *Luther and Culture*, 95-96.

[28]*The Journal of Modern History* 32 (1960): 118.

[29]*Luther und Melanchthon: Münster*, 32.

townsmen, especially those in the free imperial cities, held in common. Among the few imperial cities Grimm treated was Nürnberg and he stated that the relationship of Luther and Melanchthon to the Nürnberg townsmen was of utmost importance in the development of the whole Reformation.[30] This was so because Nürnberg adopted the Reformation early and had inordinate influence in advising Franconian, Swabian, and other imperial cities to do likewise.

Grimm returned to social themes in his presidential address to the American Society of Church History in 1962. Entitled "Social Forces in the German Reformation,"[31] it was to become his seminal interpretation of social history. As his 1940s essays were written against the backdrop of National Socialism in Germany, this address arose in part because of crises caused by missiles in Cuba and by the Berlin Wall. In times of trouble, he wrote, leaders look to the past for guidelines for the present:

> Although the dramatic conflicts of the sixteenth century were enfolded in a microcosm when compared with the extent of our own, there are sufficient parallels to warrant a renewed preoccupation with the period, its problems, its leaders, and its solutions. This becomes obvious especially when we realize that many of our political, economic, and social as well as religious institutions had their beginnings in the late medieval and early modern periods and can be examined with great profit because then they existed in relatively simple forms.[32]

Continuing, he wrote: "Too often historians treat a succession of events as *ipso facto* causes and effects and parallel movements as intrinsically related. Whereas conservative church historians tend to discuss social questions as incidental to theology, liberal historians usually point to the social-democratic characteristics of the revolts. . . and Marxists dwell on economic motives. . . ."[33] To illustrate these points Grimm presented a brief historiographical sketch, including reference to the distortions of Nazi historians, showing how ideology shapes historical understanding. He concluded that his sketch shows the need for studies to be made with "no ax to grind."

In the remainder of his presentation Grimm laid the foundations for the study of social forces. What he meant specifically was the study of social groups—nobles, knights, peasants, townsmen—and what views each group held individually and had in common with the others. This obviously meant

---

[30]Ibid., 47.

[31]*Church History* 31 (1962): 3-13, reproduced without notes in Lewis W. Spitz, ed., *The Reformation: Basic Interpretations*, 2d ed. (Lexington, MA: D. C. Heath, 1972), 85-97.

[32]"Social Forces," in *Reformation: Basic Interpretations*, 85-86.

[33]Ibid., 86.

study of political, constitutional, and economic status as well as how each group perceived itself and expressed itself on religious and other issues of the day.[34] Grimm's program was not, however, class conscious; neither was it sociological nor collectively biographical. It foresaw the attempt to understand the dynamic interplay between religion and society, or at least among the groups that accepted certain religious ideas and tried to transform society according to them. In this attempt he intended to isolate into manageable units capable of study the myriad factors that comprised the Reformation.

The direction Grimm himself desired to take was also spelled out in the address when he wrote, "Even more formidable [than the above] is the task of discovering the interrrelation of religion and social concerns among the townsmen of the Reformation. . . ."[35] Although he did not specifically mention them, he was concerned with the townsmen of the free imperial cities because they could be known by name; that is, they were identifiable. Furthermore, in the cities there existed certain common features he had discussed in his previous essay, "Luther and Melanchthon." Among these was a strong sense of corporate loyalty, independence, and freedom,[36] expressed through ethics, workable institutions, and reforming efforts. While he did not elaborate, I suspect the underlying reason Grimm concentrated on the imperial cities was that they maintained documentary repositories in the early sixteenth century and many of these still existed. As opposed to princely towns and territorial principalities, the cities that maintained their archives offered the best sources for the study of social and religious forces.

By this time in his career, Grimm had become interested in the city secretary of Nürnberg, Lazarus Spengler, early proponent of Luther and an important lay leader of the Reformation. In his presidential address, Grimm remarked that Spengler "best illustrates the complexity of interests involved in bringing the Reformation" to Nürnberg.[37] On this one man and in this one city Grimm spent much of the remainder of his career. That commitment illustrates the direction he thought Reformation research should take. Spengler was an important, educated individual who occupied an influential position in a large city that became one of the first openly to adopt Luther. The study of Spengler's environment and his relations with fellow burghers would help to explain the appeal of the Reformation. Most important, the documentary materials were available. From 1960 on, he researched Nürnberg and Spengler; the ultimate result is the monograph, *Lazarus Spengler, A Lay Leader of the Reformation.*[38]

---

[34]Ibid., 97.

[35]Ibid., 92.

[36]See *Luther und Melanchthon: Münster,* 35-40.

[37]"Social Forces," in *Reformation: Basic Interpretations,* 94.

[38]Columbus: The Ohio State University Press, 1978.

In 1967, almost as a précis of the subsequent book, Grimm wrote "Lazarus Spengler, the Nürnberg Council, and the Reformation."[39] In it he began, as always, with the importance of religion and added, "Today's great desideratum is an analysis of the various social forces of the period to ascertain reasons for the phenomenal spread of the Lutheran Reformation. . . . [We] must begin with analyses of the motives and interests of individuals and manageable groups within the social classes of that day" and not with generalizations and assumptions."[40] This work, in addition to his articles, "The Reformation and Urban Social Classes,"[41] and "Luther's Contributions to Sixteenth-Century Organization of Poor Relief,"[42] plus the Spengler monograph, were based in part on materials contained in archives, especially in Nürnberg.

Taken together, these writings constitute refinements in Grimm's concern with social history. Whereas the 1967 Spengler article was probably the most tightly knit and narrowest in terms of subject matter, Grimm's later works, including the second edition of his text, return to broader, more ecumenical themes. Such themes were not missing from the early Spengler work; rather, that one essay gave him the opportunity to put into effect the program outlined in his 1962 address. From 1967 Grimm knew where he was going with the Nürnberg secretary, and he could devote his energies to the important roles played by merchants in the spread of the Reformation and to the theological and ethical justification for the rise of secularly administered poor relief.

Grimm wrote in the preface of the second edition of *The Reformation Era, 1500-1650*:

> The similarity of the Reformation era to our space age with its rapid and profound changes accompanied by its search for truth, meaning, relevance, and identity is sufficient justificaton for telling the story of the rise of Protestantism and the renewal of Catholicism in its complete setting.[43]

In effect he was reiterating the major emphasis of both his life and his work. As Miriam Chrisman so eloquently stated in a recent address to the Sixteenth Century Studies Conference, Grimm represents more than the religiosity of a previous generation; he embodies the very essence of a continuing thread in the Western experience, namely humanist education. It is not surprising then

[39]*Luther for an Ecumenical Age*, ed. Carl S. Meyer (St. Louis: Concordia Publishing House, 1957), 108-19.

[40]Ibid., 108.

[41]Presented in 1967 and published in 1969: John C. Olin, ed., *Luther, Erasmus and the Reformation: A Catholic-Protestant Reappraisal* (New York: Fordham University Press, 1969), 75-86.

[42]*ARG* 61 (1970): 222-34.

[43]New York: The Macmillan Co., 1973, vii.

that in one of his last writings, "The Ecumenical Outlook of Martin Luther," he returned to views expressed in his first scholarship: Christian love, charity, fellowship, social service, and ecumenism.[44] In both the area of religious history and social history, Harold Grimm sought to make the Reformation meaningful to our age.

---

[44]*Semasia: Beiträge zur germanisch-romanischen Sprachforschung* 2 (1975): 83-95, especially 90, 95.

Toward a Social History of Ideas
in the German Reformation

H. C. Erik Midelfort
University of Virginia

MANY SCHOLARS ACCEPT A. G. DICKENS' ASSESSMENT of a few years ago that the two biggest changes to come over Reformation research in the last generation have been concentration on the late medieval background and emphasis on the social context in which the Reformation took place. Now we are faced with the prospect of joining together late-medieval ideas and social history. This enterprise is just beginning.

But social history is a subject that has stimulated vigorous, even bitter, controversy, and some have doubted whether American contributions have served to clarify so much as to obscure the social history of the Reformation.[1] At the basis of this particular argument is the question of what we mean by "social history." Surely no one would seriously hold that it is simply history with the politics left out; but it also seems that it is not just "the study of the human past in terms of the groups through whose interrelations a given society gets its living and reproduces its structure and culture," to use the recent definition by Thomas Brady.[2] This formula generously allows historians to pay attention to both analytic and teleological aspects of the Reformation, i.e., to the problems of who supported (or rejected) Protestant ideas, at what stage, and where, and why; and to the problem of what general impact these ideas had on the course of European history. But Brady's formula, for all its generosity, does not seem to pose the corresponding question for the social history of ideas, namely, the way in which social groups adapt, mold, change, and reform the ideas themselves. In other words, social historians, with all of their proper concern for statistical precision and interdisciplinary method, run the risk of assuming improperly that ideas are only "carried" or "introduced" by various groups. I think that ideas, even Protestant ideas, were initiated, created and modified by the very groups and individuals usually identified as mere carriers. Men in the sixteenth century carried ideas like quicksilver in their hands, inevitably imposing their own shapes upon them.[3]

---

[1] See especially Robert W. Scribner, "Is There A Social History of the Reformation?" *Social History* 4 (1976): 483-505.

[2] Thomas Brady, "Social History," in Steven Ozment, ed., *Reformation Europe: A Guide to Research* (St. Louis: Center for Reformation Research, 1982), 161-81, at 161.

[3] I am suggesting that ideas are fluid and conform, "at bottom," to their containers, i.e., to the persons who "hold" the ideas. Using this awkward metaphor allows us to avoid the exaggerations involved in seeing ideas as solids (e.g., as Cartesian lumps of wax, easily shaped but having a determinate shape of their own nonetheless) or as gases (in which an idea would so perfectly conform to its container in all dimensions as to be reducible to psychology or sociology). We can shape a fluid by changing its container but we cannot determine completely its shape.

I should like to show how recent research has tended to truncate our understanding of the social history of the Reformation by prompting many scholars to deal obsessively with an arbitrarily narrow set of questions.

Without trying to deal with all of the work on the social history of religion in the sixteenth century (in any event I am not competent to do so), I should like to single out some of the most important responses to Bernd Moeller's 1962 book, *Imperial Cities and the Reformation*. No one, I think, doubts the importance of that book over the last twenty years, even if many would hesitate before joining A. G. Dickens in his enthusiastic dictum: "The German Reformation was an urban event."[4] In 1962 Moeller did two separate things: First, he tried to explain why so many towns, especially imperial cities, adopted the Reformation or at least flirted seriously with evangelical preaching; but, second, he tried to explain why the theology of the Upper Germans, Zwingli and Bucer, appealed more directly to cities that were used to controlling cooperatively their own fates than did the theology of Luther, whose teachings apparently appealed more to princes and urban oligarchs than to guild republicans. This is not the place to assess Moeller's theses or to convict him of romantic idealism (or of any other idealism).[5] But it does seem worth saying that recent researchers have so concentrated on the first of Moeller's questions that they have almost lost sight of the second.

Two recent controversies have created this seeming oversimplification of recent research by concentrating attention on only a couple of problems in the full range of necessary questions. One concentration has been on the narrow question of who wanted the Reformation and why, while the other has dealt with the nature of early Reformation ideas and the extent to which Luther, Zwingli, and Bucer seriously disagreed in the early years.

In a pugnacious and erudite book in 1978, Thomas Brady presented his conclusions regarding Strasbourg's ruling class during the Reformation.[6] Instead of acting out of true concern for the unity and general religious welfare of Strasbourg (as Moeller would have it), the urban oligarchs apparently acted only to preserve their own privileged position in 1525, "introducing" the Reformation as a way of coopting and controlling a popular protest movement. Despite his disagreement with Moeller over the motives, ethos, and force be-

[4] A. G. Dickens, *The German Nation and Martin Luther* (London: Edward Arnold, 1974), 182. So common has Dickens's thesis become that it is now subject to scurrilous or polemical inversion, as in Peter Blickle's recent *Die Reformation im Reich* (Stuttgart: E. Ulmer, 1982), 66.

[5] See the exchange between Moeller, "Stadt und Buch: Bemerkungen zur Struktur der reformatorischen Bewegung in Deutschland," and Brady, "'The Social History of the Reformation' between 'Romantic Idealism' and 'Sociologism': A Reply," in Wolfgang J. Mommsen, ed., *Stadtbürgertum und Adel in der Reformation* (Stuttgart: Klett-Cotta, 1979), 25-39 and 40-43, respectively. And note the implicit critique in Hans-Christoph Rublack, "Forschungsbericht Stadt und Reformation," in Bernd Moeller, *Stadt und Kirche im 16. Jahrhundert* (Gütersloh: Gerd Mohn, 1978), 9-26.

[6] *Ruling Class, Regime, and Reformation at Strasbourg, 1520-1555* (Leiden: E. J.Brill, 1978).

hind reform in Strasbourg, Brady did not reject Moeller's general claim that in almost every case known to us the Reformation was popular, perhaps even a popular *movement* in the sense to which Robert Scribner has recently called attention.[7] For Moeller and Brady and Scribner (and others), "there was no *Ratsreformation*," no reform created, initiated, and imposed by urban oligarchs. A host of studies of the urban Reformation, in Stralsund, Lübeck, Basel, Ulm, Osnabrück, Konstanz, Memmingen, Frankfurt, Zürich, Bern, Geneva, Worms, and Hamburg, seemed to confirm the popular shape of reform.[8] Sometimes connected to this conclusion, even covertly or unconsciously, was either the corollary that the Reformation was a revolution no oligarchy would have initiated willingly, or the unexamined assumption that reform ideas spread so quickly precisely because they were popular, or even necessary.[9] Popular Reformation is perhaps as good a generalization about forces for reform in the Holy Roman Empire as many others, but we should stipulate that it is an empirical observation and not a necessary truth. From the very start Nuremberg has caused trouble for the popular Reformation thesis because its Reformation proceeded with surprisingly little popular demand or protest.[10] Winfried Becker pushed this troubling exception further, holding in 1974 that the urban Reformation was promulgated by town councils without social revolution and in many cases without any notable changes in the urban regime.[11] From this perspective all urban Reformations were in fact *Ratsreformationen*. Subsequent research by Wolfram Wettges has tried to lay out

[7] Robert W. Scribner, "The Reformation as a Social Movement," in Mommsen, ed. *Stadtbürgertum und Adel*, 49-79.

[8] Philip Broadhead, "Popular Pressure for Reformation in Augsburg, 1524-1534," in Mommsen, ed., *Stadtbürgertum und Adel*, 80-87; Hans R. Guggisberg, *Basel in the Sixteenth Century* (St. Louis: Center for Reformation Research, 1982); Wilhelm Rausch, ed., *Die Stadt am Ausgang des Mittelalters* (Linz: Österreichischer Arbeitskreis für Stadtgeschichtsforschung, 1974); Wilfried Ehbrecht, "Verlaufsformen innerstädtischer Konflikte in nord- und westdeutschen Städten im Reformationszeitalter," in Moeller, *Stadt und Kirche*, 27-47; Ehbrecht, "Köln, Osnabrück, Stralsund: Rat und Bügerschaft hansischer Städte zwischen religiöser Erneuerung und Bauernkrieg," in Franz Petri, ed., *Kirche und gesellschaftlicher Wandel in deutschen und niederländischen Städten der werdenden Neuzeit* (Cologne: Böhlau, 1980), 23-64; Ehbrecht, ed., *Städtische Führungsgruppen und Gemeinde in der werdenden Neuzeit* (Cologne: Böhlau, 1980); Otthein Rammstedt, "Stadtunruhen 1525," in Hans-Ulrich Wehler, ed., *Der deutsche Bauernkrieg, 1524-1526* (Göttingen: Vandenhoeck und Ruprecht, 1975), 239-76; Ingrid Bátori, ed., *Städtische Gesellschaft und Reformation* (Stuttgart: Klett-Cotta, 1980); Walter Jacob, *Politische Führungsschicht und Reformation. Untersuchungen zur Reformation in Zürich: 1519-1528* (Zurich: Zwingli-Verlag, 1970); S. Jahns, *Frankfurt, Reformation und Schmalkaldischer Bund* (Frankfort: Kramer, 1976); Hans-Christoph Rublack, *Die Einführung der Reformation in Konstanz* (Gütersloh: Gerd Mohn, 1971).

[9] For an indictment of these assumptions see W. Becker, *Reformation und Revolution* (Münster: Aschendorff, 1974).

[10] Moeller, *Imperial Cities and the Reformation* (Philadelphia: Fortress Press, 1972); Gerald Strauss, *Nuremberg in the Sixteenth Century* (New York: Wiley, 1966); Harold J. Grimm, *Lazarus Spengler: A Lay Leader of the Reformation* (Columbus: Ohio State University Press, 1978).

[11] Becker, *Reformation und Revolution*, 86-91.

schematically the important and different reformatory roles played by (1) preachers and intellectuals, (2) town councillors, and (3) the people. All three groups had to cooperate to produce the urban Reformation, filling respectively the positions of propagandists, organizers, and motors without which the reform would have lacked direction, sanction and force.[12] His studies of Nuremberg, Regensburg, and Augsburg showed the variant forms that these three forces could assume. But by now what had begun as a fruitful program of historical research was beginning to bog down in social theory. Researchers have come to concentrate obsessively on the *Trägerschichten* or *Führerschichten*. The study by Kaspar von Greyerz, otherwise fine, aims at showing that Colmar's late Reformation—and others at Aachen, Aalen, Dortmund, Essen, and Hagenau—were all dominated by concilliar action, not popular or guild rebellion.[13] Studies like this are really aiming toward a theoretical claim that the Reformation was not, and perhaps could not be, a social revolution. My objection is that, in claiming that the town council always had a vital role in sanctioning the Reformation, these scholars are surely not telling Moeller or Brady something they did not know. Their conclusion would not have seemed remarkable if previous scholars had not already distorted the terms of discourse.

The other distorting controversy has concerned the evangelical ideas themselves. Moeller described Luther's thinking in its original formulation as typically more preoccupied with the salvation of individuals than with the creation of godly commonwealths. Coming from the less culturally developed Northeast and living in small towns that lacked the corporate structures of guild rules and the communal impulses of the great imperial cities, Luther could hardly avoid producing a Reformation that was as profound and inward looking as it was unconcerned for sanctification and communal discipline.[14] The ancient urban centers of the Southwest and of Switzerland, dependent as they were on corporate organs of government and on a communal sense of unity, could hardly avoid finding the urban theologies of Bucer and Zwingli more congenial than Luther, at least until their guild constitutions were reformed and castrated by Charles V in the wake of his victories over the Schmalkaldic League.

Scholars have not been slow to attack this part of Moeller's essay, although in general it has attracted less attention than the controversy over who made the Reform. One of the sharpest critiques came from Steven Ozment, who argued that Moeller had vastly exaggerated the importance of differences be-

---

[12]Wolfram Wettges, *Reformation und Propaganda. Studien zur Kommunikation des Aufruhrs in süddeutschen Reichsstädten* (Stuttgart: Klett-Cotta, 1978).

[13]Kaspar von Greyerz, *The Late City Reformation in Germany. The Case of Colmar, 1522-1628* (Wiesbaden: Steiner, 1980).

[14]Moeller, *Imperial Cities*, relying for these points in particular on H. Schöffler, *Die Reformation* (Bochum, H. Pöppinghaus, 1936).

tween Luther and the humanist theologians of the Southwest.[15] In Ozment's view, the early reformers had a common message, one of religious liberation from the burdens of late medieval theology. The early Reformers may have had their private and learned differences, but in public, in their popular pamphlets they stressed the basic evangelical doctrine of salvation through faith and grace alone, thereby undercutting Catholic doctrines of indulgences, purgatory, sacraments, and monasticism and the elaborate Catholic panoply of pilgrimage, confession, the invocation of saints, preparation for death, celibacy, and the imitation of Christ with which the humble late medieval Christian could hope to please his God. Instead of stressing geographic or social differences among the early reformers, Ozment saw the whole dynamic of the Reformation as declension, a fall away from the original liberation of the early 1520s into the stifling embrace of territorial and urban institutions, which were as ready to burden the consciences of its local Protestant parishioners as Catholic confessors had ever been. Ozment's picture is as full of movement and irony as it is lacking in discrimination.

Heiko Oberman has correctly diagnosed the similarity between Ozment's history and that of Anabaptists, who spoke of the Constantinian fall of the Church.[16] And Oberman has also sharply rejected Ozment's attempted blending of all the early reformers into a theology of liberation, pointing to dramatic differences in training, background, strategy, and goals between the Lutheran Reform and the Southwest German and Swiss Reform. In Oberman's view the urban reformers were generally trapped in a Thomist (or via antiqua) understanding of church and state and aimed, as a consequence, at various approximations of theocracy, while Luther and the Reformation in territories such as Württemberg kept alive a keen, nominalist sense of separate spheres. Although Oberman has claimed that he rejects much of Moeller's argument, it is evident that he has preserved many of Moeller's categories (Luther vs. Upper German; princely vs. urban) even as he derives them not from the social experience of historical communities, but from late medieval scholastic debate. Ozment's strength is that he has been willing to look at popular literature; Oberman's that he has not lost his grip on the importance of theological distinctions. Even enthusiasts for Ozment's method will have to confess some discomfort when they find themselves asked to believe that Calvin was not properly a Protestant at all.[17] And Oberman's formulation seems to float in the purest ether.

Both Ozment and Oberman, however, have fundamentally broken with Moeller's original project of understanding the social origins of Reformation

[15]Steven Ozment, *The Reformation in the Cities: The Appeal of Protestantism to Sixteenth-Century Germany and Switzerland* (New Haven: Yale University Press, 1975).

[16]Heiko Oberman, *Masters of the Reformation* (Cambridge: Cambridge University Press, 1981), 276-77.

[17]Steven Ozment, *The Age of Reform* (New Haven: Yale University Press, 1980), 372-80.

ideas. This is odd since Ozment claimed that his approach was dictated by a "methodological collaboration . . . a direct confrontation of ideology and society," an effort to locate ideas in a social matrix.[18] Recently, however, Ozment has admitted that his aim was not to illuminate the specifically urban Reformation (regardless of his title) but to "argue for the social force of religion itself, in part against Moeller's earlier interpretation. . . ."[19] Instead of looking for what I have described as a social history of ideas, in which a constant tension exists between ideal and material interests, Ozment has apparently opted for the priority of intellection.[20] In Oberman's case it is even clearer that, despite his willingness to refer to various kinds of reform (monastic, urban, princely) he is nonetheless moving about the heavy lumber of scholastic theology in the academic backroom where the real structures of history are built.

It seems to me that neither critic is able to cope effectively with the fact that pre-Reformation Germany evinced a remarkable hunger for the Bible in vernacular translation while the French and English and Italians apparently did not. Mentel's 1466 edition of the German Bible underwent thirteen new editions before 1522, plus several Low German editions. There exist some 800 manuscripts of German translations of parts of the Scriptures from the fourteenth and especially the fifteenth centuries.[21] In contrast, French vernacular translations were mainly restricted to the "wealthy or even to court circles," and Italy was notoriously slow in obtaining general access to a vernacular Bible.[22] As we know, the demand was great enough in Germany to account for fifteen editions of Luther's New Testament in Wittenberg from 1522 to 1524 and sixty-six others in other towns.[23] From 1534 to 1620 Luther's translation

---

[18] Ozment, *The Reformation in the Cities*, 2.

[19] Ozment, "Pamphlets as a Source: Comments on Bernd Moeller's 'Stadt und Buch,'" in Mommsen, ed. *Stadtbürgertum und Adel*, 46-48, at 47.

[20] Although Ozment has made repeated gestures toward a more balanced approach, he continues in his most recent work to prefer large generalizations about all of society to the patient effort to tease apart specific social groups in order to find out what ideas were congenial to each. To take but one example, Ozment has argued that "the Protestant catechism, so often deplored by modern scholars as an assault on the freedom and autonomy of children, may instead have been the chief means of their liberation from the internal bonds of authoritarian religion," *When Fathers Ruled: Family Life in Reformation Europe* (Cambridge, MA: Harvard University Press, 1983), 172-73. Whatever the merits of this audacious claim, it seems to be a good case of intellectual priority since Ozment shows no interest in the question of how catechetical ideas were taught, received, digested, and distorted in different situations.

[21] G. W. H. Lampe, ed., *The Cambridge History of the Bible* 2 (Cambridge: Cambridge University Press, 1969): 434; S. L. Greenslade, ed., *The Cambridge History of the Bible* 3 (Cambridge: Cambridge University Press, 1963): 423.

[22] *Cambridge History of the Bible* 2: 451-53.

[23] Ibid., 3: 428.

of the whole Bible went through 430 editions, without counting issues of single Testaments or books of the Bible.[24] Admittedly much of the difference here between Germany and the rest of Europe depended on the success of repressive measures elsewhere, but it also seems clear that the hunger for Scripture was greater in Germany than elsewhere, and that this hunger probably did not arise from any peculiarly repressive pre-Reformation Catholicism in Germany (as Ozment might argue) or from the scholastic assumptions of German readers (as Oberman might have to argue). I do not intend to look through my fingers at these learned men, but to point to important issues for the social history of the Reformation that their approaches seem unable to resolve.

The best studies of the past few years seem to me to be aware of these difficulties and to suggest at least two ways of proceeding, one more fruitful, I think, than the other. The researchers of Wilfried Ehbrecht, Jan Juliaan Woltjer, Heinz Schilling, Hans-Christoph Rublack, Volker Press, and Peter Blickle (to name a handful) have tried to understand the Reformation as a process broken into specific phases. Clearly the reforming movement ran through a series of parallel gestures that could be studied with profit. If we could grasp several *Verlaufsformen*, perhaps we could understand the various configurations of Protestant piety from the mid-sixteenth century onward. In many towns the first recorded stirrings of religious rebellion centered on the arrival of a preacher, or less often a book or printed cartoon. In many cases we have no evidence of how the Reformation actually began, but following the initial stage of proclamation we can usually detect what Rublack has called the "interval," a phase of intense conflict in which all authority and order, religion and imperial loyalty seemed about to dissolve.[25] In Esslingen, for example, this phase was full of double binds and difficult decisions. Finally, the council opted for the evangelical message out of conviction and a sense that public order would also be strengthened by the gospel. Only in the third phase of establishment did Esslingen experience an outburst of iconoclasm (1532) of the sort that shook other towns in earlier phases. Wilfried Ehbrecht has used a similar three-phase analysis to tell the stories of reform in Cologne, Osnabrück, and Stralsund, but here the "phases" are called grievance, negotiation, and confrontation. Obviously the last stage did not always involve victory.[26] Woltjer's work on the Netherlands also detects three "phases" of (1) persecution of Protestants, (2) Protestant takeover, and (3) Protestant rule.[27]

---

[24]Ibid., 3: 432-33.

[25]Hans-Christoph Rublack, "Reformatorische Bewegung und städtische Kirchenpolitik in Esslingen," in Bátori, ed., *Städtische Gesellschaft,* 191-220, at 194-200.

[26]Ehbrecht, "Köln, Osnabrück, Stralsund."

[27]J. J. Woltjer, "Stadt und Reformation in den Niederlanden," in Petri, *Kirche und gesellschaftlicher Wandel,* 155-68.

Volker Press has divided noble responses to the Reformation into three phases of initial enthusiasm, indecision, and a late period of decision.[28]

I could multiply examples, but I think it is obvious from the work of these able historians that the notion of phases, drawn perhaps from physical wave theory, has no innate or occult power to illuminate the process of reform. Some of these learned phase detectors are saying little more than that the Reformation, wherever it prevailed (and even where it did not), had a beginning, a middle, and an end. My only quibble with this as a useful story line is that historians have too often thought that the story of the Reformation was complete once evangelical preaching obtained legal sanction. They have usually lost interest in the Reform once the Catholic mass was abolished and the monasteries sequestered, as if the Protestant message had been mainly a gospel of destruction and secularization. Recently Heinz Schilling has tried to turn phase analysis into an analytical tool in his brilliant study of the reform at Münster. He argues that Lutheran reformers succeeded in the 1520s in most other cities by riding the back of a guild-run rebellion for increased participation in city government. In Münster, however, the Lutheran movement came out of phase, ten years late, during the princely Reformation of the early 1530s. Lutheran councillors in 1533 were driven (in a critical step that Schilling does not fully explain) to deny that very communal movement on which they had risen. As a result of this shift in phases, Bernhard Rothmann was able to inherit all of the weight, authority, and tradition of the communal opposition movement. His increasingly radical theology could now join forces with a broad spectrum of Münster's citizenry to oppose the increasingly conservative, Lutheran council. Rothmann could count on so large and so general a following "because his 'radical-communal' thinking about [church] order was generally congruent with the constitutional traditions of the city."[29] Here at last the rhetoric about phases may actually clarify a situation because Schilling is not simply telling a story with a beginning, a middle, and an end. The phases of citizen opposition in Münster can be seen as problematic precisely because they ran against the waves or phases of a more common experience. This sort of analysis is potent, in other words, only when one set of waves can be seen conflicting with another. On the other hand we will have to be careful that we do not so thoroughly reify "phases" that they replace human beings as actors in our story. Phase analysis used carefully, as by Kaspar von Greyerz in his study of the late Reformation at Colmar, may turn out to be generally helpful.[30]

[28]Press, "Adel, Reich und Reformation," in Mommsen, ed., *Stadtbürgertum und Adel*, 330-83; Press, "Stadt und territoriale Konfessionsbildung," in Petri, ed., *Kirche und gesellschaftlicher Wandel*, 251-96.

[29]H. Schillling, "Aufstandsbewegungen in der stadtbürgerlichen Gesellschaft des Alten Reiches. Die Vorgeschichte des Münsteraner Täuferreichs, 1525 bis 1534," in Wehler, ed., *Der deutsche Bauernkrieg*, 193-238.

[30]Von Greyerz, *The Late City Reformation*.

However, an even more fruitful insight is that legal establishment of the gospel was not so much the end of the Reformation as the beginning. Instead of treating church history as a captive of legal and political formalities, some historians have begun to ask what really changed when a town or territory turned Protestant. Robert Scribner's recent book on pictorial propaganda for the Reformation implies at least (even if it fails to argue the point) that a major evangelical goal was simply revulsion at Roman Catholicism.[31] Weak as a means of positive instruction, Protestant cartoons were most effective in dividing the Christian world into two parts: the faithful and the demonic. Scribner may in his way reinforce Gerald Strauss's general point that doctrinal instruction was slow to seep into the parishes.[32] Linked with surprising frequency to carnival and festive buffoonery, Luther's movement may have seemed to some people to have been a jubilant or apocalyptic socio-religious inversion rather than a sober call to serious study and personal regeneration.[33]

Another work that goes well beyond the legal and official understanding of the Reformation is the recent book on printing in Strasbourg by Miriam Chrisman. Casting her net widely, she forced herself to transcend the normal and tedious categories of familiar history. She records the growth of vernacular literature in various fields in the middle decades of the sixteenth century, then the dominance of institutional and scientific works after 1570, aimed at establishing religious and academic orthodoxy.[34] Extending beyond the official dates for the Reformation in Strasbourg, her book broadens our understanding of the social shaping of ideas by exampling ways in which the demands of the book trade determined which book would be printed and sold. Book publishers clearly did not create the demand for their books, but by creating compendia, anthologies, translations, they could determine the context within which certain ideas would be understood.

Finally, a number of recent investigations are beginning to peel back the veneer of social appearance that has impeded study of the social classes in sixteenth century Germany. Volker Press's studies of the lower nobility, for example, have uncovered the vital importance of imperial policy for the very existence of the imperial knights.[35] Many nobles carefully tuned to the political realities around them and resisted making any religious decision before the

[31]Robert W. Scribner, *For the Sake of Simple Folk: Popular Propaganda for the German Reformation* (Cambridge: Cambridge University Press, 1981).

[32]Gerald Strauss, *Luther's House of Learning* (Baltimore: Johns Hopkins University Press, 1978).

[33]R. W. Scribner, "Reformation, Carnival and the World Turned Upside-Down," in Bátori, ed., *Stadische Gesellschaft und Reformation*, 234-64; Yves M. Bercé, *Fête et revolte: Des mentalités populaires du XVIe au XVIIIe siècle* (Paris: Hachette, 1976).

[34]Miriam U. Chrisman, *Lay Culture, Learned Culture: Books and Social Change in Strasbourg, 1480-1599* (New Haven: Yale University Press, 1982).

[35]Volker Press, *Kaiser Karl V, König Ferdinand, und die Entstehung der Reichsritterschaft* (Wiesbaden: Steiner, 1976).

second half of the sixteenth century. Press has correlated this long period of indecision with zones of general religious indifference in which nobles seem to have cared little for the theological storms raging among the townsmen.[36] In an age that we characterize as intensely religious, these zones of indifference cry out for further study. Despite our brave concentration on the towns, the social fact is that the landed classes dominated Germany down to the nineteenth century.[37] We cannot afford to remain locked in the formulae of textbooks and ignorant of them. Press has only begun what should become a major effort.

Not only the nobles need attention. For decades the study of peasants and religion has gyrated hysterically around the flames of the Peasants' War to the almost total neglect of other sources and other periods. The visitation articles of various territories become rich sources in the second half of the sixteenth century, and it seems amazing that we have done so little to get at them. We may discover that peasants were not simply ignorant of the formal religious principles taught in catechisms but that they had their own ideas on religious danger and health. A recent study of David Sabean, for example, argues that when villagers stayed away from communion the pastors might worry about the delinquent's soul but other villagers worried about the implicit attack on their own corporate health.[38] Staying away from communion was a form of hostility that was thought to work mysteriously. Witchcraft accusations also often showed a preter-theological concern for the mysterious bonds of community and for evil as disloyalty. We cannot proceed with these histories if we persist with the ideas of the dominant clerical and magisterial classes. Villagers did not just receive or ignore the religious ideas presented to them. Like everyone else they apprehended and modified what thoughts they found useful.

It turns out that even the much-studied burghers have surprises to offer us if we are willing to go beyond the customary legal establishment of Protestantism. Basel, for example, was an officially evangelical town from 1529 onward, but unlike some other towns it preserved an openness to intellectual ferment for another fifty years.[39] Until 1580 or so Basel was hardly a bastion of rigid Protestant orthodoxy. Nor were the "Calvinist" towns of the Netherlands. One of the most important features of the Dutch Reformation, in fact, was its

---

[36]Press, "Adel, Reich und Reformation," at 372-374.

[37]Thomas W. Robisheaux, "Peasants and Pastors: Rural Youth Control and the Reformation in Hohenlohe, 1540-1680," *Social History* 6 (1981): 281-300; Heide Wunder, "Bauern und Reformation im Herzogtum Preussen," in Peter Blickle, ed., *Bauer, Reich und Reformation: Festschrift für Günther Franz* (Stuttgart: Ulmer, 1982), 235-51.

[38]David W. Sabean, "Communion and Community: The Refusal to Attend the Eucharist in Sixteenth Century Protestant Württemburg," in *Mentalitäten und Lebensverhältnisse. Beispiele aus der Sozialgeschichte der Neuzeit. Rudolf Vierhaus zum 60. Geburtstag* (Göttingen: Vandenhoeck und Ruprecht, 1982), 95-107.

[39]Guggisberg, *Basel in the Sixteenth Century*, 45-48.

imperfection.[40] Contrary to the desires of preachers, after 1566 and especially after 1572 Catholics and other dissenters had to be tolerated even though the public church was Calvinist.[41] Throughout the seventeenth century an extremely large minority of about forty percent remained Catholic. Calvinists sustained themselves as a ruling minority in the United Provinces, a position that dictated its own conditions for public and ecclesiastical life. Similar studies might reveal similar problems and similar histories in the various *Paritätstädte* of the Empire. Even towns with a facade of unity could turn out to harbor hosts of doubts, doubters, and dubious Christians. We need to take a look before we too hastily conclude that we can end our story with the abolition of the Catholic mass.

In conclusion, I commend a closer look at the idea of phases and a more careful study of the social reality of religion in the sixteenth century. Otherwise I have no path-breaking new methodology to advertise. Adolf von Harnack doubtless was over simplifyng when he snorted, "Methode, das ist Mutterwitz!" but he was not all wrong. It is easy to become so enamored of one historical method, whether anthropological or structuralist or Marxist, that we exclude topics and perspectives from our view simply because our method doesn't handle them well. Social historians of the Reformation need to learn to read pamphlets and sermons and vernacular translations as well as tax rolls and visitation protocols. I am afraid that German historians are still far from being able to produce any worthy counterpart to Keith Thomas's *Religion and the Decline of Magic*. But the eclecticism for which I speak has no better name than erudition, a goal rather than a method. So shall we read without theory? No one can, although historical theories are often only implicit and unconscious. And clearly enough the stories we tell will have some point, if only dispersive, deconstructive, defamiliarizing, or ironic.[42] Still, we can hope to do more to shape the theories and ironies we actually use. Ideas and theories, I have suggested, are like quicksilver in our hands. We can lose an idea altogether by being too tight fisted or too open handed, but if we carry an idea we cannot avoid imposing our own shape upon it. And when we do, we ought to know what we have done, for only in this way does the practice of history raise the consciousness of us all. And this is part of the liberation I have in mind when I look forward to a social history of ideas in the Reformation.

---

[40]Woltjer, "Stadt und Reformation in den Niederlanden."

[41]Heinz Schilling, "Religion und Gesellschaft in der calvinistischen Republik der Vereinigten Niederlande: 'Öffentlichkeitskirche' und Säkularisation; Ehe und Hebammenwesen; Presbyterien und politische Partizipation," in Petri, ed., *Kirche und gesellschaftlicher Wandel*, 197-250.

[43]I am persuaded by Hayden White that most history written today is ironic if not intentionally dispersive. See his *Metahistory* (Baltimore: Johns Hopkins University Press, 1973).

Harold Grimm as a student

The Reformation, Purgatory, and Perpetual Rents in the Revolt of 1525 at Frankfurt am Main

Lawrence P. Buck
Widener University

ONE OF THE MOST WIDESPREAD GRIEVANCES in the German urban insurrections of 1525 concerned rents and rent charges. Dissidents aired complaints on the topic at Cologne, Münster, Osnabrück, Nördlingen, Mainz, Würzburg, Nuremberg, Langensalza, Boppard, Limburg, and Frankfurt am Main.[1] The universality of the problem of rent charges is sufficient justification for an inquiry into this topic. The fact that the standard surveys of the Peasants' War and the urban revolts either ignore the issue of rent charges or pass over it in vague, misleading terms makes a systematic study all the more needed. Frankfurt am Main offers one of the best cases for such a study not only because the baneful effects of rent charges were particularly severe there, but also because several different groups—city council, religious reformers, and rebel leaders—attempted to deal with the problem during the urban revolt of 1525.[2]

The early Reformation movement in Frankfurt concentrated on a group of themes that were interrelated with the topic of rent charges, specifically opposition to the doctrine of purgatory, rejection of the practice of endowing purgatory masses, and criticism of the perpetual rent charges that made up these endowments. When one realizes the especially grievous situation that existed in sixteenth century Frankfurt regarding rent charges it is quite understandable that these themes would attract the attention and support of the citizenry.

[1] Kurt Kaser, *Politische und soziale Bewegungen im deutschen Bürgertum zu Beginn des 16. Jahrhunderts* (Stuttgart: Kohlhammer, 1899), 206 n. 1

[2] The ravages of the Second World War destroyed many of the most important archival sources for sixteenth century historical research on Frankfurt. Some of the more important sources that are still extant in the Frankfurt City Archive (Frankfurt Stadtarchiv = StaFfm) include the Bügermeisterbücher (= Bmb.), which provide an elliptical record of deliberations during city council meetings, and the Ratschlagungsprotokolle (= Rsp.), which record the disposition of matters which came before the council. The most important printed sources include the journal of a canon from the collegiate Church of Our Lady, Wolfgang Königsteins Tagebuch (= Königstein, Qu. 2) contained in H. Grotefend, gen. ed., *Quellen zur Frankfurter Geschichte* (Frankfurt a.M.: Carl Jügels Verlag, 1888), vol. 2: *Frankfurter Chroniken und annalistische Aufzeichnungen der Reformationszeit*, ed. Rudolf Jung, 27-173; and the city chancellor's narrative of the revolt of 1525 known as Johann Marstellers Aufruhrbuch (= Aufruhrbuch, Qu. 2) in ibid., 174-230. Finally, Karl Euler has brought together selections from a group of important materials in the Haus-, Hof- und Staatsarchiv in Vienna in "Beiträge zur Reformationsgeschichte der Stadt Frankfurt a. M.," *Archiv für Frankfurts Geschichte und Kunst*, ser. 3, 9 (1907): 159-210 [hereafter cited as Euler, *AFGK* (1907)].

These topics were certainly not peculiar to Frankfurt. Luther himself had spoken out against rent charges in his *Von Kauffshandlung und Wucher* (1519, 1520, 1525) and in his *Ordnung eyns gemeynen kastens* (1523); he had criticized private masses and endowed purgatory masses in his *De abroganda missa privata* (1522).[3] However, what is new in Frankfurt is that the implications of these ideas were drawn up in an integrated reform program by the popular leaders of the early evangelical movement and by the urban rebels. The so-called "Evangelical Brothers" led by the shoemaker Hans von Siegen drew the logical implication from the rejection of the doctrine of the mass as a sacrifice, namely, the rejection of purgatory masses and the abolition of the rent charges that supported these endowments.

In order to understand why these themes were so relevant to the Frankfurt populace it is necessary to know the function of rent charges and to appreciate the special circumstances in Frankfurt. The generic term "rents" refers to a wide variety of payments including ground rents, life rents or annuities, and rent charges (which could be terminal or perpetual, primary or secondary). Ground rents (paid to the owner of land which was let for building upon), and life rents (annuities, paid in return for an investment of capital with interest) are still in use today. Sixteenth century ground rents and life rents were similar enough to their modern counterparts as to require little clarification. A rent charge, however, is a more archaic financial instrument, which needs some explanation.[4]

The sale of rent charges developed in the Middle Ages as a means of providing relatively large sums of money in an economy that frequently suffered

---

[3]*Luther's Works: American Edition*, ed. Jaroslav Pelikan and Helmut T. Lehmann, 55 vols. (St. Louis: Concordia Publishing House and Philadelphia: Muhlenberg Press, 1955-1972), vol. 36: *Word and Sacrament II*, ed. Abdel Ross Wentz (Philadelphia: Muhlenberg Press, 1959), 129-230; and vol. 45: *The Christian in Society II*, ed. Walther I. Brandt (Philadelphia: Muhlenberg Press, 1962), 159-94 and 231-310. Hereafter cited as *LW:AE*.

[4]On the topic of rent charges see Wilhelm Lühe, "Die Ablösung der ewigen Zinsen in Frankfurt a. M. in den Jahren 1522-1562," *Westdeutsche Zeitschrift für Geschichte und Kunst* 23 (1904): 36-72, 229-272 (hereafter cited as Lühe); Friedrich Mattausch, "Die Nürnberger Eigen- und Gattergelder: Frei Erbleihe und Rentenkauf in Nürnberg von den ersten urkundlichen Nachweisen bis zur Gegenwart," *Mitteilungen des Vereins für Geschichte der Stadt Nürnberg* 47 (1956): 1-106; W. J. Ashley, *An Introduction to English Economic History and Theory*, pt. 2: *The End of the Middle Ages* (New York: Longmans, Green and Co., 1901), 405-11 (hereafter cited as Ashley); M. M. Postan, ed., *The Cambridge Economic History of Europe* (Cambridge, England: Cambridge University Press, 1963), vol. 3: *Economic Organization and Policies in the Middle Ages*, 527-33, 542-53; Max Neumann, *Geschichte des Wuchers in Deutschland bis zur Begründung der Heutigen Zinsengesetze (1654)* (Halle: Verlag der Buchhandlung des Waisenhauses, 1865), 212-92; D. Stobbe, "Zur Geschichte und Theorie des Rentenkaufes," *Zeitschrift für deutsches Recht* 19 (1860): 178-217; Siegfried Hoyer, "Wirtschaftliche und soziale Ursachen des deutschen Bauernkrieges, Das Beispiel Thüringen," *Zeitschrift für Geschichtswissenschaft*, vol. 29, no. 12 (1981): 1106-20; Wilfried Trusen, "Zum Rentenkauf im Spätmittelalter," in *Festschrift für Hermann Heimpel* 2 (Göttingen: Vandenhoeck und Ruprecht, 1971): 140-58.

from cash shortages. A property owner or the holder of an hereditary tenancy would sell a rent charge to some wealthy person. The property owner received a sum of money from the wealthy person in return for encumbering his property with the obligation of paying rents either for a term of years or in perpetuity. Terminal rent charges were more common in the countryside; perpetual rents were more typical of cities. The one obligated to pay rents was referred to as the seller or debtor; the one who received the rents was the rent charger. Rent charges could be advantageous to both parties—the seller, who might be a merchant in need of capital for his trade, could thus acquire such capital; the rent charger could guarantee for himself and his heirs an ongoing income.

Legally, rent charges were real property which could be taxed, and sold or bequeathed by the rent charger to a third party. Thus the heirs of the original debtor frequently had to pay rents for monies that they had never seen, to persons who had no part in the original agreement. They inherited a perennial liability.

A given property or tenancy could be encumbered with more than one rent charge, that is, with secondary rent charges. In fact, in the later Middle Ages it frequently happened that the number of rent charges against a piece of property amounted to more money than the property was worth. In this circumstance the debtor (or his heirs) might simply abandon the property and, in the case of Frankfurt, move to the faubourg Neustadt to build a new house. There was thus a constant threat of urban decay. For example, in Frankfurt, the number of abandoned and burned-out properties increased from 165 in 1420 to 403 in 1463.[5] In 1541 Emperor Charles V himself referred to the bad effects of rent charges, noting decayed and deserted houses that gave "an ugly appearance to entire streets [of Frankfurt]."[6]

This urban blight was in part a consequence of the deliberate investment policies of the ecclesiastical establishment of Frankfurt. The monasteries and collegiate churches saw rent charges as a safe field of investment through which they could obtain a steady income without assuming the obligation of managing additional properties.[7] On the other hand, the ecclesiastical establishment was unavoidably driven to become a collector of rents by the very operation of the intercessory apparatus of the Church; pious men gave rents as endowments for chantries, anniversary masses, memorial masses, lights, and the like. In 1522 a wealthy merchant, Jakob Heller, left 400 fl. to the Dominican cloister for the purchase of rents to pay for daily requiem masses, special anniversary masses, and a perpetual light.[8]

[5]Karl Bücher, *Die Bevölkerung von Frankfurt am Main im XIV. und XV. Jahrhundert,* Sozialstatistische Studien 1 (Tübingen: H. Laupp, 1886), 202 (hereafter cited as Bücher).

[6]Lühe, 240. See also Aufruhrbuch, Qu. 2, 272 ff.

[7]Ashley, 406.

[8]Hermann Dechent, *Kirchengeschichte von Frankfurt am Main*, vol. 1 (Frankfurt a. M.: Kesselringsche Hofbuchhandlung [E. v. Mayer] Verlag, 1913), 54 (hereafter cited as Dechent). In 1521 Johann de Castro, the dean of the St. Leonhard's chapter, left his church 400

Rents in support of intercessory institutions were certainly not peculiar to Frankfurt, but there were many more clerical rents in Frankfurt than in other cities.[9] Sixteenth century inventories of ecclesiastical rent charges show thousands of rents owed to the collegiate and monastic churches.[10] The growth of the number of ecclesiastical rent charges threatened the city's financial stability, for since 1299 clerical properties in Frankfurt had enjoyed tax exempt status. Approximately one-third of all real estate in the city was held in mortmain, and the ever-expanding number of clerical rent charges not only burdened the citizenry and contributed to urban blight, it also deprived the city of part of its tax base.[11]

The council was fully cognizant of the problem posed by ecclesiastical rent charges and had worked throughout the later Middle Ages to resolve the issue. It ultimately failed to do so because of the recalcitrance of Frankfurt's own clergy. As early as 1376 Emperor Charles IV ordered that lands or rent charges used as endowments for intercessory institutions be sold to laymen within one year, and that any new grants likewise be secularized within a year of receipt.[12] In 1407 the council negotiated an agreement with the Archbishop of Mainz that restated Charles IV's order, but with a new cut-off date: ecclesiastical rents acquired after 1407 had to be secularized within a year. This part of the agreement, however, was not enforced and the expansion of mortmain properties continued apace.[13] The period from 1420 to 1463 saw a 144 percent increase in the number of abandoned properties in Frankfurt. Convinced that

fl. for a rent to support requiem masses in his name, Georg Eduard Steitz, "Reformatorische Persönlichkeiten, Einflüsse und Vorgänge in der Reichsstadt Frankfurt a. M. von 1519-1522," *AFGK*, n.s. 4 (1869): 138 [hereafter cited as Steitz, *AFGK (1869)*]. On endowed intercessory institutions in general see K. L. Wood-Legh, *Perpetual Chantries in Britain* (Cambridge, England: Cambridge University Press, 1965), passim; and Alan Kreider, *English Chantries: the Road to Dissolution* (Cambridge, MA: Harvard University Press, 1979), passim (hereafter cited as Kreider).

[9]Georg Ludwig Kriegk, *Frankfurter Bürgerzwiste und Zustände im Mittelalter* (Frankfurt a. M., 1862; reprint ed., Frankfurt a. M.: Verlag Sauer und Auvermann KG, 1970), 142 (hereafter cited as Kriegk). In a response to the council in 1526 on the question of rents the Frankfurt clergy stated: "Dweil die Ewige Zinns in allem rechten geistlich und weltlich der Kirchen und irer Dienern zugelassen sein und sonderlich in Frankfurt merertheils alle stifftungen uff solche zinns gemacht / wo die dan abgeloest sollten werden wurde aller gotts dinst inwendig kurtzen jaren niedergelegt / die stifftungen und letzsten willen der Verstorben zerprochen." Hans Wolter, "Die Gravamina des Klerus gegen den Rat von Frankfurt am Main im Jahre 1526," *Archiv für mittelrheinische Kirchengeschichte* 25 (1973): 222 (hereafter cited as Wolter).

[10]For example, see StaFfm, Leonhardstift, Buch 5a; Leonhardstift, Akten 386a; Liebfrauenstift, Städtische Akten 53; Barfüsserkloster, Urkunden und Akten, No. 121, Items No. 1 and 2; Bartholomaus-Stift Urkunden No. 3876 (1525).

[11]Kriegk, 105 n. 2.

[12]Ibid., 106.

[13]Dechent, 38-39. The agreement of 1407 served as a kind of ecclesiastical constitution for Frankfurt. Since it had been negotiated with Archbishop Johann of Mainz it was known as the *Rachtung Johannes*.

clerical rents were to blame, the council issued a stern decree in 1439 prohibiting future sales of perpetual rents; henceforth only extinguishable rents could be laid on properties in the city. To enforce this decree, the council ordered that all new rent charges had to be sealed in the city chancellory in the presence of the burgomaster and another council member. The clergy, however, circumvented the council's order by sealing new rents with the seals of their collegiate churches. Thus they foiled another attempt at reform.[14]

The problems created by rent charges continued to worsen through the fifteenth century. In 1470 Emperor Frederick III renewed Charles IV's order of 1376; in 1477 even Pope Sixtus IV issued a bull affirming the imperial order.[15] The council, however, found all of these orders unenforceable.

In the sixteenth century the city government took a slightly different approach. Rather than prohibit the sale of perpetual rents, it attempted to make all clerical rents redeemable. At a meeting with other cities in Esslingen in 1522, Frankfurt's delegates unsuccessfully tried to arrange for a cooperative urban policy on rents at the upcoming imperial diet at Nuremberg.[16] In 1523, in response to popular protests at the Frankfurt village of Bornheim, the council tried to make all rents, both clerical and secular, redeemable.[17]

The year 1524 saw the develoment of a vociferous evangelical movement in Frankfurt and in its hinterland. Protesters demanding a reform preacher in the village of Sachsenhausen provided the council with the opportunity of opening discussions with superior church officials at Mainz on a variety of topics, including rent charges. The episcopal officials of the archdiocese, however, rejected all of Frankfurt's suggestions for reform, leaving the city fathers in a weak position for facing the unrest of 1525.[18]

The city council was not alone in its opposition to rent charges, for the early evangelical reformers in Frankfurt also treated this topic. At times they attacked the institution of rent charges directly; at other times they aimed their attacks at the theology that justified the intercessory institutions which many of the rents supported. To appreciate the interconnection between rent charges and the Frankfurt evangelical movement, it is necessary briefly to consider the theology that supported the endowed chantries.

Two tenets were chiefly responsible for the theological foundations supporting the establishment of intercessory institutions: the Catholic doctrine of the Mass and the teaching on purgatory. According to the latter, the souls of those who died penitent were made fit for paradise by expiation of venial sins

---

[14]Lühe, 43; Bücher, 201-202; and Friedrich Bothe, *Geschichte der Stadt Frankfurt am Main*, 3d ed. (Frankfurt a. M.: Englert und Schosser, 1929), 182 (hereafter cited as Bothe).

[15]Kriegk, 106.

[16]Bothe, 298.

[17]Euler, *AFGK* (1907), 165-66.

[18]Ibid., 207.

through punishment in purgatory. According to the former, the Mass was seen as a reenactment of Christ's original sacrifice which could accrue merit for the souls of the departed, suffering in purgatory. As a consequence of these teachings it became customary for those who could afford to do so to endow chantries where stipendary priests could say services in the name of the departed to shorten his stay in purgatory. The clergy who performed these services were known as "stipendary priests," "Mass priests," "chantrists," "intercessory priests" or "purgatory priests."[19]

The early evangelical movement in Frankfurt concentrated on the themes of endowed masses and rent charges. The man who preached the first evangelical sermon in Frankfurt was Hartmann Ibach, a native of Marburg and a former Franciscan monk. The reform-minded patrician trustees of the St. Catherine's nunnery brought Ibach to Frankfurt to preach a series of Lenten sermons at the cloister church in 1522. On March 11 he spoke against perpetual rents, urging his listeners not to pay their rents, but rather to use this money for poor relief.[20]

Ibach's attack did not go unnoticed by the Frankfurt clergy. The archconservative parish preacher, Dr. Peter Meyer, personally attended Ibach's sermon on rents and was so disturbed that he went to Maniz to urge archepiscopal officials to take action against him. The council, fearing that the Lenten sermons might cause some sort of civil disturbance, entreated Ibach to leave Frankfurt.[21]

Ibach departed in 1522. Sometime around mid-year 1523 the secular administrators of St. Catherine's arranged for another advocate of reform, Diethrich Sartorius, to come to Frankfurt. Formerly a cleric at the parish of St. Ignatius at Mainz, Sartorius came to Frankfurt as a preacher at St. Catherine's. From his chancel there he attacked the doctrine of the Mass as a sacrifice, and the traditional teaching on purgatory, both of which were essential for the meaningful operation of endowed intercessory institutions. Officials at Mainz complained about Sartorius' sermons, but he withstood archepiscopal opposition much longer than Ibach; he preached regularly at St. Catherine's

---

[19]Kreider, 19, 32. Kreider uses the term "intercessory institution" to cover a variety of endowed services—requiems, anniversary masses, memorial masses, and lights. Anniversary masses are said on the 8th, 30th, or 365th day after the death or burial of an individual, or annually on the anniversary of the death or burial. Memorial masses are performed in memory of a deceased person. Lights are wax tapers placed on altars or before images of saints in hope that passersby will be reminded of the departed and pray for his soul. See *LW:AE* 45: 180 n. 37.

[20]Dechent, 84-88; Georg Eduard Steitz, "Der Humanist Wilhelm Nesen," *AFGK*, n.s. 6 (1877): 123 [hereafter cited as Steitz, *AFGK* (3877)]. The secular administrators of St. Catherine's were Hamman von Holzhausen and Johann Frosch, two very influential patricians in the city.

[21]Steitz, *AFGK* (1869), 114-17; Karl Bauer, "Der Bekenntnisstand der Reichsstadt Frankfurt a. M. im Zeitalter der Reformation," *Archiv für Reformationsgeschichte* 19 (1922): 210.

from about mid-year 1523 until November 1524. During this year and a half he exercised considerable influence upon the populace of the city.[22]

The citizenry soon began to organize its own protests against the doctrine of purgatory and against perpetual rent charges. Sartorius' ministry had led to the founding of groups calling themselves "Evangelical Brothers" or "lovers of the Word of God and Christian truth" in Frankfurt, in Sachsenhausen, and in Oberursel.[23] The Evangelical Brothers came to the council's attention after they became embroiled in a dispute with the Dominicans over the doctrine of purgatory. On November 6, 1524, three of the Evangelical Brothers of Frankfurt had a verbal exchange with the Dominican lector over a sermon he had preached on All Souls' Day. Later these same men presented the Black Friars with five articles that they had drafted to provide scriptural proof for the rejection of the doctrine of purgatory. The altercation was serious enough to prompt the Dominicans to ask the council for protection against these men.[24]

The leader of the Evangelical Brothers in this dispute was the shoemaker, Hans von Siegen. He was also the most important leader of the popular rebellion in 1525. At that time one of his most adamantine demands concerned the extinguishment of perpetual rent charges and the conversion of the revenues for intercessory institutions into monies for the common chest.[25]

The Evangelical Brothers remained organized and active through the winter and spring of 1524-1525. November 24, 1524, they submitted a petititon to the city council asking that Sartorius be allowed to continue his ministry in Frankfurt. (The council had forced him to stop his preaching in November.)[26] In April 1525, just before open revolt broke out in the city, they submitted to the council Eleven Articles in which were articulated ecclesiastical, political, and economic grievances. These articles were eventually incorporated into the much larger Forty-six Articles of the Frankfurt insurgents. Of particular interest for this study are points 3 and 10 of the Eleven Articles, which called for perpetual rents to be made extinguishable, and for undocumented rents to be declared null and void.[27] The actions of the Evangelical Brothers clearly demonstrate the interconnection of concerns about purgatory, intercessory institutions, and perpetual rent charges.

---

[22]Euler, *AFGK* (1907), 189, 195; Dechent, 103; Sigrid Jahns, *Frankfurt, Reformation und Schmalkaldischer Bund*, Studien zur Frankfurter Geschichte 9 (Frankfurt a. M.: Verlag Waldemar Kramer, 1976), 36 (hereafter cited as Jahns); Johannes Kübel, *Die Einführung der Reformation in Frankfurt a. M.* (Frankfurt a. M.: H. L. Brönners Druckerei und Verlag, 1933), 26.

[23]The Oberursel group did not form until 1525 when Sartorius moved there.

[24]Euler, *AFGK* (1907), 189-91.

[25]Aufruhrbuch, Qu. 2, 193.

[26]Euler, *AFGK* (1907), 192-95.

[27]Rudolf Jung, "Zur Entstehung der Frankfurter Artikel von 1525," *AFGK*, ser. 3, 2 (1889): 200-201[hereafter cited as Jung, *AFGK* (1889)].

In late fall or winter of 1524 the Evangelical Brothers were joined by Gerhard Westerburg, a native of Cologne, and a doctor of Roman and canon law, who had become a dedicated follower of Andreas Carlstadt. City chancellor Johann Marsteller recorded in his so-called Aufruhrbuch that Westerburg's home became the meeting place of the evangelical brothers, and that Westerburg conferred and intrigued with Hans von Siegen and his cohorts "by day and by night" but "especially at night."[28] Westerburg's influence was of special significance, for he is best known for his opposition to the doctrine of purgatory. In fact, his only known publication up to this time was a work entitled *Vom fegefewer und standt der verscheyden selen. . . .*[29]

Westerburg did not found the Evangelical Brothers, as has sometimes been argued, for he did not even come to Frankfurt until after they had already had their altercation with the Dominicans.[30] However, he himself need not have been in Frankfurt to influence the Evangelical Brothers, for when he published his anti-purgatorial treatise in 1523 he sent the available copies to Cologne, to the Netherlands, and to Frankfurt.[31] Thus it is quite possible that the Evangelical Brothers had read his work before he arrived in their midst. In any case he joined the Evangelical Brothers after November 1524. His presence thus helps to explain popular attitudes toward the doctrine of purgatory, intercessory institutions, and the endowed rents that supported them.[32]

[28]Aufruhrbuch, Qu. 2, 196.

[29]Copies of Westerburg's treatise are in the British Museum and in the rare book room of the University of Pennsylvania Van Pelt Library. I have made use of the latter copy.

[30]Georg Eduard Steitz, "Dr. Gerhard Westerburg der Leiter des Bürgeraufstandes zu Frankfurt a.M. im Jahre 1525." *AFGK*, n.s. 5 (1872): 71 [hereafter cited as Steitz, *AFGK* (1872)] holds that Westerburg founded the Evangelical Brothers. This, however, is very unlikely. Because of his close association with Andreas Carlstadt, he was included in the order that exiled Carlstadt and Martin Reinhard from Saxony. On November 26, 1524, Westerburg wrote to Duke John of Saxony in an attempt to get the order against him lifted. His appeal was unsuccessful, and he left Saxony for Frankfurt. Westerburg did not learn of the order against him until October or November 1524 when he returned to Jena from Zurich. The fact that as late as November 26 he was still seeking to maintain Jena as his home suggests that he had not yet taken up permanent residence in Frankfurt. Since it is possible to date the Evangelical Brothers in Frankfurt as early as November 6, at the time of their altercation with the Dominicans, it is unlikely that Westerburg could have founded the group.

[31]Steitz, *AFGK* (1872), 21.

[32]There are some interesting similarities between Westerburg's treatise and the ideas of the Evangelical Brothers. He began with an introduction addressed to the government of his native Cologne, urging the city council to do away with the "useless, expensive, and satanically ostentatious" practices that resulted from the doctrine of purgatory. (Westerburg's phrase was "unnutz, unkost und teufflichs bracht," *Vom Fegefewer. . .* , University of Pennsylvania, fol. 1v.) When, in 1525, Hans von Siegen was negotiating for the council's acceptance of the Frankfurt Articles he added a point of his own (number 43) that "henceforth no ostentatious display shall occur at requiems and anniversary masses" (es soll nun hienfuro kein gebrenge mit seelmessen und begegnnuss gehaltenwerden) Aufruhrbuch, Qu. 2, 190. In the actual exposition of his tract Westerburg began by establishing the primacy of scriptural authority and then argued that there was no scriptural foundation for

Westerburg's influence extended well into the famous urban revolt of 1525. In fact, in an attempt to end the revolt the council expelled him from the city. The events of 1525 clearly demonstrate the importance of the topic of perpetual rents in the minds of the Frankfurt populace.

The insurrection broke out on April 17, 1525, during the high point of the Peasants' War. About noon on Easter Monday dissidents from the faubourgs of Sachsenhausen and Neustadt assembled in the St. Peter's churchyard in Neustadt to protest perpetual rents and excise taxes.[33] Although Hans von Siegen was not one of the original organizers of this protest, he quickly emerged as the most important leader of the dissidents. That day the protesters attacked the Dominican monastery and the nearby Fronhof (where St. Bartholomew's chapter stored the rents it collected in kind). The council's immediate response to the protesters, on April 18, was to order the collegiate churches[34] and the monasteries to make complete inventories of their rents and other incomes,[35] "damit der gemeine Mann gestillt werde."[36] This was not enough, though, for the street demonstrations continued. On April 18 the rebels armed themselves and occupied the city gates; April 19 they elected a sixty-one member committee to negotiate with the city council.[37]

The Committee of Sixty-one drafted a statement of grievances, which it presented to the council on April 20. But before the concessions could be sealed and formally adopted, Hans von Siegen and his cohorts added three more points of their own (that is, articles 43, 44, and 45). With the concluding statement the council thus agreed to forty-six points; hence the document is known as the Forty-six Articles.[38]

After the rebels forced the council to accept the Forty-six Articles, they formed the Committee of Ten to oversee the implementation of reforms. This

the doctrine of purgatory. This was, of course, precisely the approach that the Evangelical Brothers took in their argument with the Dominicans, Euler, *AFGK* (1907), 190. Westerburg concluded his treatise with a denunciation of all the intercessory institutions and burial practices related to the doctrine of purgatory: he condemned exequies, requiems, anniversary masses, memorial masses, lights, commendations of souls, catafalques, canopies, death bells, and the consecration of graves, *Vom fegefewer. . .*, University of Pennsylvania, fol. 10v. He suggested that the money used to support these institutions and practices should be used instead to provide welfare for the poor. Here again his tract stated an idea that was identical to the demands of Hans von Siegen and the Evangelical Brothers, Aufruhrbuch, Qu. 2, 193. Clearly Westerburg exercised a strong influence on the Evangelical Brothers of Frankfurt.

[33]Kriegk, 506-7 n. 108; Königstein, Qu. 2, 84; Aufruhrbuch, Qu. 2, 175.

[34]St. Bartholomew's, St. Leonhard's, and the Church of Our Lady.

[35]See above n. 10. These inventories provide a direct insight into the operation of ecclesiastical rents.

[36]Quoted in Kriegk, 156.

[37]For a contemporary narrative of events see Königstein, Qu. 2, 84-89; and Aufruhrbuch, Qu. 2, 174-93.

[38]Aufruhrbuch, Qu. 2, 176-78 and 184-90. See also Günther Franz, *Quellen zur Geschichte des Bauernkrieges* (Munich: R. Oldenbourg, 1963), 455-61.

committee (which included Hans von Siegen) drafted three supplemental articles, two of which treated rents and their extinguishment.

Altogether, articles 6, 11, 14, and 43 of the Forty-six Articles,[39] and articles 1 and 3 from the Committee of Ten[40] dealt with rents and their use for endowment of intercessory institutions. Article 6 abolished undocumented rents; article 11 made documented perpetual rents extinguishable; article 14 placed all future endowed alms in the common chest and abolished intercessory institutions such as anniversary or memorial masses; article 43 proscribed all "ostentatious display" (*gebrenge*) at requiem masses. The additional articles from the Committee of Ten simply clarified the above points. One declared invalid all rents which were contrary to these concessions; another held that no rents need be paid until their legality was documented. The Committee of Ten also asked the council to consider transferring the revenues of confraternities and endowed anniversary and memorial masses to the common chest.[41]

It would be misleading to imply that perpetual rent charges and intercessory institutions were the only matters of concern for the Frankfurt dissidents, for the Forty-six Articles treated a variety of political, economic, and religious issues. However, it is fair to say that, judging from the negotiations over the implementation of the concessions, no issue was more sensitive or more hotly contested than the question of rent charges. The reforms posed problems of implementation, for the rents that they treated might be documented with legal or illegal seals, owed to local or foreign rent chargers, and paid to support secular or ecclesiastical interests. They therefore needed extensive clarification. During the months of May and June ongoing deliberations between the council and the citizenry attempted to make the necessary interpretations.[42]

The steps taken toward implementation ultimately went for naught because Frankfurt's noble neighbors forced the cancellation of all concessions to the citizenry after the defeat of the Peasants' Revolt. On July 2, 1525 the council had to comply with the demands of Archbishop Richard of Trier, Elector Ludwig of the Palatinate, and Bishop Wilhelm of Strasbourg (representing the Archbishop of Mainz) that the Forty-six Articles be declared null

---

[39]Aufruhrbuch, Qu. 2, 185, 186, 190.

[40]Ibid., 192-93.

[41]Ibid., 193.

[42]The council feared punitive countermeasures against Frankfurt rent charges if it interfered with the incomes of foreign investors, and therefore hoped for a coordinated policy in conjunction with other cities. The clergy rightly feared that articles 6 and 11 would undermine the economic base of the ecclesiastical structure, Wolter, 222, and therefore tried to block execution of rent reforms. The populace, however, remained intransigent in its demand for speedy and comprehensive implementation of these articles. Kriegk, 185 ff.; Aufruhrbuch, Qu. 2, 204-12; StaFfm, Rsp. 2 (1517-1533), fol. 96v, 101r, 102r,103v, 105, 106v, 107r; Bmb. 1524, fol. 120v, 121r, Bmb. 1525, fol. 9v, 10r, 18r, 18v, 25r, 25v, 28r, 39r, 39v, 45v-46r, 46v, 56v, 58v-59r, 64r, 754, 79, 87r, 98r, 101v, 105v, 111r.

and void.[43] Thus the idealistic reforms of the Frankfurt rebels ended in a disheartening defeat. The council felt that the Forty-six Articles went too far, but it still wanted to correct the destructive effects of the expansion of ecclesiastical rent charges within the city. However it did not succeed in makng perpetual rents extinguishable until 1561, and then only after extensive diplomatic negotiations.[44]

It is obvious that the Frankfurt reformers, dissidents, and clergy alike perceived the interconnection of the doctrines of purgatory and the Mass with the endowed intercessory institutions and the perpetual rent charges that provided for Mass priests. If the Mass were not a meritorious work and if there were no purgatory, then there would be no need for the intercessory clergy nor the payment of rents that supported them. The rebel leader Hans von Siegen and the Evangelical Brothers understood this all quite well, for they supported Diethrich Sartorius in his attack on the Mass and purgatory; they clashed with the Dominicans over the same issues; and they drafted articles of grievance demanding the aboliton of perpetual rents and the conversion of revenues for intercessory institutions into monies for the common chest.

The council and the citizenry further realized that there was a direct connection between the expansion of ecclesiastical perpetual rent charges on the one hand and the erosion of the city's tax base and the spread of urban blight on the other. The council tried to resolve the problem by working slowly and deliberately with the Archbishop of Mainz and the emperor to find a way of making perpetual rents extinguishable and to find a way of stopping the spread of ecclesiastical rent charges. The rebels tried to accomplish a similar goal by using force instead of diplomacy and by attacking not only the symptom (perpetual rents) but also the cause (endowed chantries and the theology of purgatory). In 1525 neither approach succeeded, though by 1561 the council's efforts finally paid off.

The events of the years 1524-1525 clearly demonstrate the potential for revolutionary change contained within the ideas of Luther and his early followers. Luther's criticism of rent charges, his condemnation of private masses, and his rejection of the doctrine of purgatory are reflected in the demands of the evangelical reformers and urban rebels of Frankfurt. Hartman Ibach, Diethrich Sartorius, Gerhard Westerburg, and especially Hans von Siegen and the Evangelical Brothers focused their attacks on the doctrine of the Mass as a sacrifice, on the doctrine of purgatory, on the endowment of anniversary masses, and on the destructive effects of rent charges. They used ideas that they held in common with the Lutheran Reformation in their attempt to achieve far-reaching religious and economic reforms in Frankfurt am Main.

[43]Kriegk, 189-194; Aufruhrbuch, Qu. 2, 225; Jahns, 39; StaFfm, Bmb. 1525, fol. 34v, 35r, 38r, 39r, 39v, 40v-41r, 48r, 50r.

[44]Lühe, 263; Max Quarck, *Soziale Kämpfe in Frankfurt am Main vom Mittelalter bis an die Schwelle der grossen Revolution* (Frankfurt a. M.: Verlag der Buchhandlung Volksstimme, Maier & Co., 1911), 20.

Harold Grimm as a student in Europe

Protestantism, Divorce, and
The Breaking of The Modern Family

Thomas Max Safley
Wabash College

"AND HENCE IS CONCLUDED," WROTE MARTIN BUCER in his *De Regno Christi* (1557), "that matrimony requires continuall cohabitation and living together, unless the calling of God be otherwise evident; which union if the parties themselves dis-joyn either by mutual consent, or against the others will depart, the marriage is then brok'n."[1] Later in the same chapter, the author expanded his idea:

> that God requires of them both so to live together, and to be united not only in body but in mind also, with such an affection as none may be dearer and more ardent among all the relations of mankind, nor of more efficacy to the mutuall offices of love, and loyalty. They must communicate and consent in all things both divine and human, which have any moment to well and happy living. . . . Thus they must be to each other, if they will be true man and wife in the sight of God, whom certainly the Churches ought to follow in their judgement.[2]

These sentiments seem strangely anachronistic. They suggest two relatively modern phenomena: a companionate marriage based on affection and a complete divorce by mutual consent.

It is not surprising that virtually no one—theologians, jurists nor magistrates—accepted Bucer's suggestions regarding divorce or his vision of marriage.[3] Matrimony in early modern Europe was much more than an emotional and physical union of individuals. It was also a union of families and fortunes, the recognized foundation upon which society and economy rested.

Divorce, as understood and initiated by Protestants, was necessarily a strictly regulated institution. The process of obtaining one was arduous.

---

[1] *The Judgement of Martin Bucer Touching Divorce Taken Out of the Second Book Entitl'd Of the Kingdom of Christ*, trans. John Milton, in *The Complete Prose Works of John Milton* (1643-1648), reprint ed., New Haven: Yale University Press, 1959) 2:464.

[2] Ibid., 465.

[3] "No one was more forceful on the subject than Martin Bucer, by all accounts the most 'liberal' sixteenth century Protestant on the subject of divorce." Steven E. Ozment, *When Fathers Ruled* (Cambridge, MA: Harvard University Press, 1983), 84. Wendel put forward this opinion as well, adding that Bucer had but limited influence on the marital ordinances of Strasbourg. Francois Wendel, *La mariage à Strasbourg à l'epoque de la reforme, 1520-1692* (Strasbourg: Imprimerie alsacienne, 1928), 160.

Grounds were limited to a few objective, verifiable circumstances. The proceedings themselves were time-consuming and expensive. Remarriage was permitted only by consent of court. At every point, divorce excited the most intense magisterial scrutiny; marital dissolution could not be a matter of individual whim.

Divorce epitomizes the tension between individual and communal concerns in the formation and dissolution of marriage. Despite the fact that it was closely controlled for communal and disciplinary purposes, divorce was and remains a quintessentially individualistic act. One person, driven by a determination to escape an intolerable union, began the procedure by petitioning the competent court. By so doing, that individual risked estrangement from his or her family, disruption of the domestic economy, and alienation from the community. It is at least arguable that individual self-sufficiency and self-fulfillment were by no means generally accepted principles of early modern society.

Today the individual aspects of divorce are for the most part obvious and unchallenged. The availability of divorce by mutual consent reduces the bond between couple and community, attenuating the social responsibilities of the married pair and hindering the expression and exercise by the community of its concerns in the matter. The extraordinary frequency of divorce is weighty proof of the isolation of the modern nuclear family and the self-sufficiency of its members.

This self-sufficiency, this independence from kin and community, is the endpoint described by modern historians for the development of marriage and the family.[4] Even the most recent of these analyses, however, have failed to examine fully the consequences of divorce for pre-modern domestic history and modern historical theory.[5] An act of self-determination in a society whose values were essentially communal could only confuse existing concepts of marriage and family. Furthermore, the nature of early modern divorce suggests

[4]"But the four key features of the modern family—intensified affective bonding of the nuclear core at the expense of neighbors and kin; a strong sense of individual autonomy and the right to personal freedom in the pursuit of happiness; a weakening of the association of sexual pleasure with sin and guilt; and a growing desire for physical privacy—were all well established by 1750 in the key middle and upper sectors of English society. The nineteenth and twentieth centuries merely saw their much wider social diffusion." Lawrence Stone, *The Family, Sex and Marriage in England 1500-1800* (New York: Harper & Row, 1977), 8-9. "[T]he father-mother-children triad acquired an ever-increasing independence with respect to the *lignage* and to the servants, until in the nineteenth century it became the fundamental nucleus of our society." Jean-Louis Flandrin, *Families in Former Times* (New York: Cambridge University Press, 1979), 9. The most recent study of the early modern family to win attention accepts the basic terminology and characteristics established by Stone. See Ozment, *When Fathers Ruled*, 2.

[5]Only Ozment devotes an entire section to the issue of divorce. His worthwhile analysis, however, is not convincingly integrated into his general thesis regarding marriage and the family during the Reformation. See Ozment, *When Fathers Ruled*, 80-99.

that the rise of the individual, self-sufficient family was, contrary to the impression gained from magisterial studies, neither unopposed nor linear. A study of marital dissolutions, therefore, should contribute to our understanding of domestic history. Beyond further defining relations between family members and between family and community, such a study should clarify the dynamic between individual and communal values.

Modern scholars tend to associate the rise of the family as a self-sufficient, affective unit with the influence of Protestant marital and familial doctrines.[6] One may attribute this, at least in part, to the importance granted the writings of Protestant theologians and canonists. Their understanding of marriage and divorce grew from their opposition to Catholic sacramental theology and Catholic glorification of celibacy.[7] Protestants inveighed against the practice of celibacy which, they claimed, denigrated the marital state and promoted carnal sin.[8] While denying that marriage was a sacrament, a divinely ordained institution through which the faithful might win grace and achieve salvation, they recognized it as a highly religious state created by God to allow humans to practice their created sexual natures without sin.[9] Protestant theologians thus concluded that marriage was one key to a Christian life; it formed a refuge from sin for the corrupt and weakened spirits of humankind. In this context, marriage—and, by extension, divorce—became events in the pilgrimage of the individual soul. They were institutions uniquely oriented toward the spiritual needs of husband and wife.

[6]Ozment makes this connection overtly. "While it cannot be claimed that Protestants were unique in achieving loving marriages, their new marriage laws, especially those that recognized for the first time a mutual right to divorce and remarriage, became the most emphatic statement of the ideal of sharing, companionable marriage in the sixteenth century. The domestic legislation of the Reformation encouraged both spouses to be more sensitive to the other's personal needs and vocational responsibilities, thereby enhancing the status of both men and women." Ozment, *When Fathers Ruled*, 99. Stone acknowledged this connection as well. "This shift of emphasis toward the nuclear family was given powerful support by Reformation theology and practice." Stone, *The Family, Sex and Marriage*, 135. While insisting that there was very little difference between the attitudes toward marriage of Puritan and Catholic moralists, J.-L. Flandrin admitted that "the Puritans were already more insistent than the Catholics on married love as a duty." Flandrin, *Families in Former Times*, 166. Even Peter Laslett, reviewing family structure in certain Calvinist villages in trans-Danubian Hungary, seems to find departures from this association between Protestantism and the nuclear family exceptional and idiosyncratic. "Since Calvinism has been often thought of as the harbinger of rationalism, modernism, the capitalist way of life, the facts from the Danube lands serve to show how complicated yet fascinating the familial historical geography of Europe turns out to be." Peter Laslett, *Family Life and Illicit Love in Earlier Generations* (New York: Cambridge University Press, 1977), 17.

[7]Martin Luther, *De captivitate Babylonica ecclesiae praeludium*, (1520), in *D. Martin Luthers Werke*, 100 vols. (Weimar: H. Böhlau, 1883-1966), 6: 550, 554. Henceforth cited *WA* (Weimare Ausgabe). Ulrich Zwingli, *De vera et falsa religione* in *Huldrychi Zvinglii Opera*, 8 vols. in 10 (Zurich: F. Schultheis & S. Hohr, 1832) 3: 231.

[8]Zwingli, *De vera et falsa religione*, in *D. Huldrychi Zvinglii Opera* 3: 227.

[9]Luther, *Vom ehelichen Leben* (1522) in *WA* 10²: 276. Zwingli, *De vera et falsa religione* in *D. Huldrychi Zvinglii Opera*, 3: 227.

Again, the tension between communal and individual interests is apparent. Although forced to consider marriage and family in terms of individual sin and salvation, Protestant theologians remained very much aware of the concerns and values of society in such domestic issues. Martin Luther, Ulrich Zwingli, and their followers did not encourage complete individual freedom either in marital formation or in marital dissolution.[10] Through their discussions of the legitimacy of divorce, the few acceptable grounds for divorce, and the possibility of remarriage after divorce, it is possible to infer their ultimate conviction that these were social institutions which fulfilled social functions.

That marriage was an ideal state and a refuge from temptation for the vast majority of human beings suggests that it was a necessary precondition of orderly society. Carnal sin not only manifested individual corruption but also violated social norms. Therefore, a marriage in which husband and wife failed for whatever reason to comfort one another physically, emotionally, and materially threatened their salvation and social order. Divorce and remarriage proved obvious remedies.

Protestants were nearly unanimous in their affirmation of the legitimacy of divorce.[11] Quite apart from social imperatives, Protestants and Catholics alike recognized that divorce was sanctioned in scripture.[12] Beyond the issue of legitimacy, however, their unanimity dissolved over considerations of the licit grounds for divorce and the possibility of remarriage for one or both spouses thereafter.

Adultery was the only ground for divorce clearly cited in scripture and the only ground on which all reformers could unreservedly agree.[13] Nevertheless, all magisterial reformers found ways to recognize other grounds.

Luther advocated divorce and remarriage for both spouses in cases of adultery, malicious abandonment, and *impotentia antecedens*.[14] In these instances, marriage failed to protect the spouses from sin as a result of crime, absence, or disability.

Later apologists for Lutheran marital doctrine, among whom Johannes Brenz and Johannes Bugenhagen were most influential, proved more conservative on the issue of divorce than the master himself.[15] Both accepted adultery and impotence but found abandonment distinctly problematic. For them, abandonment could only serve as grounds for divorce when one spouse was absent, could not be located, and was presumed dead.[16] Under any other circum-

---

[10]Ozment, *When Fathers Ruled*, 85.

[11]Ibid., 83.

[12]Matt. 19:9.

[13]Hartwig Dieterich, *Das protestantische Eherecht in Deutschland bis zur Mitte des 17. Jahrhunderts* (Munich: Claudius Verlag, 1970), 70.

[14]Luther, *Vom ehelichen Leben* (1522) in *WA* 10²: 288.

[15]Ozment, *When Fathers Ruled*, 85.

[16]Dieterich, *Das protestantische Eherecht*, 105.

stances, the marriage remained intact. Brenz admitted the fact that imperial law offered further grounds for divorce. He argued that, while a Christian could not accept these as valid, they remained necessary for the ordering of society.[17] Brenz clearly recognized the communal facets of divorce.

On the issue of remarriage, Brenz and Bugenhagen permitted it for the innocent or injured spouse but were vague, again departing from Luther, regarding the guilty. Bugenhagen did not raise the issue, and Brenz spoke only of punishment and excommunication.[18] Here too, Brenz, at least seems clearly cognizant of the need for discipline and restitution, both of which are communal concerns.

Swiss reformers proved more liberal on the issues of divorce and remarriage than their Lutheran counterparts. In theory, they recognized a broader array of grounds for divorce and advocated remarriage for both spouses. Zwinglian Protestants insisted that divorce be considered not only in the light of scripture but also according to the essential purpose of marriage and the precedents of Roman and Mosaic Law.[19] Ulrich Zwingli, therefore, joined Luther in his denial of marriage as a sacrament, his criticism of the practice of celibacy, and his conception of marriage as a crutch for human weakness.[20] Yet, he went a step further by recognizing not only adultery, abandonment, and impotence but also contagious disease as valid grounds for divorce.[21] In all but the last two circumstances, where physical infirmity prevented marriage from fullfilling its essential purpose, both parties could and should remarry. Zwingli's colleague in Basel, Johannes Oecolampadius, advocated divorce but feared the potential consequences of degenerating public and private morality.[22]

Divorce brought individual and communal needs and values into close association and potential conflict. Although Protestant theologians approached the issues of marriage and divorce in the context of the individual soul, their concerns, as Oecolampadius made clear, extended well beyond the married couple and the nuclear family. By arguing the disciplinary necessity of marriage and divorce, by limiting the grounds for divorce, and by advocating remarriage, they revealed the communal aspects of their concerns. For Protestant theologians, though doctrine might change, the existence of a *corpus Christianorum*, the unity of individuals and authority in one great community, did not. Protestants did not promote self-interest or self-sufficiency.

[17]Ibid., 107.

[18]Ibid., 104.

[19]Adrian Staehelin, *Die Einführung der Ehescheidung in Basel zur Zeit der Reformation* (Basel: Helbing & Lichtenhahn, 1957), 50.

[20]Zwingli, *De vera et falsa religione* in *D. Huldrychi Zvinglii Opera*, 3: 227-231.

[21]Ibid.

[22]Staehelin, *Die Einführung der Ehescheidung*, 51.

Rather, they sought to define explicitly the rights and responsibilities binding husband to wife and couple to community.

Theologians viewed domestic issues in terms of individuals, their souls and salvation. The context changes dramatically and necessarily when jurists and magistrates consider divorce. Their concerns are even more overtly social and communal.

Protestant jurists tended to be more conservative than theologians on divorce and remarriage.[23] This may be attributed in part to their legal training, the insistence on establishing validity through precedence, and in part to their vision of stable society, communities governed by law and tradition. To them, divorce and remarriage could not be easily reconciled with a traditional, Christian society. Jurists insisted that marriage was essentially indissoluble and that only the gravest circumstances justified divorce.[24] While displaying general agreement that adultery was such a circumstance, legal experts could not agree regarding malicious abandonment and never considered abuse or life-threatening situations.[25] Likewise, they were divided over the issue of remarriage for the innocent spouse and never raised the question about the guilty spouse's rights.[26] In the latter's case, death or banishment were the legal responses of precedent, obviating any remarriage.

The noted Protestant jurist, Bonifacius Amerbach, serves as an excellent case in point. He joined the Reformation only after considerable hesitation and developed opinions concerning divorce that were relatively conservative.[27] Scripture offered clear justification for divorce on grounds of adultery. Remarriage, for the innocent spouse only, was justified according to Roman and Mosaic Law but could not be derived easily from scripture. The only other ground for divorce, to which Amerbach would agree, was malicious abandonment. Insanity and disease, cases in which no crime had been committed, could not, according to Amerbach, be admitted as grounds for divorce.[28] He insisted not only on scripture but also on some criminal act as justification for granting a divorce. Amerbach clearly associated divorce with communal order rather than individual well-being.

Theologians and jurists—theorists all—limited divorce in various ways. They restricted both the reasons and grounds to a relatively small corpus based on precedents established in scripture and statute. Viewing the actual ordinances, the rules by which magistrates regulated divorce and remarriage, it becomes clear that practice took the matter forward, establishing principles where theorists remained silent.

[23]Dieterich, *Das protestantische Eherecht*, 243.

[24]Ibid., 142.

[25]Ibid., 143.

[26]Ibid.

[27]Staehelin, *Die Einführung der Ehescheidung*, 52.

[28]Ibid., 53.

For the cities of southern Germany and German-speaking Switzerland, the most influential marital code was that of Zurich.[29] Written in 1525, it became a model for the cities of Basel, Bern, St. Gall, and Schaffhausen and influenced marital legislation from Ulm and Augsburg to Strasbourg and the Duchy of Wurtemberg. The marital ordinance of Zurich provides a general outline for the Protestant governance of marriage and divorce.

The magistrates of Zurich, influenced by Zwingli, took a practical approach to marital dissolution. Apart from arguments for the legitimacy of divorce based on scripture, the authorities reasoned that marriage could not exist when spouses failed to observe their physical and material responsibilities to one another.[30] The magistrates, therefore, viewed circumstances which impaired sexual fidelity and harmonious, conjugal life as legitimate grounds for divorce. The Zurich marriage court granted divorce in cases of proven adultery and impotence.[31] Judicial discretion made conviction of a capital crime, malicious abandonment, contagious disease, and deadly assault potential grounds for divorce as well.[32] By the same token, the magistrates of Zurich treated remarriage for divorced persons as a necessary means of preventing further sins and offense. The innocent or injured spouse could remarry without further ado, while the guilty party could remarry only upon good behavior over a period of time.[33]

The magistrates, by virtue of their daily governmental responsibilities, engaged more directly in ordering society than theologians or jurists. The debate concerning the legitimacy of divorce, grounds for divorce, and remarriage after divorce were less important than establishing workable means by which disrupted marriages could be dissolved, spouses could be punished or protected according to their merits, and community order could be maintained. For these reasons, marital ordinances do not rehearse long theological or juridic debates. Rather, the codes furnish practical, even functional reasons for innovations such as divorce. Likewise, grounds for divorce are more numerous, and greater latitude is given the magistrates in order to fit law to individual circumstances. Sanctions against marital offenses tend to be less extreme—fines replacing corporal or capital punishment—in the hope that reconciliation might be achieved and order preserved.[34] Strict rules governed the settlement of property after divorce, a topic few theoreticians broached.

The magistrates knew that marriage involved property as well as persons and established a new unit of production and consumption in the community.

[29]Walther Köhler, *Zürcher Ehegericht und Genfer Konsistorium* (Leipzig: M. Heinsius Nachfolger, 1932, 1942), 231.

[30]Ozment, *When Fathers Ruled*, 84.

[31]Köhler, *Zürcher Ehegericht und Genfer Konsistorium*, 74-75.

[32]Ibid., 76.

[33]Ibid., 113.

[34]Ozment, *When Fathers Ruled*, 86.

Divorce dissolved these units necessitating a careful redistribution of property to punish malefactors and protect the innocent.

In Strasbourg, property laws were strict in order to nullify any advantage the guilty spouse might hope to enjoy from the divorce. Gifts exchanged at marriage were returned to the donors. Hence, the *Morgengabe* reverted to the husband or to his heirs, and the dowry reverted to the wife. Usufruct of the dowry, however, passed to the children.

Communal property, the property gained during the marriage, was divided into shares. The innocent spouse received his or her customary share immediately. The guilty lost all direct control of his or her share. That person's share became the property of the children or the nearest heirs. The city inventoried the guilty party's share and determined the usufruct of one-third as a pension for the support of the guilty person. If no communal property existed, the city could provide a pension for the guilty spouse as an act of charity.[35] The purpose of such tight regulation was twofold: to punish the guilty and to protect the rights of the innocent. As with remarriage, these ordinances protected public order and furthered communal goals. Indeed, these rules could act both as a deterrent to marital offenses by raising the potential costs of a divorce and as an inducement to divorce by insuring the injured party a generous property settlement.

The marital ordinances of Basel, enacted in 1533, offer further proof of the functional, communal concerns of the Protestant magistracy. In justifying divorce, the magistrates of Basel abandoned all arguments from religious scripture or legal theory. Instead, they asserted that divorce was necessary to prevent private repudiation and remarriage, to prevent individuals from judging their own cases.[36] To punish the guilty, to prevent illicit advantage and to control the formation and dissolution of marriages, the Basel city council legalized divorce. Explicit grounds for divorce were stated: proven adultery, malicious abandonment, impotence, capital crime, deadly abuse, and contagious disease.[37] Remarriage proved as difficult an issue for the city fathers of Basel as it did for theologians and jurists. In the final analysis, the magistrates acted conservatively, denying remarriage to the guilty party and permitting it for the innocent after an interval of one year.[38] Again, the purpose was to punish the offender and prevent anyone from taking illicit advantage of a divorce. Property settlements, as in Strasbourg, were draconian. The innocent spouse

---

[35]Wendel, *La mariage à Strasbourg*, 170.

[36]"Item so haben wir geordnet, das kein ehegemahel (auch von offentlichs ehebruchs wegen) den andern seinen ehegemahel aigens gwalts verlossen oder von im schlagen mög, dieweil in aigner sach niemants sein selbs richter sein soll . . . ." *Ehegerichtsordnung*, 27 October 1533, *Gerichtsarchiv* Ue2, Staatsarchiv des Kantons Basel-stadt, 23. Henceforth cited SaKBs.

[37]Ibid., 22.

[38]Ibid., 24.

retained control of all of his or her private property as well as the dowry. Furthermore, that person acquired outright control of two-thirds of the communal property acquired by the couple during their marriage. The guilty spouse lost all independent control of his or her private property. The remaining one-third of the communal property passed to the city, which inventoried and administered it in trust. From the proceeds, the city provided a minimal pension sufficient to cover the guilty party's basic necessities and nothing more.[39] By assuring a minimal income, the magistrates hoped to avoid still greater crimes and disorders resulting from want on the part of the guilty spouse.[40] When the guilty party died, the property devolved to his or her nearest heirs.

The Basel divorce ordinances extended the power of divorce as a means of communal oversight and regulation. The reasons for divorce stated specifically that it was a means to prevent private, individual action and to strengthen the prerogative of the community to review domestic affairs. The grounds served not only to limit the range of marital dissolution but also to reveal those offenses which the magistrates thought sufficiently grave to justify the risks of divorce.[41] Property settlements were so organized as to assure that the innocent spouse would continue to enjoy the same standard of living while the guilty party would be reduced to a ward of the state. The communal goals of orderly marital life within the purview of the community seem to have been foremost in the minds of the Basel magistrates.

Theologians, jurists, and magistrates were keenly aware of the risks posed by divorce. Beyond whatever scriptural, legal, or practical justification might exist for it, divorce encouraged a sort of private initiative which could threaten communal order and discipline. Protestant leaders felt bound to recognize divorce, but none of them encouraged it. Rather, they sought to define the relationships—the rights and responsibilities between husband and wife and between couple and community. Most important, they tied the married pair closely to the community by making marital formation and dissolution matters of communal oversight and regulation, matters that only the community could legitimize. This constituted a unique extension of communal authority and communal values. It is true that early modern states had exerted themselves since the 1400s to control the institutions responsible for marriage and morality.[42] Yet divorce legislation went beyond concerns about institutional coherence or political autonomy to place the very existence of marriage under the control—one might even say in the service—of the state. The theoretical consideration of divorce suggests that the Protestant Reformation, far from

[39]Ibid., 27.
[40]". . . und damit das brüchig theil durch mangel leiblicher narung nit in grosser sinden falle." Ibid.
[41]Thomas Max Safley, *Let No Man Put Asunder: The Control of Marriage in the German Southwest, A Comparative Study, 1550-1600* (Kirksville, MO: Sixteenth Century Publishers, Inc., 1984), 6. Permission granted by publisher to reprint information on divorce.
[42]Köhler, *Zürcher Ehegericht und Genfer Konsistorium*, 236.

promoting self-interest or self-sufficiency on the part of individuals, sought to bind them more firmly to the community.

Historical studies of divorce have concentrated attention for the most part on doctrine and legislation. As has been suggested, this poses a problem not only for the understanding of divorce but also for theories concerning marriage and the family in general. Much less is known about the public practice of divorce and the private experience of marital dissolution. Few studies have analyzed divorce litigation from the period of the Reformation, and fewer still have penetrated personal attitudes and reactions as recorded in private correspondence and diaries.

Studies of litigation are generally hampered by narrow chronological limits. The recognition of revealing patterns of court activity requires longer periods of study. Nevertheless, Protestant divorce litigation in the sixteenth century suggests some intriguing possibilities. In Zurich during the years of Zwingli's dominance (1525-1531), the marital court heard seventy-two petitions for divorce on grounds of adultery,[43] twenty-eight on grounds of impotence,[44] and 107 on grounds of abandonment.[45] In Calvinist Geneva, between 1559 and 1569, the Consistory heard nine divorce petitions, but granted only three: two on grounds of abandonment and one on grounds of impotence.[46] The Massachusetts Bay colony granted twenty-seven divorces between 1639 and 1692, thirteen on grounds of desertion and adultery, nine for a variety of reasons ranging from adultery to abuse to abandonment, and five for which no specific grounds were recorded.[47]

These statistics are too superficial to reveal much concerning the experience of divorce. Abandonment consistently proves the most frequent cause for dissolution, suggesting perhaps that domestic arrangements in early modern Europe were subject to great stress. One might conclude that magistrates were concerned for the appearance of stable, harmonious marriage in the form of uninterrupted cohabitation. Only under these circumstances could such larger communal goals as sexual fidelity, material sustenance, and the orderly devolution of property be achieved.

More detailed and lengthy studies have been conducted in the city of Basel.[48] These should support firmer conclusions on the individual and communal aspects of divorce.

[43]Ibid., 109.

[44]Ibid., 115.

[45]Ibid., 120.

[46]E. William Monter, "The Consistory of Geneva, 1559-1569," in *Bibliotheque d'Humanisme et Renaissance* 38 (Geneva: Droz, 1976): 473.

[47]Edmund S. Morgan, *The Puritan Family: Religion and Domestic Relations in Seventeenth-Century New England* (New York: Harper & Row, 1966), 37.

[48]See Staehelin, *Die Einfuhrung der Ehescheidung*, and Safley, *Let No Man Put Asunder*.

Unlike Zurich, where there was an initial rush of divorce cases in the first years of the court's activity, Basel exhibited a more steady flow of divorce litigation. Between 1529 and 1554, the Basel marital court granted 148 divorces: 99 on grounds of adultery, 21 on grounds of abandonment, 14 on grounds of a capital crime, 6 each on grounds of impotence and disease, and 2 on grounds of deadly abuse.[49] From 1550 to 1592, the pace slowed somewhat. The marital court granted 226 divorces: 114 on grounds of adultery, 84 on grounds of abandonment, 19 on grounds of deadly abuse, 7 on grounds of impotence, and 2 for uncertain causes.[50]

Divorce litigation over the first sixty years of the Basel court's existence forms a wave-like, harmonic pattern with a period of brisk activity followed by a period of inactivity and finally returning to greater activity. Between 1529 and 1550, divorce levels ranged between five and ten cases annually. Exceptional maxima occurred in 1534 and 1535, with twelve and thirteen divorces respectively, and exceptional minima occurred in 1533, with one divorce, and in the period 1546 to 1548, with one, two, and three cases per year.[51] The period 1550 to 1570 saw relatively few divorces in Basel. Cases rarely exceeded five per year except in 1551 when seven divorces were granted.[52] From 1570 to 1590, the Basel marital court experienced its period of greatest divorce litigation with annual case levels ranging between six and fifteen.[53]

Divorce litigation in Zurich and Basel differed in two fundamental regards. First, magistrates in the two cities did not emphasize the same offenses. On the basis of divorces granted, Zurich authorities emphasized abandonment, setting uninterrupted cohabitiation as a value. Basel magistrates granted more divorces on grounds of adultery, thus showing greater concern for sexual fidelity. This emphasis diminished relative to other marital responsibilities after 1550. Second, Zurich experienced an initial burst of divorce litigation between 1525 and 1531, while Basel divorce litigation was more consistent at a lower frequency. In Zurich, the magisterial attitude toward divorce may have been more relaxed and liberal. Zurich offered somewhat broader grounds for divorce and gave both spouses the right to remarry. The innocent party could do so immediately, while the guilty spouse had to wait for a period of time (usually one year) to prove good behavior. Thereafter, he or she could petition the court for permission to remarry.[54] Given this relative liberality and availability of divorce, individuals and couples rushed to the court to ligitimize through divorce some other arrangement, pursued privately or through a

---

[49]Staehelin, *Die Einführung der Ehescheidung*, 181-98.

[50]Safley, *Let No Man Put Asunder*, 142.

[51]Staehelin, *Die Einführung der Ehescheidung*, 181-98.

[52]Safley, *Let No Man Put Asunder*, 134.

[53]Ibid.

[54]Köhler, *Zürcher Ehegericht und Genfer Konsistorium*, 113.

Catholic official, to dissolve their marriages.[55] The immediate peak of activity, were it the result of such behavior, would decline slowly thereafter to more "normal" levels. In Basel, the harmonic pattern suggests an initial burst of litigation between 1529 and 1559—suggesting a pattern of behavior similar to that in Zurich albeit at much lower levels— to legitimize *de facto* separations, followed by the expected decline between 1550 and 1570. The recovery after 1570 remains to be explained. Taken as a whole, the trends in divorce litigation in Basel resemble a reasonable pattern of adjustment by community and magistracy to a new legal institution.[56] The magistrates employed statutes and procedures to frustrate divorce, promote reconciliation, and preserve marriage. This being the case, it follows that fewer people would have approached the court to validate extra-legal separations and that patterns of litigation would be more constant over time.

The authorities of Basel did not encourage divorce. Rather, they employed a considerable legal arsenal to prevent marital dissolution, granting divorce only as a last resort. Reconciliation was the constant goal.[57] As noted, the grounds for divorce were limited to a few objective, verifiable circumstances. When proper grounds existed, however, the marital court could still be dilatory. It imposed special fees (the *Scheidgulden*) in cases of divorce and ordered mandatory jail sentences for those people petitioning for divorce but unable to afford the fees.[58]

The court often brought pressure to bear on the plaintiff to forgive an erring spouse.[59] If the plaintiff proved determined to proceed, the magistrates often ordered extended negotiations, in the presence of friends, relatives, and officials, to resolve the conflict and preserve the marriage. In the case of *Misslin v. Heidellin*, Lienhart Misslin sued for divorce from his wife of fourteen years, Salome Heidellin.[60] He accused her of being an alcoholic. In his words, she could not seem to drink enough wine. He alleged that she sold his property in his absence to support her habit and recently committed adultery. Salome admitted her offenses and begged forgiveness. She pleaded that Misslin was often away on business and her problems stemmed from loneliness. The case was introduced on 1 September 1591. The court ordered negotiations aimed at reconciliation on five occasions, delaying a final decision until 17 March 1592.

[55]Such reasoning has been convincingly applied to the city of Rouen during the French Revolution. See Roderick Phillips, *Family Breakdown in Late Eighteenth-Century France* (Oxford: Oxford University Press, 1980), 46.

[56]Safley, *Let No Man Put Asunder*, 133.

[57]Köhler, *Zürcher Ehegericht und Genfer Konsistorium*, 63. Monter observed similar values practiced by the Consistory of Geneva. See Monter, "The Consistory of Geneva, 1559-1569," 474.

[58]*Ehegerichtsordnung*, 27 October 1533, 21.

[59]Staehelin, *Die Einführung der Ehescheidung*, 64. Ozment noted that Lutheran canonists insisted that attempts be made to reconcile a couple before permitting them to divorce one another. See Ozment, *When Fathers Ruled*, 85-86.

[60]Protocol, 17 March 1592, *Gerichtsarchiv* U7, 159r-159v, SaKBs.

In the end, the divorce was denied, despite failure to reconcile the couple, and they were ordered to resume cohabitation.

On 9 February 1591, Margreth Shaffner entered a petition for divorce from Jacob Ulmann, a miller, on grounds of abuse.[61] She claimed that he beat her so frequently and severely that she bore their first child prematurely and that she had to fear for life and limb. Ulmann received a procedural delay to prepare his response and, finally, claimed that the premature birth was due to his wife's poor health. He denied abusing his wife but did admit one instance of adultery which, he claimed, his wife knew and forgave. Again, the court ordered prolonged negotiations but, when these failed, granted the divorce on 8 May 1591.

As demonstrated in both these cases, the Basel magistrates could prolong a divorce, and increase its expense, by ordering negotiations. With the same ends in mind—avoiding divorce and preserving marriage—the judges could delay a hearing to allow a given problem time to resolve itself, or they could hold special sessions to examine the probity of particular evidence. Barbel Schonbergerin sued Rudolf Hasslin for divorce on 21 August 1571.[62] She claimed that she suffered a prolonged illness two years after her marriage. During that time, Hasslin beat her despite all her efforts to please him. He eventually sold all his property leaving her ill and destitute. Hasslin admitted the rightful sale of his property but denied anything beyond verbal abuse. He claimed his wife was often impudent and moved him to anger. The court ordered a one-month waiting period in the hope that the dispute might resolve itself. Whether it did or not is unknown; the couple did not reappear in court.

Delays could be more involved. On 28 November 1581, Katharina Hug sued for divorce from Fridlin Frickher, accusing him of abuse and adultery.[63] Frickher responded that the adultery had occurred long ago. He had confessed and been forgiven, and he now wished to live with Hug as husband and wife. The court ordered a six-month trial separation to allow time for the couple to forgive and forget. They did neither, reappearing before the marital court on 29 May 1582 to renew their divorce. Hug claimed there was no improvement in Frickher's behavior; he continued to abuse her and commit adultery. Frickher denied any wrongdoing but claimed he had no wish to live with Hug if she was determined to leave. After reviewing the case and hearing witness testimony, the court granted a divorce.

At the end of a long procedure, often extending over months at great expense to the litigants, involving accusation and counter-accusation, requiring extended witness testimony, and including forced negotiations, the court reached a verdict. While most decisions simply granted or denied the divorce, some could be surprising in their sophistication. If there was any glimmer of

---

[61]Protocol, 9 February 1591, *Gerichtsarchiv* U7, 154v-156v, SaKBs.

[62]Protocol, 21 August 1571, *Gerichtsarchiv* U6, 36r-36v, SaKBs.

[63]Protocol, 28 November 1581, *Gerichtsarchiv* U7, 74v-76r, 78r-78v, SaKBs.

hope for a reconciliation, the court would deny a divorce and order the couple to resume married life. Such was the case in *Misslin v. Heidellin*. To such a verdict, the magistrates occasionally attached orders for special action to put aside some material threat to marital harmony. In the case of *Kriegin v. Zell* the residence of the married couple in the home of in-laws was the cause of the dispute.[64] The court ordered the couple to establish their own domicile within fourteen days. On 15 January 1590, Peter Eckhlin sued for divorce from Anna Adell.[65] Married eighteen months, Eckhlin became fearful of his wife's strange, threatening behavior. She slept with a knife at her side, giving him cause to fear for his life. He claimed she pledged allegiance to the devil and had, on occasion, tried to commit suicide by throwing herself in the Rhine. He wished to divorce her because she was a danger to herself and others. Adell denied pledging allegiance to the devil and attempting suicide. She claimed that Eckhlin beat her so savagely that she slept with a knife to protect herself. She hoped the court would grant the divorce on grounds of abuse. After considering these claims and the testimony of witnesses, the court denied a divorce. Instead, it permitted a four-year separation, during which time Eckhlin was to support his wife while she received psychological treatment. Insanity was valid grounds for divorce according to Basel law. That the court was willing to risk an extended separation and order therapy for the afflicted spouse, rather than simply grant a divorce, is eloquent testimony to its desire to avoid the dissolution of marriage.

If a divorce was granted, the court faced the issue of remarriage. Basel denied remarriage to spouses found guilty of some marital crime; the city allowed an innocent spouse to remarry only by petitioning the court after a one-year waiting period. Unlike Zurich, where the innocent spouse could remarry at will and the waiting period was intended to determine contrition and good behavior on the part of the guilty spouse, Basel used the waiting period to foster reconciliation. The city fathers might shorten or dispense with the waiting period if there was objective danger of immorality as a result of enforced celibacy or if there was no hope for reconciliation.[66] Otherwise, they generally held to the letter of the law. Between 1550 and 1592, following 226 divorces, there were only 57 petitions to remarry lodged by divorced persons. Nearly all of these petitions included the observation that reconciliation was impossible, and the court granted the vast majority of them.

Basel marital court sought to preserve marriages and granted divorces only when absolutely necessary. The magistrates insisted on marriage as the preferred state for their citizens. The paucity of remarriage petitions suggests that the citizens may not have agreed. Whether they remarried without court consent, emigrated from the community, or chose to remain single is unclear.

---

[64]Staehelin, *Die Einführung der Ehescheidung*, 69.

[65]Protocol, 15 January 1590, *Gerichtsarchiv* U7, 145r, 157v, SaKBs.

[66]Staehelin, *Die Einführung der Ehescheidung*, 102.

Yet, the tantalizing possibility remains that individuals either did not generally share the Protestant commitment to matrimony as a facet of social doctrine and discipline or did not feel obliged to expose further their personal
affairs in a public forum.

Such patterns of litigation as these give some evidence of public behavior
on the parts of public officials and private individuals. They reveal the values
and concerns of the authorities and, perhaps, of a broad cross-section of the
community, but they obscure the personal experience of divorce. Court protocols are inevitably compromised by the hand and eye of the magistrate. Nevertheless, they permit some observations on individual perceptions of and
responses toward marital dissolution.

Protestant authorities, in Basel and elsewhere, did not encourage divorce
but sought to preserve marriages whenever possible. When divorces were
granted, they were based on specific grounds as listed in the apposite statutes.
Written by the authorities, these laws were the result of their marital concerns
and values. The granting of divorce, therefore, tells much about the ideals of
those in authority. In Basel, adultery, abandonment, and abuse, the three
grounds most frequently cited in specific divorce cases, were the offenses
which the authorities considered most threatening to proper marital life. Sexual fidelity and peaceful, continuous cohabitation were the hallmarks of a
proper Christian marriage. Offenses against any of these forced the magistrates to disregard their advocacy of marriage.

The grounds accepted for divorce and the frequency with which they appear in the litigation reveal communal values and norms. But they indicate aspects of divorce as a private event too. Divorce was a petitory procedure in
which no action was taken by the authorities unless initiated by private petition. Therefore, the grounds alleged in a divorce petition reveal part of the pe-
titioner's experience. Adultery, abandonment, and abuse effectively dissolved
marriages in the minds of the plaintiffs. The very fact that they occurred broke
the bonds between husband and wife. One might argue with some justification that these grounds appear because they alone would yield the desired legal
result. Yet such reasoning suggests a level of both sophistication and duplicity
that cannot be found in the documents. In all events, the Basel magistrates
were sufficiently painstaking in divorce litigation to detect and deny the majority of spurious petitions. It is much more likely that these grounds corre-
spond to the experience of the majority of married persons. A violation of
sexual fidelity, cohabitation, or harmonious conjugality effectively ended a
marriage, and an injured spouse went to court to attain communal acknowl-
edgement of the fact.

Apart from the grounds for divorce, the details of testimony offer a number of observations concerning married life and the causes of its dissolution in
early modern Europe. One striking circumstance is the fluidity of marital life.
Private repudiation and remarriage were common aspects of divorce in Basel.
On 13 December 1558, for example, Catharina Muspachin sued for divorce

from Heini Shnyder.[67] She testified that she married Shnyder after the death of her first husband. Eight days later Shnyder abandoned her and never returned. Muspachin had since learned that Shnyder had married again and was living with his other wife in a nearby village. The plaintiff offered proof of her allegations, and when Shnyder refused to appear in court the magistrates granted the divorce. Similar was the case of *Suter v. Keller*.[68] In 1577, Barbell Suter petitioned for a divorce from Rudi Keller. She claimed that they had married while in service. Keller abandoned her for some time but later returned saying he had established himself in business in the community of Weil am Rhein. They moved there, but he soon disappeared again. For seven years she had heard nothing of him and wished to remarry. Keller's father testified that he believed his son was dead. The court cross-examined Suter and learned that she had no proof of Keller's demise, beyond the father's suspicion, and that she had engaged in sexual relations with her intended second husband. Suter was arrested and fined but granted the divorce and allowed to remarry immediately to prevent further immorality. A final example is the case of *Hepperlerin v. Steiger*[69] In 1581 Anna Hepperlerin sued for divorce from Ulrich Steiger. Steiger, she charged, was a poor provider and, after ten years of impoverished marriage, he left her to fight as a mercenary. Her dire poverty forced her to commit adultery for which she was duly punished. Having returned from war, Steiger refused to live with her. Steiger confirmed all that his wife said adding only that he could not forgive her misdeed and refused to live with an adulterous wife. The court granted the divorce. In these and many other cases, the extended absence or uncertain fate of one spouse created difficulties for the other. Failure to cohabit robbed a marriage of the appearance of stability and created a situation in which poverty, immorality, and bigamy were frequent events.

Another strikingly frequent circumstance of divorce litigation is the complexity of the marital dispute. Although the protocols abbreviate most of the circumstances of a divorce case, omitting what the magistrate believed to be extraneous details in favor of legally significant points, they cannot hide the fact that most marital disputes extend over a long period of time and include circumstances beyond the immediate grounds. In the case of *Schnytzeri v. Heylmann*, initiated on 5 March 1566, Sophia Schnytzeri claimed that she had tolerated numerous offenses over her years of marriage.[70] Her husband violated her marriage contract (seizing and selling her property without compensating her), abused her physically, and refused to cohabit with her. He finally committed adultery, and she decided to sue for divorce. Heylmann fled Basel rather than appear in court, and Schnytzeri received her divorce. On 2 March

[67]Protocol, 13December 1558, *Gerichtsarchiv* U5, 178r, SaKBs.

[68]Protocol, 30 July 1577, *Gerichtsarchiv* U7, 18r, SaKBs.

[69]Protocol, 5 September 1581, *Gerichtsarchiv* U7, 71v, 72v, SaKBs.

[70]Protocol, 5 March 1566, *Gerichtsarchiv* U5, 228v-229r, SaKBs.

1581, Elssbeth Klein sued for divorce from Hans Huober.[71] She charged that he failed to support her, forcing her to suffer such poverty that she could neither keep house nor feed her children. Huober lodged a counter-accusation that for the past four years she had refused to fulfill her conjugal debt. The court dismissed both accusations—his as unfounded, her's as invalid—and ordered the couple to resume cohabitation. Catherina Offenburgin sued for divorce from Claudi Dorchamps on 15 January 1566.[72] She testified that they had moved to Basel three years earlier. Since that time he had alienated all her property without compensating her and had given her no money with which to keep house. After the recent death of their son, he had refused to abide by their marriage contract, failed to cohabit with her, and committed adultery on numerous occasions. Speaking through his representative, Dorchamps claimed that he could not submit to the court because he no longer resided in its jurisdiction. The divorce was granted. Property disputes figure in these, though by no means in all, divorce cases. More striking is the fact that in many cases the actual dispute is more complex than the alleged grounds for divorce.

Again, the tension between communal and individual interests is obvious. The community embodied its values in law and set the court to administer and defend them. Yet, the problems of individuals or couples were frequently much more involved and could be neither fully assessed nor resolved by the marital court. The court could act only when certain violations occurred. Those couples whose problems fell outside the pale of legally recognized offenses were without recourse and could only wait for their marriage to improve or worsen. In such circumstances, extra-legal separations, such as the popular practice of wife-selling or simple repudiation and remarriage, would flourish. The relative unavailability of divorce in Protestant communities—Basel counts as an example of particular conservatism—may explain the infrequency of litigation.[73] It certainly suggests a fundamental incompatibility between Protestant communal interests, which regarded marriage as a social discipline and an ideal way of life, and individual interests, which required efficacious means to redress and resolve marital disputes.[74]

[71]Protocol, 2 March 1581, *Gerichtsarchiv* U7, 65v, SaKBs.

[72]Protocol, 15 January 1566, *Gerichtsarchiv* U5, 227v-228v, SaKBs.

[73]In revolutionary France, divorces were easily obtainable. The courts were not centrally located. Thus litigants did not have to travel far. Fees were minimal. Grounds were generous, including divorce by mutual consent. Settlements protected the material interests of all parties. Under such circumstances, it comes as no surprise that the frequency of divorce was high. See Phillips, *Family Breakdown in Late Eighteenth-Century France.* During the Reformation, Strasbourg was one of the most liberal cities in its treatment of divorce. It is a great pity that no records of divorce litigation there are extant. Scholars have noted the increasing conservatism of Protestant views toward marriage and divorce. Studies should be undertaken to determine the reasons for such a shift, its influence on litigation and on married life. See Wendel, *La mariage à Strasbourg*, 156.

[74]The tension between religious doctrine (especially when raised to a social principle) and socio-economic imperatives has been noted in *ancien régime* France. The matter deserves further evaluation. See Flandrin, *Families in Former Times*, 210.

Legislation and litigation provide copious evidence concerning the pretexts and process of divorce. Relatively little evidence has yet come to light regarding the consequences of divorce. Legal documents necessarily fall silent as soon as a case is closed, and only a very few scholars have found records detailing the private experience of divorced people.[75]

Divorce must have shattered the bonds of affection binding husband to wife and greatly complicated those of children and kin. Yet, as was noted in the cases from Basel, these bonds may have been strained by a complex and extended dispute long before the couple proceeded with a divorce. After a divorce was granted, what became of the family as an affective unit? A marital dissolution could create emotional complications affecting the spouses and especially the children of a truncated family. The potential conflicts of children and step-parents are well documented in early modern France.[76] They have even passed from folk wisdom to folklore in a variety of stories featuring wicked step-mothers.[77] The hatred of the step-mother may have been inspired by the fact that her husband's children competed with her for his affection or competed with her children for the father's estate. In any event, the step-mother of folklore might be interpreted as a metaphor for the truncated family. Bernard Zink, an affluent Augsburg merchant, writing in his diary, remembered his step-mother as a young, proud woman who treated her step-children badly.[78] He added, however, that she was dear to his father and pleased him well. Later in his life, after the death of his first wife, Zink recounted the selection of a second spouse.[79] One of the reasons for marrying Dorothea Kuelinbecklin was that she promised to love and honor Zink's children by his first wife as if they were her own.

Divorce and remarriage could compromise affective solidarity among spouses and children. By the same token, it could strengthen ties with other kin. Hermann von Weinsberg related how he and his brother stood by their sister, Sibilla, during her protracted divorce from Conrad Eck.[80] Hermann defended her in court and loaned her money to support her. His frequent com-

---

[75]Ozment's consideration of the divorce of Sibilla von Weinsberg from Conrad Eck, taken from the diary of Hermann von Weinsberg, is an important exception. See Ozment, *When Fathers Ruled*, 80-83.

[76]Flandrin, *Families in Former Times*, 42.

[77]Ingeborg Weber-Kellermann, *Die Familie: Geschichte, Geschichten und Bilder* (Frankfurt am Main: Insel Verlag, 1976), 22-28.

[78]"Die was ain junge stolze Frau, die was uns Kinden nit günstig und hett uns hert und tet uns übel; aber sie was unserm Vater lieb und geviel im wol, als noch oft und dick alten Mannen jung Weib wol gevallen, dem sei als im ist." Horst Wenzel, *Die Autobiographie des späten Mittelalters und der frühen Neuzeit 2* (Munich: Wilhelm Fink Verlag, 1980), 51.

[79]"Des ward sie vom Hertzen fro und sprach sie wolt mich gern haben und wolt alles das tuen, das ich wolt, und wolt mich undertenig und gehorsam sein und nichts von mir begeren, dann was mein freier und gueter Will war, und wolt mich und alle meine Kind in Eren haben und ir sie lassen empfohlen sein als ir aigne Kind." Ibid., 67.

[80]Ozment, *When Fathers Ruled*, 80-83.

ments on the matter suggest considerable concern and affection for Sibilla and outrage at the treatment she received from Eck. Indeed, the divorce was as much a matter of family honor as of his sister's marriage. Studies of divorce in France during the *ancien régime* suggest that kin could often shelter and comfort the victimized spouse in cases of marital dissolution.[81] Not only did authorities insist on the responsibilities of married couples to community and kin, the couples themselves depended on such ties in time of stress. The evidence of solidarity within the extended family, a solidarity which is not exceptional in the twentieth century, indicates that historical theories insistent on the isolation of the modern nuclear family may suffer the weakness of generalization.

The pre-industrial family was more than an affective unit. In an age in which household and workshop were often identical, the family was a unit of production. Bernard Zink told in his diary the story of his first marriage.[82] Both he and his wife were destitute servants, who had to work at home day and night to make ends meet. They provided both moral and material support for one another and eventually built a considerable fortune through their mutual efforts.

It is certainly no surprise that an established Augsburg merchant would, decades after the fact, attribute his success to hard work and economic self-sufficiency. To acquire wealth, a degree of independence was necessary. Enterprise and prosperity in pre-industrial society required self-sufficiency and choice just as they do in capitalist society.[83] The ability of a family unit to make self-interested decisions, to plan for its future, an ability some authorities see closely connected to Protestant ideals,[84] involves the same independence necessary to dissolve the family unit. Divorce, as a self-sufficient action on the part

---

[81]Alain Lottin, *La desunion du couple sous l'ancien régime: L'exemple du nord* (Paris: Éditions universitaires, 1975), 162.

[82]"Item als ich bei meinem Herrn was da nam ich mein Weib. Die was ainer armen Frawen, ainer wittben Tochter von Moringen. . . . Mein Weib heiss Elisabeth und was auf dasselbmal meins Herrn Jos Kramers Magt, so was ich auch sein Diener. . . . Und als wir nun Hochzeit mit ainander hetten gehapt, da west ich sicher nit was ich tuen solt, dann ich hett nichts, so hett ich mein Herrn Huld gar nit und hett die Huld verloren, dann es was im laid, dass ich mein Weib genomen hett und in darumb nit ratgefragt und wolt mir weder ratten noch helfen. Also west ich nit, was ich anfahen solt. Doch was mir das Weib lieb und was gern bei ir, und bedacht mich mit meiner Hausfrawen. Die was mir auch hold und trost mich und sprach: 'Mein Burkhart, gehab dich wol und verzag nit, lass uns ainander helfen, wir wollen wol ausskomen; ich will an dem Rad spinnen und will alle Wuchen . . . woll ausspinnen, das is 32 Dn.' . . . [D]a erkecket ich auch und gedacht: Nun kan ich doch ain wenig schreiben, ich will besehen, ob ich mug ainen Pfaffen haben, der mir zu schreiben geb; so wenig du dann verdienst so gewinnt dein Weib 32 Dn., so ist noch Wohlfail, villeicht geit Got zu, dass wir wol ausskoment. . . . Und mein Weib und ich sassen zusamen und ich schrib und sie span . . .; doch seien wir oft bei ainander gesessen die gantzen Nacht. Und gieng uns gar wol und gewunnen was wir bedorften." Wenzel, *Die Autobiographie*, II, 57-58.

[83]Natalie Z. Davis, "Ghost, Kin and Progeny: Some Features of Family Life in Early Modern France," *Daedalus* 2:1977, 88.   [84]Ibid., 96.

of individuals, not only complicated the corporate life of a community but also threatened the prosperity and productivity of the nuclear and extended family.

Many divorces involved property disputes, but a divorce could also destroy a family as a productive unit. The laws regulating property settlements in Strasbourg and Basel effectively robbed the guilty party of financial independence and transferred large proportions of the patrimony to the state.[85] The ruin of a family business through divorce affected not only husband and wife but also the community, by reducing some people to poverty or making them wards of the state, and the kin, by transferring property in which they had an interest.

Recent studies suggest that divorce becomes truly plausible only when the affective and productive functions of the family are separate.[86] When work shifted physically to a distinct, specialized workshop and employment became separated from traditional family constraints, divorce became a feasible option for couples suffering chronic marital distress. If this is true, recourse to divorce should follow socio-economic class distinctions. Such seems to have been the case in Rouen during the French Revolution where non-laborers were overrepresented among divorce litigants.[87] Unfortunately, no such data has yet been discovered for the sixteenth and seventeenth centuries.

Given that divorce threatened patrimony and prosperity, persons living in localities with legalized divorce may have taken steps to prevent such a disaster. One tactic might have been to draft marriage contracts without clauses specifying universal communality of property. Since private property often devolved to each spouse in a divorce, minimizing communal property reduced the amount that the state could sequester or redistribute. Francois Wendel discovered a trend away from universal communality in marriage contracts in Strasbourg after 1560.[88] Since no divorce litigation survives in Strasbourg, it is not possible to determine whether changes in property customs are related to changes in marital dissolution. Divorce studies would reveal the property interests of married couples and their tendency to pursue individual or communal interests.

Both as a unit of affection and as a unit of production, the family was the foundation of early modern society. So it is proper to consider the family, among its other functions, as a social unit.

Divorce certainly compromised the ability of a family to socialize the next generation. Yet in a period when remarriage after the death of one spouse was

---

[85]Similar laws existed in Zurich. See Köhler, *Zürcher Ehegericht und Genfer Konsistorium*, 257.

[86]Phillips, *Family Breakdown in Late Eighteenth-Century France*, 97.

[87]Ibid., 91

[88]Wendel, *La mariage à Strasbourg*, 176.

not uncommon and when children left the household early to enter service, the circumstances presented by divorce may not have been so unusual.

Marital dissolution may have had a greater influence on a family's standing in the community. No evidence suggests that divorce created a stigma for the parties involved. The magistrates did not favor divorce but were willing to grant it under compelling circumstances. How the community at large viewed divorce is a matter of some speculation. Studies of wife-selling indicate that the community often reacted negatively to such actions.[89] Yet, the crowd directed its corporate ire most often at the wife and her purchaser, suggesting that adultery (the purchaser was often the wife's lover), the marital offense, disturbed communal values more than the "divorce" itself. Communities often directed *charivari* against marital offenders or those who permitted marital offenses—the cuckold, the beaten husband, the adulterous or shrewish wife—but not, so far as is known, against divorced or separated spouses.

Divorce may not have compromised a family's social standing, but it challenged social authority, especially the partiarchal authority of the husband. With a divorce, or the threat of one, a wife could undermine the traditonal *imperium* of her husband. That this did not happen frequently should come as no surprise in a traditional, partriarchal society. In Zurich, from 1525 to 1531, husbands initiated nearly sixty per cent of all divorces on grounds of adultery or abandonment.[90] In Basel the figures were less striking. Between 1529 and 1550 husbands sued for divorce in about sixty per cent of all cases.[91] From 1550 to 1590, wives initiated the bare majority of divorces, just over fifty per cent.[92] Not until the revolutionary regime in France, with its very liberal divorce laws, do women initiate the vast majority of divorces, creating a *de facto* challenge to domestic patriarchal authority.[93]

The unity of family as affective and productive units reenforced a partiarchal image of the world.[94] This image was dissolving in the late eighteenth century but not necessarily in the sixteenth and seventeenth centuries. The partiarch was still the symbol of authority and the source of security (legal, material, and emotional) for the members of the early modern family. Divorce weakened this image, but, given the magisterial reluctance to divorce and the relatively low frequency of divorce cases initiated by women, representative elements of society still clung to this vision.

The significance of divorce in early modern society must be assessed not in terms of statistics but in terms of language and ritual. As a public ceremony,

---

[89]Samuel P. Menefee, *Wives for Sale: An Ethnographic Study of English Popular Divorce* (New York: St. Martin's, 1981), 127.

[90]Köhler, *Zürcher Ehegericht und Genfer Konsistorium*, 109, 120.

[91]Staehelin, *Die Einführung der Ehescheidung*, 181-98.

[92]Safley, *Let No Man Put Asunder*, 175.

[93]Phillips, *Family Breakdown in Late Eighteenth-Century France*, 56.

[94]Weber-Kellerman, *Die Familie*, 68.

divorce signalled the legitimacy of marital dissolution, a self-interested, individualistic action. The language of magistrates and litigants indicates public and private perceptions of such action. A close evaluation of Protestant divorce theory indicates that theologians, jurists, and magistrates rejected this individualism and sought to strengthen the bonds between husband and wife, couple and kin, family and community. Among the means chosen were a limited range of grounds for divorce and legal tactics designed to prevent marital dissolution. It is one of the ironies of Protestantism that it could simultaneously encourage and frustrate individualism and its expression. The reaction of private persons remains obscure. Popular attitudes toward divorce—its legitimacy and necessity—cannot be evaluated through court protocols and legal codes. The tendency of Protestants to become more conservative on the issue of divorce and the tendency of divorce litigation to hold at low levels may suggest that married couples faced with a domestic crisis tolerated the situation or sought extra-legal solutions. For private citizens as well as public officials divorce was a last, worst resort.

Marriage, divorce, and remarriage have always had communal and individual aspects. Divorce creates a tension between the interests of kin and community and the individual interests of the couple. To evaluate fully this dichotomy, a model of early modern marital dissolution—its causes, course, and consequences—should provide valuable information on the emotional content of marriage, its social and economic functions, and its links to kin and community. Until such a model is developed, it is premature to connect the modern nuclear family with early modern Europe.

Women, Marriage, and Magisterial Reformation: The Case of Malmø, Denmark

Grethe Jacobsen
Copenhagen

I

TRADITIONALLY, THE REFORMATION IN SCANDINAVIAN countries is seen as a typical expression of Lutheran doctrines and church organization established by the rulers to further their dynastic policies and secure their power.[1] This certainly is true for Denmark after 1536. However, the years prior to 1536 in fact saw a more gradual and varied movement ranging from the princely backed Lutheran Reformation, carried out in the duchies by preachers from Wittenberg, to a magisterial humanist-inspired reform in the Scanian town of Malmø, where the preachers and the urban magistrates worked together in order to establish a Christian commonwealth.[2]

Danish historians have until now focused on the theological content and political results of the Reformation. This emphasis on theology and politics, formulated and acted upon by men, has meant that the role of women in the Danish Reformation and the role of the Reformation in the history of Danish women has not been studied. This article will attempt to remedy the situation by analyzing the changes wrought in Malmø by the Reformation and their impact upon the lives of women.

Women may have worked actively to bring about the Reformation but no source mentions their contribution except a brief reference in a letter from 1576.[3] The lack of source material thus forces us to look at the impact of developments of the 1520s and the 1530s. The major immediate change appears to be in the regulation of marriage, an important factor in the lives of most women. I shall not be arguing that this shows a different attitude toward marriage as an institution and was in itself an improvement; rather, changes in the regulation of marriage offered women for a while the opportunity to make changes and improvements in their marital conditions.

---

[1]Harold J. Grimm, *The Reformation Era, 1500-1650*, 2nd ed. (New York: Macmillan, 1973), 189-90.

[2]*Den danske kirkes historie*, 8 vols. (Copenhagen: Gyldendal, 1950-1966), 3: 345-51.

[3]The letter of June 19, 1576, by a canon in Viborg, describes how, during a sermon in 1526, the reformer Hans Tausen was threatened by the bishop's servants and protected by the male citizens after their wives had brought weapons from their homes "aliis uxores arma ex ædibus asportant," cited in Ole Grell, "Det verdslige øvrighedsbegreb, som det fremtræder i Malmølitteraturen 1530-36," *Kirkehist. Saml.*, 1981: 11, printed in *Kirkehistoriske Samlinger* 1 (1849-1852): 376. Henceforth cited *Kirkehist. Saml.*

II

Strategically located on the West coast of Scania, across the Sound from Copenhagen and on the Baltic trade routes, Malmø · was, in the later Middle Ages, a thriving commercial city and, with some 5,000 inhabitants, the second largest in the kingdom of Denmark. German and Dutch trading partners also transmitted impulses from central Europe, including news of religious stirrings during the second and third decade of the sixteenth century. According to a contemporary chronicler, merchants from Stralsund and Stettin first introduced evangelical preachers to Scania and gave the population a taste for new religious ideas.[4] In Denmark the climate was in general favorable to the ideas of a reform within the church, not in the least because King Frederik I (1523-1533) favored the evangelical preachers, though officially he remained a Catholic. He supported the reformers as much as he could without alienating the secular nobility who might become allies of the bishops, the archbishop-elect and other high-ranking prelates who, with one or two exceptions, were noble.[5] Frederik's oldest son, Duke Christian of Slesvig and Holsten, was openly Lutheran and supported the Reformation in the Duchies, implemented by reformers from Wittenberg.[6]

In Malmø the reform movement was initiated by the mayor, Jorgen Kock, who asked a native son, Claus Mortensen, to return from Copenhagen where he had studied. In 1527 Claus Mortensen began preaching, first outside the city, drawing huge crowds, later in a chapel inside the walls, and finally in the main church of St. Peter. He was followed by other preachers and in 1528 a printer arrived. During the following years Malmø was one of the two main centers of reform activities in Denmark. The archbishop-elect of Lund attempted in 1528 to stop the preachers, but in vain.[7] In October of that year, the king, upon the request of the city council, gave permission for the city to take over the monasteries of the Franciscans and the Order of the Holy Spirit in town. The buildings were to be used as a hospital and a town hall when the brothers had left. The letter included the proviso that the priests and

---

’An excellent analysis of Frederik I and his policies is found in Suno W. Scharling, "Frederik 1.s kirkepolitik," *Kirkehist. Saml.*, 1974: 40-88.

"A. D. Jørgensen, "Reformationen i Sønderjylland indtil Foråret 1526," *Kirkehist. Saml.*, ser. 4, vol. 1 (1889-1891): 577-620; Bjørn Kornerup, "Fra Hertug Christians Reformation i Tørning Len," ibid., ser. 6, vol. 5 (1945-1949): 545-48.

For the reformers of Malmø see C. Sonnenstein-Wendt, "Om Reformatorerna i Malmø och de första lutherska presterna derstädes. Några personalhistoriska bidrag til Danmarks kyrkohistoria," ibid. 4 (1860-1862): 128-235; for a general account of the reformation in Malmø see Gösta Johannesson, *Den Skånska kyrkan och reformationen*, Skånsk senmedeltid och renässans, 1 (Lund: Gleerup, 1947): 158-77.

the monks were not to be forced out.[8] This was blithely ignored. After eighteen months of verbal and physical harassment, the last monks left in May of 1530.[9]

In 1529, again acting upon a petition from the magistrates, the king issued another letter allowing the city council to take over the property belonging to the altars, confraternities and vicariates in town and use the income for the hospital, for supporting an evangelical preacher and for a school for "simple" clerics where these could be taught the Holy Writ.[10] In 1532 the archbishop-elect resigned and his successor had to promise not to hinder in any way the work of the preachers in Malmø.[11]

Early in 1533, Frederik I died and the Council of the Realm, dominated by the bishops and the conservative Catholic nobles, refused to elect his son, the Lutheran Duke Christian, as his successor. During the interregnum (1533-1534) the Catholic party sought to regain lost territory and stop the reform in Malmø and elsewhere. The pressure on Malmø to give up its political and religious goals mounted until in May, 1534, the citizenry rose against the Council of the Realm and declared itself for the imprisoned Christian II. A civil war broke out which lasted for two years. In the summer of 1534 Duke Christian was acclaimed king by the Jutish nobility and he began the successful reconquest of his kingdom. In April, 1536, Malmø surrendered to him after a ten-months siege and, in July, Copenhagen was the last town to give up the fight. In August, 1536, the bishops were imprisoned and though most of them were released shortly after, none were allowed to return to their former offices.

The new leaders of the church were the non-noble superintendents, some of them fresh graduates from Wittenberg; others were veterans of the reform movement, like the Malmø reformer, Frans Vormodsen, who became the superintendent of Scania (the former archdiocese). Under the guidance and supervision of Johannes Bugenhagen, the Lutheran *Fürstenkirche* was established with the Church Ordinance of 1537.[12] The participation of Malmø in the civil war on the side of the jailed Christian II did not impair its relations to his cousin, King Christian III. The town retained its privileges and control over

[8]*Kong Frederik den Førstes danske Registranter*, ed. Kr. Erslev and W. Mollerup (Copenhagen: Selskabet for Udgivelse af Kilder til dansk Historie, 1879), 181 (8 October 1528). Henceforth *Fr. 1 reg.*

[9]The major source is the anonymous chronicle *De expulsione Fratrum Minorum*, written 1532/33. The fourth chapter deals with the Franciscans in Malmø. The chronicle is printed in *Scriptores Historioe Danicæ Medii Ævi*, ed. M.Cl. Gertz, (Copenhagen: Selskabet for Udgivelse af Kilder til dansk Historie, 1922; repr. 1970) 2: 326-67. Henceforth *De expulsione*.

[10]*Fr. 1 reg.*, 207 (5 June 1529).

[11]Scharling, "Frederik 1.s kirkepolitik," 73-74.

[12]Johannesson, *Skånska kyrkan*, 181-260; C. T. Engelstoft, "Kirke-Ordinantsens Historie, en Undersøgelse," *Kirkehist. Saml.* 4 (1860-1862): 1-110, 369-442.

local church affairs and its secular leaders remained or were with one exception back in their mayoral and counciliar offices within a few years.[13]

As noted, the Danish reform movement had two distinct fronts: one in the Duchies and Western Denmark influenced by Luther and spearheaded by reformers from Wittenberg, the other in Eastern Denmark influenced by Christian evangelical humanism and led by students of the Carmelite teacher and humanist, Poul Helgesen (Paulus Helie). Helgesen remained a Catholic in Copenhagen while his students broke with the Church and established their base in Malmø.[14]

In many towns the city council and the burghers supported the evangelical preachers. However, in Malmø the magistrates initiated the reform and they participated in the movement to an extent not found elsewhere. The close cooperation between the council and the preachers as well as the actions taken by the magistrates reveal that, in effect, we find in Malmø before 1536, an urban-magisterial reformation comparable to that of Strasbourg which Williams in his work on the Radical Reformation uses as a prototype for this development.[15] Not only are the dates for the decisive period identical (1529-1533) but the political views of the leaders were the same. What the mayors in Malmø envisioned was a status for their town within the Danish monarchy similar to that enjoyed by the Imperial Free Cities in the Empire.[16] Christian II (1513-1523) had supported the citizens against the nobility and thus fueled the political aspirations of the burgher leaders. Frederik I could not afford quite so openly to advance the political influence of the civic elite but he bestowed favors on the cities, including Malmø.[17]

The two different orientations in the reform movement did not cause a split between the Lutheran and the humanist preachers, and in 1530, at a time crucial for Protestants, they cooperated in the formulation of the *Confessio*

---

[13]Jørgen Kock, leader of the party of Christian II, returned to Malmø in 1539/40 as the royal moneyer, then from 1540 until his death as a mayor. The three other mayors continued in their offices as did all but one of the councilors. A general assessment of Malmø's position after 1536 is in Johannesson, *Skånska kyrkan*, 231-235; Ole Peter Grell discusses Jørgen Kock in "Jørgen Kock: en studie i religion og politik i reformationstidens Danmark," in *Profiler i nordisk senmiddelalder og renaissance: Festskrift til Poul Enemark på tresårsdagen 13. April 1983* (Arhus: Arusia, 1983), 113-26.

[14]An important source for the Reformation in Malmø is the *Skibykrønike*, written around 1533 by Poul Helgesen in which he levels acrimonious attacks on the Protestant preachers, in particular his former students. The chronicle is printed in *Skrifter af Paulus Helie*. 7 vols. (Copenhagen: Det danske Sprog- og Litteratur Selskab, 1932-1948), vol. 6, ed. Marius Kristensen and Hans Ræder (1937), 51-149.

[15]George H. Williams, *The Radical Reformation* (Philadelphia: The Westminster Press, 1962, 1975), 234-98.

[16]Johannesson, *Skånska kyrkan*, 209-11.

[17]*Danmarks Historie*, ed. Aksel E. Christensen, et al. (Copenhagen: Gyldendal, 1977-) 2: 295-96. See also n. 20.

Hafniensis which was their challenge to Catholic theologians.[18] This may partly explain why the magistrates in Malmø experienced no problems in carrying out their program without damaging their relations with the king. Furthermore, the city council clearly wanted an orderly reform. The political and religious program of the Malmø politicians and reformers carried no threatening seeds. They wanted reform but not revolution. The magistrates wanted evangelical liberty but stressed their loyalty and obedience to the monarch.[19] They wanted control over ecclesiastical property in their town in order to utilize the income more efficiently in charity toward the poor and sick, but had no intention of distributing income among the poor. The magistrates also curbed the more radical of the reformers, adapting the reform to suit the wealthy bourgeoisie of Malmø.

Theological debate and missionary preaching were the functions of the preachers while the magistrates took care of the civic and political questions that arose when the ecclesiastical institutions disappeared. The magistrates, numbering twelve councilors and four mayors,[20] were drawn from the merchant class as no artisan or retail dealer was eligible for counciliar office.[21] The city government was, however, careful not to alienate the common citizenry, especially not the artisans organized in guilds.[22] Leading artisans, as for example Oluf Bødker (Cooper), the stepfather of Claus Mortensen, were given certain public offices. These included church wardens and *rodemestre*, officials in charge of administering the military duties and obligations of the citizens.[23]

Evidence for magisterial activities during the first half of the sixteenth century is found primarily in the Rådstueprotokol, the record of actions taken by the city council as governing body and as one of the two urban courts.[24].

---

[18]For a thorough discussion of the dogmatic sources and contents of the *Confessio* and the Protestant writings see Niels Knud Andersen, *Confessio Hafniensis, Den københavnske bekendelse af 1530. Studier i den begyndende reformation* (Copenhagen: Gad, 1954).

[19]Johannessen, *Skånska kyrkan*, 128-46; Scharling, "Frederik 1.s kirkepolitik," 61-62.

[20]In 1526, Frederik I issued two privileges which permitted the city governments of Copenhagen and Malmø to expand from two mayors and ten councilors to four mayors, elected by the citizens, and twelve councilors who appointed their own successors, *Fr. 1 reg.*, 122.

[21]Mackeprang, *Dansk Købstadstyrelse fra Valdemar Sejr til Kristian IV (Forordn. af 1619)* (Copenhagen: Det nordiske Forlag, 1900), 53-60.

[22]Grethe Jacobsen, "Guilds in Medieval Denmark: The Social and Economic Role of Merchants and Artisans," (Ph.D. diss., University of Wisconsin-Madison, 1980), chap. 7.

[23]*Malmø Rådstueprotokol (Stadsbok) 1503-1548*, ed. Erik Kroman, Ældre danske rådstueprotokoller og bytingsbøger, (Copenhagen: Selskabet for Udgivelse af Kilder til dansk Historie, 1965), Henceforth *MRP. Rodemestre* are mentioned on 289, 55, 121-22, 168, 144, 146-47 and Oluf Bødker's public offices on 55, 86, 113.

[24]The oldest urban court was the *byting*, presided by the royal reeve with jurors selected from the citizenry. In 1292 a second court, presided by the members of the city council, is mentioned; this court became an important element in the judicial structure during the

The *Rådstueprotokol* shows how income from the former ecclesiastical properties was used as a loan to the printer, Olaf Ulricsson, later as wages for the
preachers, the schoolmasters, and the staff at the hospitals.[25] It records the letter of resignation of the last Catholic parish priest on October 11, 1529, in
which he left it to the councilors to elect the pastor and the preacher "they
deem useful."[26] Above all, the *Rådstueprotokol* records how political and institutional changes affected the half of the city's population not mentioned in the
theological writings of the time, namely women. Affected in particular was
the major event in the lives of most women: marriage either to clergymen or
to laymen.

III

The issue of clerical marriage versus clerical celibacy was not new in 1527
when Claus Mortensen began preaching. During the fifteenth century several
prohibitions against the concubines of the clergy were issued.[27] In 1497 the
archbishop promulgated a set of synodal statutes of which paragraphs 23 and
24 forbade priests and clerics to have concubines and to bring them or their
children to gatherings or confraternities. Also strictly prohibited was the birth
of children in the houses of clergymen.[28] The real tenor of these paragraphs is

fifteenth and sixteenth centuries. The lack of extant court records, however, makes it impossible to determine the exact relationship between the jurisdiction of the two courts,
Kulturhistorisk leksikon for nordisk middelalder fra vikingetid til reformationstid 22 vols.
(Copenhagen: Rosenkilde og Bagger, 1956-78), 17, cols. 7-8; 18, cols. 362-63. The records
of the city council court in Malmö (the earliest extant records) indicate that this court took
care of cases dealing with trade and craft production, including debts and violations of the
city's regulations concerning trade and the monopoly of the craft guilds. It also, in some
cases, functioned as an appellate court for the *byting*.

 MRP, 83 (loan to the printer); 145-46, 181-82 (wages to clergy and hospital staff).

 [26]"som thennom tøckes nøtteligh at være," ibid., 83. The original letter of resignation in Malmö Stadsarkiv, B:nr. 362 (1529, 29/9). Henceforth MSA. In March, 1529, Frans
Vormodsen had borrowed from the magistrates a five-volume edition of the Bible, a volume
with "anotationibus Ieronimi," a concordance of the Old and New Testaments and an edition of the letters of Paul and James, along with a folding table from the rectory, *MRP*, 80-
81. One wonders how pleasant the six months prior to his resignation had been for the
priest.

 In 1440, the bishop of Slesvig forbade priests and clerics to keep concubines,
Repertorium diplomaticum regni Danici mediævalis, (Copenhagen: Selskabet for Udgivelse af
Kilder til dansk Historie, 1894-1912), nr. 7085. In general, celibacy was never popular in
Denmark. In 1241, celibate priests were specifically given tax exemption, as discussed in N.
H. Holmqvist-Larsen *Møer, skjoldmøer og krigere*, (Copenhagen: Museum Tusculanum,
1983), 20-21.

 Diplomatarium diocesis Lundensis, ed. Laurits Weibull (Lund: Lindstedts Univ.
Bokh., 1900-39), 5: 314: "De concubinis. Item mandamus, qvod nullus sacerdos in domo
vel habitatione sua publicam teneat focariam et concubinam . . . ne qvis sacerdos ad convivia
vel invitationes concubinam suam aut infantulos suos, si qvam vel qvos habuerit, qvod absit,
secum adducere aut qvovismodo habere presumat. . . . De puerperiis. Item ut scandala in

that a concubine and children were, of course, forbidden to any priest, canon or other member of the clergy; and if one ignored this, he should at least exercise discretion to avoid scandal.

How common clerical families were is difficult to say but they were not an unusual phenomenon. Poul Helgesen argued that the most eager defenders of the Lutheran doctrines were the sons of priests.[29] Admittedly, he is a biased source but there seems to be some truth to his charge. For a woman involved, being the concubine of a priest was an insecure position, even if she were tacitly accepted by society. The ecclesiastical authorities, whatever their private lifestyle, were decidedly against the practice. To be the lawful wedded wife of a clergyman with a recognized social function in society was clearly an improvement in status and security. On this issue the Reformation brought a change for the better to some women.

The earliest signs of change appear in the law code issued by Christian II in 1522. Paragraph 17 forbids any priest or cleric to purchase landed property "unless they want to follow the teachings of St. Paul as he writes in his first letter to Timothy, chapter 3, advising them to take wives and live in holy matrimony as their ancient forefathers have done."[30] After the flight of Christian II in 1523, his laws were declared invalid. Yet the idea of allowing the clergy to marry did not disappear. The reformers took up the issue and their arguments received royal support indirectly when in 1526 Frederik I married his daughter, Dorothea, to Albrecht of Brandenburg, formerly Grand Master of the Teutonic Knights, now Duke of Prussia.[31] In 1529 the king made the new bishop of Roskilde swear that he would permit monks and nuns to marry and the same promise was extracted in 1532 from the new archbishop-elect.[32]

In Malmø, clerical marriage was supported by the city council. The first to be recorded is that of the priest, Per Lauritsen, who married a woman named Mette sometime before December 18, 1525. On that day the magistrates summoned to their court a citizen who had harassed with words and deeds the

---

clerico publica evitentur districtius prohibemus ne qvis sacerdos in domo sua puerperia suorum infantulorum aut introductiones concubinarum suarum sub qvavis solennitate aut invitatione facere presumat sub pena qvatuor marcarum argenti."

[29]"Nulli magis faverent impie secte quam sacerdotium spurii, inter qvos erant plerique michi noti, sed multi plures pluribus," *Skrifter af Paulus Helie* 6: 180.

[30]*Samling af gamle danske Love*, ed. J. L. A. Kolderup-Rosenvinge, 5 vols. (Copenhagen: Gyldendal, 1821-46) 4: 9-10: "Skall ingen Prelathe, Prest eller Clerck . . . kiöbe thill sig noget Jordegodtz, Kiöbstedtzguodtz eller Landtzguodtz effter thenne Dagh. . . . uden the ville effterfölge St. Pauli Lærdom, som hand skriifuer utii syn förste Epistel Cap. 3 ad Timotheum, raader thennom, ath the thager Hustrue och leffuer utii thenn hellige Echteskab, som theris gamble Forfædre giort haffue."

[31]Andersen, *Confessio*, 205.

[32]Scharling, "Frederik 1.s kirkepolitik," 66, 73-74.

priest and his wife. He was told to abstain from further harassment of the couple "until they are legally separated in the court of Lund."[33] The couple had apparently not suffered in silence as they in turn had to promise not to retaliate. Whether their case ever reached the episcopal court is uncertain. Barely a year and a half later, Claus Mortensen arrived in Malmø and the city council began cutting all ties to the archbishop. Claus Mortensen married shortly after his arrival as did most of the reformers who followed him.[34]

The support of the city council in this issue is evident from an incident related in the *Chronicle of the Expulsion of the Franciscans*. During one of the many disputes between the preachers and the friars, the guardian angrily charged his opponents with leading immoral lives. The preacher, Frans Vormodsen, who led this dispute and who had recently married, became so furious that he could not speak. Then the mayor, Jøergen Kock, stepped forward and exclaimed, "What are you saying, is matrimony immoral?" To this accusation the friar had to back down.[35]

Clerical marriage indeed became one of the central issues in the debates between Catholics and Protestants, in particular between Poul Helgesen and his former students in Malmø.[36] The effect of the dispute was that a radical view on clerical marriage came to be espoused by the latter. While stopping short of demanding that priests marry, the reformers argued that, as practically nobody was capable of living in celibacy and as God forbade fornication and instituted marriage as a guard against sinning, everybody actually had an obligation to marry. The reformers did not discuss the positive aspects of marriage and the role of the wife in marriage except to translate Luther's writings on the subject. Ironically, the debating parties were not really as far apart on this issue as they seemed. As a reform Catholic, Poul Helgesen was not against clerical marriage as such; indeed he favored a modification in the demands for celibacy as a means to end this debauchery in the church. What he did oppose was the fact that the reformers openly broke their vows of celibacy, thereby defying Rome. To Poul Helgesen any church reform had to come from the pope, not from the preachers in Malmø.

The debates leave the impression that, to the reformers, marriage was a statement of principle rather than the formal expression of a bond between two people. One may speculate what it meant to their wives to be living principles. It is worth noting that in Strasbourg also, debates concerning the marriage of priests focused on the husband and the effect of marriage upon his life

[33]*MRP*, 314. This Per Lauritsen is not the same as Peder Laurentius, a prominent theologian and reformer, who arrived in Malmø in 1529, where he married Anne, sister of Claus Mortensen.

[34]Sonnstein-Wendt, "Reformatorerna," 183-87.

[35]*De expulsione*, 348: "Quid . . . ais? Est matrimonialis status spurca? Respondit guardianus sese excusando, quod non appellasset matrimonii statum spurcam; proconsul vero contrarius ei improperavit."

[36]Andersen, *Confessio*, 204-14.

and character. Only the exceptional Katherine Zell drew attention to the wife of a priest.[37] As the wives presumably were too busy to write about their own feelings and opinions on the subject—or if they did, since nothing is preserved—we are limited to knowing only the conditions under which they lived.[38]

In Denmark, the first generation of priests' wives were exposed to the wrath of relatives or neighbors who opposed this innovation in clerical life-style and consequently considered these women concubines regardless of the marriage ceremony performed. The case of Per and Mette Lauritsen has been mentioned. Another example is the reformer Frans Vormodsen who in 1529 married a woman against the will of her relatives and the advice of his friends.[39] In 1533 Christiern Pedersen, a former canon of Lund, and his fiancée suffered harassment from her brother.[40]

This happened in Malmø where the magistrates backed the reformers and their actions. One may imagine the pressures upon the wives of clergymen in other cities or in rural parishes where support would be altogether lacking and a hostile bishop outright threatening. Not only were women who married priests subject to trouble when they married, they also risked losing their widows' rights if their in-laws sought to exploit the uncertainty surrounding the new institution of clerical marriage. The troubles of one wife we do know about. A minister in Jutland, Søren Svendsen, married sometime before 1533. Between 1533 and 1536 the bishop of Børglum declared this marriage illegal and the children born to the couple illegitimate. This decision was overturned by the county court, but after Søren's death, his brother used it to disinherit the widow and the children nevertheless. In 1537 the king's court confirmed the decision of the county court, firmly stating that the marriage was valid and the widow and children were legitimate heirs.[41]

[37] Miriam U. Chrisman, "Women and the Reformation in Strasbourg, 1490-1530," *Archiv für Reformationsgeschichte* 63 (1972): 143-167, esp. 147-154.

[38] We do know that women continued to rent Our Lady's (bridal) Crown for the weddings of their daughters after the Reformation, so the wives of clergymen could now enjoy this female ritual. MSA. LIa: Räkenskaper för kyrka. Andliga godsens räkenskaper 1 fol. 16v (1532): "Upbørelsze af thennem som haffue hafft wor fruess krone tilleye." Among the women who rented the crown were wives of councilors, Mette Per Harckes and Gertrud (Hans) Byngers.

[39] *Skrifter af Paulus Helie* 6: 116: "Duxit et ipse puellam quandam uxorem, inuitis eiusdem puella curatoribus, omnibusque amicis reclamantibus."

[40] *MRP* 110-11. The incident apparently wrought havoc in the family and among their friends. The brother, Vincent Jacobsen, had four men stand surety for his pledge to abstain from harassing the couple. One of the four was his father, Jacob Nickelsen, a mayor. Vincent had also harassed his stepmother, his father's mayoral colleague, Jep Nielsen, and Frans Vormodsen, the reformer. The incident is strongly reminiscent of the problems surrounding the marriage of Hedio into the Drens family in Strasbourg in 1523, Chrisman, "Women. . . Strasbourg," 153-54.

[41] *Det kgl. rettertings domme og rigens forfølgninger fra Christian III's tid*, ed. Troels Dahlerup (Copenhagen: Selskabet for Udgivelse af Kilder til dansk Historie, 1959-69) 1:

The second generation of ministers' wives were accepted members of society in Malmø and elsewhere. Concurrently, the attitudes of the Malmø reformers changed or rather broadened. In 1544 Frans Vormodsen, now superintendent of Scania, promulgated his first synodal statutes. He also outlined in them the qualifications for becoming a minister's wife. Clergymen were not allowed to marry prostitutes or corrupt women of ill repute. They were to seek out women who had a respectable background and were endowed with proper manners.[42] One example of the new activities of clergymen's wives is found in the accounts of the St. Petri Church. In 1532 "Master Oluf's wife in Greyfriars" was paid two and one-half marks for "an altarcloth she sewed and she supplied the silk and the silk thread."[43] Oluf Jensen was a preacher at the hopsital housed in the former Franciscan monastery.

Of the social background of the first generation of clerical wives in Malmø not much is revealed. We may safely assume that none were prostitutes or women of ill repute as Poul Helgesen would have been certain to use that in his writings against the reformers. The Franciscan chronicle recounts how the guardian accused Claus Mortensen of having engaged in debauchery with a whore for three days.[44] What in fact the friar was referring to was the wedding of Claus Mortensen. The epithet, whore, describes Claus' wife in her married and, in the eyes of the friar, illegal status rather than her unmarried status. She seems to have been a respectable peasant girl from a village near Malmø.

Other reformers married women from the middle ranks of urban society.[45] Only one, Christiern Pedersen, married into the merchant elite of Malmø. His wife was the daughter of a mayor and the widow of a merchant.[46]

64-65. There is an ironic twist to this case. The bishop, Stygge Krumpen, who condemned the clerical marriage, was openly living with a concubine, who was a married woman and his first cousin to boot. J. Oskar Andersen,"Krumpen, Stygge," *Dansk biografisk leksikon*, ed. Poul Engelstoft, 27 vols. (Copenhagen: Schultz, 1933-44) 13: 398-400. The cousin had received permission to live apart from her husband. *Kgl. rettertings domme* 1: 337-39.

[42]*Monumenta Historiæ Danicæ. Historiske Kildeskrifter og Bearbejdelser af dansk Historie, især fra det 16. Aarhundrede*, ed. Holger Fr. Rørdam (Copenhagen: Gad, 1873-87) 2,2: 331: "Uxores quales ducendæ pastoribus. . . non e lupanaribus, prostibula, aut aliqua corrupta et infamia scorta, sed ex honestis familiis honeste educaticis, morumque probitate ornatas." In a letter written in 1551, Peder Laurentius repeats these views and rebukes the canons at Lund Cathedral for having clung to their old ways and kept their "concubinas sive scorta . . . in dominibus." They should at once send them away and instead marry "honestas mulieres vel virgines." The letter is printed in *Peder Laurenssen. Malmøbogen*, ed. Holger Fr. Rordam Copenhagen: Det kongelige danske Selskab for Fædrelandets Historie og Sprog, 1868) lxvii. In Malmo, a priest's concubine (*præstedeje*) was renting a house from the church in 1532, but she is not listed in the rental records from 1536 onward. MSA. LIa: Räkenskaper f. kyrka 1: fol. 14r: "Bodil Prestedeye."

[43]"iij mck her Oluffss hwstrv uti graabrødre for et altere klæde hwn sydde og lodt hwn selff sylcke til oc saa meget sylcke som hwn sydde medt." Ibid., fol. 20r.

[44]*De expulsione*, 343.

[45]Sonnenstein-Wendt, "Reformatorerna," 148, 183, 208, 210, 224-26, 230, 231.

It has been suggested that the uncertainty surrounding the status of the first generation of clergymen's wives may have been a deterrent to girls of the upper ranks of society.[47]

IV

The city council of Malmø sought to usurp the jurisdiction of the Catholic Church and its courts by gaining the right to decide on matters concerning the marriages of the citizens of Malmø. The *Rådstueprotokol* records seventeen cases of marital disputes involving fourteen couples between 1529 and 1540, along with five grants of divorce between 1538 and 1540, that were settled or issued by the city council.

The first case occurred on November 29, 1529.[48] Anders Kedelsmed, an artisan, was summoned to the city council court where he swore that he would behave decently and in a Christian manner toward his wife as a goodman[49] should do, and further abstain from abusing with words and deeds three other men who, apparently, had intervened in the household quarrels; one of these was the brother-in-law of the wife. Anders broke his pledge and on July 11, 1530, the court issued an injunction against his entering his house unless his wife permitted it.[50] Thereafter he seems to have behaved, as there is no further record of his marital behavior.

The case established a precedent for the city council court to intervene in and decide on matrimonial matters. This move was supported by the king who, in 1532, referred a suit concerning the legality of a marriage to the preachers in Malmø. The case involved a farmer and his second wife, who was a cousin in the fourth degree of his first wife. The parish priest had put a ban on the couple, declaring their marriage to be illegal.[51] By removing the case from the archbishop's court to Malmø, the king clearly showed who, in his eyes, should decide on matrimonial matters. Besides its attempts to settle marital problems between Anders Kedelsmed and his wife, the city council also witnessed the sworn testimony of a citizen that five years earlier he had given a vow of marriage to the woman with whom he now had three children.[52] Having this recorded in the *Rådstueprotokol* meant that this relationship was considered legal, at least by the secular authorities and the preachers in Malmø.

[46]See above, n. 40.

[47]Johannesson, *Skånska kyrkan*, 326.

[48]*MRP*, 85.

[49]I have translated the recurring phrases *dannemand* and *dannekvinde* with goodman and goodwife, indicating respectable citizens.

[50]*MRP.*, 95.

[51]*Fr. 1 reg.* 449.

[52]*MRP*, 90-91.

The example of Malmø may have inspired the paragraphs in the Church Ordinance of 1537 which declare that the clergy should not concern itself with matrimonial matters except to perform the wedding ceremony and give spiritual advice. "Everything else belongs to the secular authorities."[53] These are defined as the mayors and the city council in the towns or the royal administrator in rural areas. The urban magistrates were to have the responsibility for settling "matters concerning matrimony, whether it is a question of quarrels, known shameful vices or behavior that otherwise would offend the commonalty."[54] Again it is stressed that the preachers may give advice and comfort but may not make the actual decision. The paragraphs do not explicitly permit the authorities to grant divorces but they do not prohibit this, either.

In Malmø, the city council in 1538 acted upon a case in a manner that showed it assumed legal power to include the dissolution of marriages. On April 1, 1538, the city council ended the trials of a citizen of Roskilde by granting him a divorce and giving him the right to remarry. His wife, it is told, had some years earlier left him and gone to Malmø, where she lived with another man and had children by him. The husband had then complained to the preachers in Malmø who "because of some small fault in him" had told him to behave as an honest man should and take his wife back. She was also ordered to leave her lover and follow her husband, which she had refused to do. The second time the husband returned to Malmø he went to the magistrates. They interrogated the woman who outright declared that she would have nothing to do with him or any other man for that matter after this day except for the man with whom she had been living. Her husband was then given the divorce by the magistrates in the presence of Claus Mortensen.[55]

This case has several interesting features. For one, the only preacher present in court did not participate in the decision. For another, the magistrates showed themselves to be more liberal than the preachers, who refused the divorce the first time. Only Claus Mortensen was in favor of divorce, as shall be discussed below. Thirdly, the authorities cited as reasons for the decision ". . . the law [but not specifically which law], Christian reason and evangelical liberty."[56] Fourthly, the woman was not prosecuted for adultery. Instead it was stressed that she had been living for more than a year with her lover, with

---

[53] *Danske Kirkelove, samt Udvalg af andre Bestemmelser, 1536-1683*, ed. Holger Fr. Rørdam, 3 vols. (Copenhagen: Selskabet for Danmarks Kirkehistorie, 1883-89) 1: 74: "Alt andet hører werdszlig øffrighed till" (cited from the Danish translation, printed 1539).

[54] "Men Ecteskabs sager maa de foruise till oss sielff eller wor Leensmand oc (om det er aff Kiøobstederne) til Borgemestere oc Raad, saa frampt som der er saadan trette emellom to eller flere. At der wil siiges offuerliust dom aff, eller om der er nogen skamelig last offuerliust witterlig, Eller oc mand frycter for nogen forargelse ebland almoen," ibid., 108.

[55] *MRP*, 135-36.

[56] "effter logen oc effther cristeligt skel oc den ewangeliske friihedt," ibid., 136.

whom she had children and shared table, bed and company—a phrase used in medieval Danish secular laws to define a legal relationship.[57] In short, the magistrates seemed sensitive to the problems of the couple and decided accordingly. The decision could encourage women who found their marriage intolerable to leave their husbands and seek a better partner. As long as they otherwise behaved as a goodwife and a proper wife, as the woman in this case seems to have done while living with her lover, divorce was a reasonable solution, at least in Malmø during the 1530s.

The liberal attitude of the magistrates is sharply contrasted with those presiding in the king's court in the city of Ålborg in Northern Jutland a year earlier.[58] A citizen of Ålborg accused his wife and her lover of deceiving him, making him a cuckold, stealing his property, and attacking him physically. The lovers argued in defense that she had obtained a witnessed divorce from the reeve some years earlier, that she had bought the property she possessed from the king's mercenaries during the war and that she had not had any further dealings with the husband. Although the couple had the divorce decree and the purchase of the property in writing and could produce witnesses to swear that the husband had not been attacked as he had claimed, their defense was for nought. The couple was condemned to death for adultery, he to be hanged, she to be drowned in a sack "according to the Emperor's law [the *Carolina*] in order that others hereafter should know that they will be punished for such monstrous deeds."[59] Actually, the *Carolina* did not specify capital punishment for adultery but it was interpreted that way by the royal chaplain.[60]

In Malmø the magistrates continued their own course. Four more divorces were granted in 1539.[61] They shared three common characteristics: the woman instituted the suit each time, Claus Mortensen and the two preachers were present and gave advice and consent but each decision was issued by the magistrates, and the reason for each decision was "evangelical liberty and Christian reason." Two of the women charged their husbands with impotence: "He is not the man whose bed any woman need seek when nature demands what is proper and natural between husband and wife."[62] Both

---

[57]*Jyske Lov* from 1241 states in Book I, chapter 27, that a woman who has lived with a man for three years and openly sleeps with him, has charge of his keys, and shares his table is to be considered his lawful wife and mistress of his house. *Danmarks gamle landskabslove med kirkelovene*, ed. Johs. Brøndum-Nielsen and Poul Johs. Jørgensen (Copenhagen: Det danske Sprog- og Litteraturselskab, 1932-61), vols. 2-4.

[58]*Danske domme 1375-1662: De private domssamlinger*, ed. Erik Reitzel-Nielsen (Copenhagen: Det danske Sprog- og Litteraturselskab, 1978-), 1: 192-97.

[59]"epther keyser logen, paa thet att andre her epther skulle wiide at straffes for sliig whørlige gerninger," ibid., 195.

[60]Ibid., 197 n. 35.

[61]*MRP*, 158-59, 161-63, 176-77.

[62]"hand icke er then mandt, ther nogen quinde haffuer behoff at søge seng met paa naturens vegne, som tilbørligt oc naturligt er emellem husbonde oc høstruff," ibid., 161, 162.

husbands admitted that the charge was justified. One of them asked his wife to forgive him for deceiving her, adding that she in every way ha. 1 behaved as an honest, faithful, and respectable woman. The other tried to defend himself by claiming that his impotence had begun only after he married her as his second wife. But she was able to prove that his first wife also had complained about him and, on her deathbed, implored him not to deceive another woman. This the husband admitted was right. Both wives were permitted to remarry while no such permission was given to the husbands.[63]

The two other divorces concerned women who had been deserted by their husbands, who were now said to be living in adultery in Germany. The wives initially had asked for help from the preachers in Malmø, who had admonished the husbands by letters, urging them to come back; meanwhile, the city council had issued safe-conducts. The husbands had indeed returned, but only for a brief spell, again leaving their wives in Malmø to fend for themselves and their children. The women then turned to the magistrates, appearing frequently in court to petition for divorce. This was granted and the women were freed to marry when three years had passed since their husbands left. Again the magistrates seemed more willing than the preachers to issue divorce decrees.

Most of the marital disputes mentioned in the *Rådstueprotokol* were heard without the presence of a clergyman as the city council appears in the role of arbitrator.[64] The records of these suits are very brief and it is not possible to say who instigated the suit. In most cases, however, it is the husband who has to promise to behave as a decent Christian goodman should towards his wife in all respects, sharing company, food and beer with her. One husband is also told to keep away from another man's wife.[65] It seems reasonable to conclude that in these cases the wife brought the suit in order to curb her husband's bad behavior. In every case, the magistrates instructed the wife to return to their court if her husband broke his pledge. In several instances he also had to appear with four citizens who were willing to stand surety for his pledge.

The husband was not always the one at fault. Sometimes the wife, too, had to promise that she would behave as a decent Christian goodwife should do.[66] One couple seems to have been a regular in court.[67] Another was admonished

---

[63]In 1537, a woman in Odense was granted a divorce on the grounds of impotence by the king's court, and among the judges was the superintendent of Funen. In this case the husband swore that his wife was still a virgin. Furthermore, he also admitted to having mistreated her and chased her away (from the marital bed?). The divorce decree permitted the woman to remarry "with the advice of her friends" whereas the man could only marry again if he informed his new wife of his defect. *Kgl. rettertings domme* 1: 203-205. These qualifying statements are not included in the Malmø decisions.

[64]Marital disputes prior to 1542 in *MRP*, 105. 112, 114, 115, 118, 132, 133, and 191, 137, 174, 183, 191   [65]Ibid., 118.   [66]Ibid., 112, 137, 183.

[67]On February 8, 1538, Oluf Tømmermand was reconciled with his wife "as has happened so often before" and he swore that he would behave decently and christianly toward his wife under the threat of losing his life, ibid., 133. Two months later, he was given

that one spouse misbehaving in the future would be punished but if both misbehaved they would be exiled.[68]

In this sentence lies the clue to the policy chosen by the magistrates. Their implicit goal, it seems, was to consolidate their own position by maintaining an orderly and stable society, using their court as a means to that end. Their explicit aims were to ensure evangelical liberty and undermine the authority of the archbishop and other outside prelates who could otherwise disrupt the Christian commonwealth under the leadership of the magistrates of Malmø. Through decisions and actions taken in the city council court, they set guidelines for civic and Christian behavior within marriage while seeking workable solutions to marital problems rather than enforcing moral standards. Their actions regarding marital disputes after 1529 were as they had been throughout the later Middle Ages regarding business disputes, debts, libel, and other litigation brought to their court. Magistrates were not averse even to make a decision against one of their own colleagues if he had not acted with fairness, even though his action could be legally defensible.[69]

It was less by design than by expediency that the magistrates appear to be liberal to the benefit of women in issues concerning marriage. During the first half of the sixteenth century women were able to use the courts much more freely than during the succeeding periods. As adults, women were in principle legally capable of appearing in their own right as long as they acted on their own behalf. A wife could also be given the power of attorney for her husband if he was prevented from appearing in court. If a woman needed a legal guardian, she could appoint a relative to plead her case or ask one of the city councilors to do so.[70] Given the opportunity, women used the city council court, a venue that agreed with the aims of the city council, to settle marital disputes as they used it to settle other civic suits.

There were, of course, limits to the liberality of the magistrates. They may have aimed at being fair as a practical way of maintaining order but they were not for equality. In settlements of marital disputes after 1538, the adjectives "humble" and "obedient," are sometimes added to "Christian" and "decent" in describing the proper wifely behavior.[71] Similarly, the husband's right to discipline his wife physically, albeit within reason, is made explicit in two cases.[72]

a fine of 140 grams of silver because he had behaved unchristianly toward his wife. The fine was payable to the city council and the king, MSA D.VIII a: Borgmästare och råds saköreslängd 1 (1527-45): 48. On January 21, 1541, Oluf and his wife, Bente, were once more reconciled and promised to live together. The spouse who broke the agreement would lose his or her life, the court told them. *MRP* 191. Apparently the threat was effective this time as there are no more records of their marital behavior.

[68]Ibid., 183.   [69]Ibid. 143-44.

[70]Inger Dübeck, *Købekoner og konkurrence. Studier over myndigheds- og erhvervsrettens udvikling med stadigt henblik på kvinders historiske retsstilling* (Copenhagen: Juristforbundets Forlag, 1978), 41-263.

[71]*MRP*, 137, 183.   [72]Ibid., 132, 174.

This subtle change in the formulaic description of settlements in marital disputes may have had its origin in the case of Niels Kuntse, a merchant who in 1539 became a councilor and in 1549 a mayor. His marital problems involved members of the mercantile and counciliar elite, and the case was ultimately settled by the king. All other marital cases settled by the magistrates involved couples from the middle class of Malmø society.

The case began in 1539 when Niels Kuntse returned from a business trip abroad.[73] He was met at the ship by one of the mayors who, obviously embarrassed, told him that his wife had locked their house and forbidden him to enter. She had also been at the city hall petitioning for a divorce, accompanied by Claus Mortensen and a sister. The spouses met shortly after at the home of the mayor and Niels asked his wife to tell him in what way he had wronged her. She began to cry and Claus Mortensen stepped forward and began scolding him in such a manner that, as Niels wrote in his petition to the king, "I am ashamed to write this to your Grace; however, I did tell your Grace's chancellor about it. Dearest, most gracious Lord, if this is Christian teachings, then may God in Heaven look upon."[74] Then Claus Mortensen and the sister took Niels' wife home and kept him out of the house.

The magistrates sought to reconcile the spouses or make Niels agree to a divorce. Failing that, they told him that they had no authority to make a decision in his case and that he had to take it to the superintendent and the preachers. Niels refused to thus let Claus Mortensen decide in part on the future of his marriage, as he had obviously done his best to break it up. Instead, Niels approached the new superintendent, Frans Vormodsen, who was clearly sympathetic to his plight but could not or would not do more than try to reconcile the spouses. Niels finally petitioned the king, who restored him to his wife and his property.

We have only Niels' account of the affair, but it is apparent that Claus Mortensen may have caused "strife and quarrels and uproar in the entire

[73]The undated document of the case is printed in *Danske Magazin* 4,4 (1886): 339-44. The editor suggests a date of 1538 but it may also be 1539. Niels' father-in-law was alive in January of 1538 but had died before January 1539, *MRP*, 132, 153; also, Niels recounts how his father-in-law gave him a piece of property shortly before he married, two years earlier, *Danske Magazin* 4, (1886): 341, 343. From the list for 1537 of rents paid for property formerly belonging to the altars it appears that Niels received the property during 1537, as his father-in-law's name is crossed out and Niels' added to the entry. MSA. LIa: Räkenskaper f. kyrka 1: fol. 68v. Niels Kuntse is mentioned as a councilor in January 1539. *MRP*, 151, but he did not sign an important letter issued October 30, 1539, by the mayors and the councilors of Malmø and the Scanian nobility, so he might have been away on business at that time. If his troubles began after his return, his petition would have been written early in 1540, after the five divorces had been granted by the magistrates (April 1, 1538; January 31, 1539; March 14, 1539 [2]; and March 8, 1540).

[74]"Meg skemmes at scriffue till eders naade the rom, dog haffuer ieg giffuet eders naadis canceller, her Johann Friis, noget tilkiende ther om. Allerkeriste naadigste herre, skal thet være cristeligen wnderuisning, thaa sse her gudt y hemelen till," *Danske Magazin* 4,4 (1886): 341.

town," as Niels charged, by urging the wife to ask for a divorce and by trying to intimidate Niels into agreeing to it.[75] At least it was an acutely embarrassing situation for the magistrates, one that could prove a threat not only to their political positions in town but also to the stability of their own marriages. Interestingly, the *Rådstueprotokol* contains no reference to this case.

Claus Mortensen was not acting on his own account, but had the support of Niels' in-laws. They may have been acting out of resentment toward an upstart foreigner who had married into family and property and whose late father-in-law had been a mayor.[76] In the end, Niels and his wife were reconciled and in 1554 made a reciprocal will.[77]

The episode did not prevent the magistrates from continuing their policy of dealing with marital cases, but no more divorces were granted and the cases all involved couples from the middle class.[78] Meanwhile, the relationship between the magistrates and their foremost reformer and preacher deteriorated rapidly, aggravated by haggling over wages and tithes due the pastor.[79] In 1541 Claus Mortensen was removed from his office as chief pastor of Malmø and provost of Oxie county. He received instead a small rural parish where he remained until his death in 1575.[80]

The next year, jurisdiction over marriage was taken away from city council courts. According to the Riber Articles, issued by the king in 1542, all matters concerning marriage and adultery should be judged by the royal, secular administrator of a diocese and the cathedral chapter. In difficult cases the superintendent should participate. The reason for this change was "the great impropriety in matters of marriage and adultery" that had existed.[81] One may speculate whether the case of Niels Kuntse had been in the minds of the lawmakers. To women in Malmø and elsewhere in the Scanian diocese this meant fewer chances as the superintendent, Frans Vormodsen, only favored divorce

---

[75]"tweest, twedrecht oc upror y then ganske Staadt," ibid.

[76]On Niels' life prior to his marriage and settling in Malmo, see ibid., 337-39.

[77]*Malmø Stadsbog, 1549-1559. Rådstuerettens, bytingets og toldbodrettens protokol,* ed. Einar Bager, Ældre danske rådstueprotokoller og bytingsbøger (Copenhagen: Selskabet for Udgivelse af Kilder til dansk Historie, 1972), 190-91. Henceforth *MSB.*

[78]See above n. 73. The *MRP* does not indicate if any petition for divorce was brought.

[79]*MRP*, 144-46, 181-82.

[80]Sonnenstein-Wendt, "Reformatorerna," 221-224. In 1555-1557 Claus Mortensen was again involved in an attempt to force a separation, this time between his own sister, Anna, and her second husband. In spite of the fact that Anna as well as her children seemed to have suffered in the marriage, the Lund chapter and the king's court refused to grant a divorce, *Danske Magazin* 4, 4 (1886): 345-48. The marriage did not last long, however, as the husband died in 1558, *MSB*, 427-28.

[81]*Danske Kirkelove* 1: 198: "eftherthii ther och findes stoer wskickelighedt wdj i Echteskaff och Huor sager."

under very special circumstances.[82] His actions show that divorce was not granted by him for reasons of incompatibility and maltreatment.[83]

The magistrates were left with marital disputes, which they sought to settle as before, preferring to ensure stability through reconciliation over setting moral examples through punishment. In 1545 the court reconciled a couple in a case where the wife had been the transgressor. Her offense is not stated but it was serious enough to warrant capital punishment if she did not keep her pledge to improve herself, live in a Christian manner with her husband, and behave as a decent goodwife should do. She may have committed adultery. To make certain that the reconciliation worked out, the husband also had to promise to live with her as a Christian and decent man should do.[84]

Another unfortunate husband was Hans Pryssing, whose legal wife was frequently unfaithful to him and who, with her lovers, consumed all that he acquired. In spite of his frequent complaints to the city council and to the chapter in Lund, he did not obtain a divorce but did get a separation. Then he lived with another woman with whom he shared bed, board and table and who carried his keys and behaved as a wife should. He publicly maintained that she was his wife although they had not had a church ceremony. In an inheritance dispute in 1554 the magistrates declared the second woman to be considered his lawful wife because of her long relationship with Hans and her proper behavior.[85]

The city council also confirmed the separation of two couples but the main issue in court was the division of property after the couple had agreed to live apart.[86] Similarly, the magistrates confirmed the proclamation of marriage vows made in private.[87] As long as the parties were agreed on either separation

[82]Ibid., 2: 14-15, Synodal statues for the Scanian diocese 1546, chap. 10: "disertis proinde verbis pronunciat Dominus, eos non liceri separari quos Deus conjunxit. Jam deprehendas multos, quos ebrietas, lenonum illicebræ et alia, quorum author est diabolus, conjunxerunt. Quare censere debemus, requiri quidem consensum uniuscujusque partis, ne videamur coacta matrimonia probare atque tyrannidem stabilire."

[83]*Kirkehist. Saml.* ser. 5, vol. 2 (1903-05): 461-463, contains the documents of a case from 1550 concerning a woman who had been beaten, scolded, and accused of witchcraft by her husband. Frans Vormodsen's decree gave her the right to live apart from her husband but she could not remarry, and the superintendent expressed the hope that they might be reconciled. As the woman had married her farmhand, probably a man without property, this also meant that he was entitled to take half of her property that had become common property during the marriage.

[84]*MRP*, 220. Other examples of marital disputes settled between 1549 and 1559 are found in *MSB*, 222, 361, 390, 398, 428, 445, 446.

[85]*MSB*, 34-35, 177-78.

[86]Ibid., 146-47, 429

[87]Ibid., 175-177: confirmation of a vow, made in 1554 by a merchant from Rostock on his deathbed. The pastor, who attended him, had reminded him of his vow to "the poor woman, Barbara, who lives with you and with whom you have your lovely children." The couple were then married by the pastor in the presence of witnesses. The letter issued by the magistrates was meant as an aid to Barbara in claiming her and her children's share in her husband's property in Rostock.

or marriage, the magistrates dealt with them, but contested vows or divorces were referred to the chapter in Lund.[88] To women in Malmø this meant that attempts to change their marital situation significantly were decided in a court presided by men who did not know their circumstances personally and who were more interested in judging cases on moral, legal, and religious authorities and ideologies than in settling disputes in the way most practical to all involved.

V

The course of events leading up to the Reformation in Malmø was to some extent similar to that which other towns in Denmark followed but nowhere do we find the magistrates as intimately involved with the reformers, deliberately attempting to change the religious and institutional structure to ensure evangelical liberty and, at the same time, political independence from all powers except the monarch. The magistrates of Malmø succeeded in severing ties to the Catholic Church and its influence on the lives and affairs of the Malmø citizenry. For women, one major importance of the reform in Malmø laying in the usurpation by the city council court of jurisdiction over matrimonial affairs of lay as well as clerical inhabitants. Because of the liberal attitude of the magistrates on these issues, this development proved beneficial to women, albeit for a short time. However, the benefit was a by-product of magisterial policy aiming at establishing control through legal jurisdiction exercised by their court. Their liberality stemmed from efforts to reach practical and workable decisions that would further the stability of the social structure. They did not intend to set examples of moral behavior, which might have alienated some of the citizens. Furthermore, there was little opposition to their actions within the city and practically none after the friars had been forced out. There were no sectarians or radical reformers[89] either, nor any urban nobility who might sabotage the religious and political goals of the reformers and the magistrates. Opposition came from outsiders, such as the Catholic clergy and the Scanian nobility; significantly, these parties posed a threat to the entire citizenry and its political and economic activities.

---

[88]Ibid., 68, 388-89.

[89]Claus Mortensen was a radical in his actions, but not in his teachings. His role during the early years was to preach and stir up popular support for the reform movement and in this he was, as a great orator, very effective. The theological debates and the formulation of the Protestant program were handled by the more learned and more moderate Frans Vormodsen and Peter Laurentius, Johannesson, *Skånska kyrkan*, 176-77. There are no indications that Claus Mortensen before or after 1536 held opinions that were not in accordance with the *Confessio Hafniensis* or the Church Ordinance. It is noteworthy that Frans Vormodsen in the case of Niels Kuntse obviously had another opinion on the issue than Claus Mortensen. Yet, he did not attack the latter but sought to work out a reconciliation.

The preconditions for the positive effect of the magisterial Reformation in Malmø on women had little to do with the reform itself. For one, there seems to have been no particularly negative attitude towards women nor an undue stress on the subordination of the female sex to the male. We do not find examples of the misogynism expressed, for example, by the early humanists in Strasbourg.[90] For another, women in general enjoyed a rather unrestricted lifestyle in late-medieval Danish towns. They were active and visible in the economic life of the city and they enjoyed quite extensive legal rights.[91] They were familiar with the city court, to which they brought suits arising from their economic activities, and with the magistrates who belonged to the society in which the women lived, worked, and married.

In the final analysis, however, these conditions rested on shaky foundations, namely, the goodwill of the all-male ruling elite. When its views on women's role and place in society changed, so did the rights of women. The case of Niels Kuntse, and the subsequent loss by the magistrates of the right to decide on matrimonial issues, was followed by a subtle change in attitudes towards women. "Humble" and "obedient" were adjectives attached to the definition of wifely behavior. In 1549 the first ordinance to attempt circumscribing the lifestyle of single women was issued by the magistrates.[92] In Malmø as elsewhere in Denmark, the following century witnessed a steady deterioration in the rights of women, culminating in the *Danish Law* of 1683.

One may, in view of the distinct character of the early Reformation in Malmø, argue that this was due to the establishment of the Lutheran *Fürstenkirche* and the subsequent development of an increasingly orthodox and inflexible church which had absorbed Luther's very restricted views on women and their role in society.[93] It is doubtful, however, if the conditions of women in Malmø could have remained unchanged had the magistrates been able to continue their political and religious line after 1536. The city council likely would have faced internal as well as external opposition and would have resorted to a stricter policy, including making decisions designed to define limits of permitted and preferred behavior. Such was done, for example, by the Consistory of Geneva.[94] The benefit to women of the male magistrates' policy

---

[90]Christman, "Women . . . Strasbourg," 144-46.

[91]Dübeck, *Købekoner, passim*; Grethe Jacobsen, "Women's Work and Women's Role: Ideology and Reality in Danish Urban Society, 1300-1550," *Scandinavian Economic History Review* 30, 1 (1983): 3-20.

[92]*MSB*, 35-36. The ordinance demanded that all self-supporting maidens (*pigher szom ere szelffødinge*) should take work as servants or be exiled from town.

[93]Merry Wiesner, "The Death of Two Marys: Images of the Female and Feminine in Luther," paper presented at Church and Society History Workshop, London, July 8, 1983.

[94]E. William Monter, "Women in Calvinist Geneva (1500-1800)" *Signs: Journal of Women in Culture and Society* 6 (1980/81): 189-209.

was a by-product rather than an integral part of the ideology governing their society. Consequently, it was bound to be insecure and temporary. As women were given neither the tools nor the opportunity to participate in the theological and political debates, they were prevented from influencing changes in ideology and society. They had to make the most of those moments in which they could make at least some decisions affecting their lives. One such moment came during the magisterial reformation in Malmø in matters concerning marriage. Women of Malmø seemed to have exploited it as long as it lasted.

Harold Grimm as a young instructor at Capitol University

Making Ends Meet: The Working Poor in Early Modern Europe*

Merry E. Wiesner
Augustana College

EVERY YEAR AT CORPUS CHRISTI, from medieval times until well into the modern period, a procession of craftsmen, all dressed in their guild livery and carrying small drums, tambourines and other musical instruments, wound its way through the streets of many European cities. The order in which the guilds marched depended on which crafts had organized first in the town and which were most economically and politically powerful. These matters had been determined over centuries of time. In Munich, for example, the procession began with clothcutters, tailors, and leatherworkers; continued, among others, with carpenters, tinsmiths, and wagon-makers; and ended with cooks, dice-makers and woodcutters. After all of the guilds, however, came another large group of people, identified in Munich as "widows, daughters, and other poor people who work in the city."[1]

Just who were all these people? They were not craftsmen nor those training to be craftsmen. They were not merchants, officials, professionals, shopkeepers, or even market women, for all of these groups had already marched by. But neither were they beggars or vagrants, for such people did not take part in Corpus Christi parades. They were, as the Munich records call them, the working poor. They were people who were attempting to survive in Munich—and indeed in every city—by doing any work that was available.

This group warrants special attention during the early modern period because they were present in nearly every city. They were vulnerable as economic, social, and intellectual changes affected them more keenly than they did those who were better off. Bad harvests, the decline of the guilds, changes in production methods, new attitudes toward charitable giving, and inflation all had direct and immediate effect. Most of all, the working poor evidenced a remarkable durability and adaptability in their efforts to support themselves and their families.

To look at this group more closely we must first identify them. Who were they? What circumstances brought one into, and then kept one in, these ranks? Other questions then arise. What employment options and opportunities were open for them? How did they view themselves, and how were they

*Research for this essay was made possible by grants from the American Council of Learned Societies and the Deutsche Akademische Austauschdienst.

[1]Munich, Stadtarchiv, Ratsitzungsprotokoll (hereafter cited RSP), 1484. This study is based on material found in the city archives of Munich, Frankfurt am Main, Strasbourg, Memmingen, Augsburg, and Stuttgart, and the state archives in Stuttgart and Nuremberg. As each archive has its own system of organizing material, I have given references in the terms by which the items may be most easily found. All translations are my own.

viewed by those around them, for example, by those who had marched in the main body of the parade?

To begin with, these were people who for one reason or another were excluded from the guilds or similar craft organizations. The earliest guild ordinances in most cities required that all members be of legitimate birth, and the number of documents required to prove legitimacy increased steadily. A simple parish record was often acceptable only if it was backed up by the testimony of two honorable citizens.[2] Not only the guild member himself, but also his wife and often his parents had to be legitimate and to have maintained an "honorable" life-style.[3] Any hint of misconduct, such as association with prostitutes or women suspected of being prostitutes, or living with one's wife after she was found guilty of adultery, could result not only in exclusion, but also in expulsion if one were already a member.[4]

Additionally, the descendants of people who had certain occupations were categorically excluded from guild membership. Children or grandchildren of executioners, prostitutes, night-soil collectors, brothel managers and, in some cities, bath operators could never remove the blemish from their past or hope to join the ranks of the truly honorable. By the mid-sixteenth century, guilds in many cities had restricted membership even further, allowing one to become a member only if married to the widow or daughter of a master.[5] Widows and daughters themselves were no longer allowed to continue operating shops on their own, nor were women accepted independently into most guilds. City councils consistently tried to fight all such restrictions, which they felt were not for the "common good," but in matters of membership they had little power over the guilds.

Exclusion from guild membership or from marriage to a guild member did not automatically drop one to the ranks of the working poor, however. If one had enough capital, one could purchase or rent an inn, a wine cellar, a shop selling variety merchandise, a brothel, a cart or boat for transporting goods, or at least a permanent stand at the public market. All of these were occupations open to and practiced by persons of both sexes and all ages, citizens and noncitizens, though the former were preferred. As long as one paid one's taxes and

[2]E. g., Frankfurt, Stadtarchiv, Zünfte (hereafter Z) C-53, Ff 4 (1587); Bürgermeister-buch (hereafter BMB) 1590, fol. 175a; 1535, fol. 73a; UGB D-11, (Schlosser) Z, No. 7.

[3]Rudolph Wissel, *Des Alten Handwerks Recht und Gewhohnheit* (Berlin: Colloquium Verlag, 1974), 1: 254.

[4]E.g., Frankfurt woolweavers (1455), Frankfurt stonemasons (1521) quoted in Karl Bücher and Benno Schmidt, *Frankfurter Amts und Zunfturkunden bis zum Jahre 1602* (Frankfurt: Joseph Baer, 1914), 87; Strasbourg, Archives Municipales, Statuten (herafter S) 1619, fol. 186; Frankfurt BMB 1505, fol. 95a.

[5]G. K. Schmelzeisen, *Die Rechtstellung der Frau in der deutschen Stadtwirtschaft* (Stuttgart: 1935), 53.

didn't bother one's neighbors, few questions were asked. The hitch, however, was that one have the initial capital; for the penniless and near-penniless, these were not options. Orphans, widows, war refugees, recent immigrants into the city, third and fourth daughters (or third and fourth sons for that matter) could rarely have gathered together enough money to purchase or even rent a permanent establishment or equipment such as a cart and horses.

As we might expect, the working poor consisted of a disproportionate share of women, they being generally excluded from the guilds and having fewer opportunities to amass capital. Studies of the tax lists in Schwäbisch-Hall, Frankfurt am Main, Trier, Wismar, and Munich indicate that while widows and single women made up ten to twenty percent of the heads-of-households, they made up thirty to forty percent of those paying the least taxes.[6] Such women often were described as living in a cellar, a shack, or a single room, though they were technically heads of households for tax purposes.

These same tax lists can also give us some idea of the total number of working poor in a city. Though there is a great deal of discussion among urban historians as to where to draw the line marking the poverty level, most would agree that those identified in the records as "habnichts"—have-nothings—or as owning less than 30 fl. worth of goods were definitely poor.[7] This group numbered from ten to twenty percent of the population in most cities, and their numbers increased during times of famine or war, when people flocked in from the countryside.

Tax records list only heads of household; therefore, they do not include servants, apprentices or journeymen who lived in a master's house, nor vagrants and itinerant beggars, all of whom may also be considered poor. This ten to twenty percent, consequently, represents that share of the poor who could not rely on someone else to fed and house them, as servants and apprentices could, but who lived solely by their own labor, with occasional aid from church or municipal charities during extremely bad times.

Thus our group of working poor, which could make up as much as a fifth of a city's population, was disproportionately female, was bunched at the old and young ends of the age scale, and came from questionable or suspect family backgrounds. What could they do and what did they do in order to survive?

The simplest answer here is: practically anything, and a wide variety of different things at once or in quick succession. These varied according to the

---

[6]Gerd Wunder, "Die Bewohner der Reichsstadt Hall im Jahre 1545," *Württembergische Franken* 49 (1965): 34 ff.; Friedrich Bothe, *Frankfurts wirtschaftliche-soziale Entwicklung vor dem 30. Jährigen Krieg und der Fettmilchaufstand (1612-1616), 2,* Statistische Bearbeitung (Frankfurt: Joseph Baer, 1920); Annette Winter, "Studien zur sozialen Situationen der Frauen in der Stadt Trier nach der Steuerlisten von 1364," *Kurtrierisches Jahrbuch* 1975, 20-45; Erich Maschke, *Gesellschaftliche Unterschichten in den südwestdeutschen Städten,* Protokolle über die V. Arbeitskreises für südwestdeutsche Stadtgeschichtsforschung (Stuttgart: Kohlhammer, 1967), 27; Munich, Stadtarchiv, Steuerbucher (herafter SB).

[7]Maschke, passim.

structure of the economy in each city and according to the age, sex, and abilities of the person. Even so, we can trace several patterns which may be considered typical.

On first coming into a city, young people of both sexes often sought permanent employment as household servants. In Nuremburg, Strasbourg, and Munich they went to an official employment agent (typically a woman), identifying her by the sign on her stand or house. If the applicant hadn't worked anywhere before and thus did not have a letter of recommendation, she was to judge the young persons' character and skills and attempt to find them appropriate positions.[8] Once hired, an employee was expected to stay at that position for at least a year unless there could be proven gross misconduct on the part of the employer. In cities without official employment agents, market women or neighborhood leaders probably handled this kind of thing informally.

If no permanent domestic positions were available—and by the mid-sixteenth century many cities required that all native young people be hired before any foreigners could be taken on—one could still work in someone's home on a temporary basis. Large households frequently hired laundresses by the day or week for the heavy laundry, seamstresses for special repairs or alterations, and repairmen to fix roofs and walls. For such work, one either would be paid completely in cash or be given several meals and a few pennies extra to take care of housing somewhere.

If one were young and strong, a number of other opportunities as a day laborer could also be available. City residents often hired people to work in their vineyards or fields, paying them by the day according to the kind of work done. Those who weeded or gleaned were paid less than those who worked with sickles, hoes, or other tools; these in turn received less than those who mowed or reaped with a scythe. According to municipal wage regulations, women were paid half of what men were paid; if they were fed on the job they were to receive no alcohol and decidedly less protein than men received.[9] The city itself occasionally hired manual laborers for repairing its fortifications and similar tasks; it also paid women roughly half what it paid men.[10]

Frederick Bothe has figured the purchasing power of day laborers' wages in Frankfurt for both 1587 and 1611. In the former year, a male vineyard worker could purchase three pounds of beef or five pounds of flour or 32 eggs if he spent his entire day's wages; a female vineyard worker could buy only half that. By 1611 the situation had worsened: male wages could purchase only

[8]Nuremberg, Staatsarchiv, Amts und Standbucher (hereafter ASB), No. 101, fols. 558-67; Munich, Stadtarchiv, Gewerbeamt (hereafter GA) No. 2569 (1580); Strasbourg S, vol. 18, fols. 30-34 (1557).

[9]Stuttgart, Hauptstaatsarchiv, A-58, Landwirtschaftordnung (1550); A-39, Generalreskripta, Taglohnerordnung (1550); Frankfurt, Ordnung für Weingarten und Feldarbeit (1604); Munich, Bussordnung, vol. 419, Taglohnerordnung (1511).

[10]Strasbourg S, vol. 10, fol. 79, Taglohner Taxe (1633).

two pounds of beef, four pounds of flour, or seventeen eggs, and female wages, again, could manage only half that. Those who did lighter garden or domestic work received even less.[11]

Along with agricultural and construction work, in many cities there were opportunities for piecework of one kind or another, particularly in textile production. The large number of weavers in a city like Augsburg or Frankfurt or Ulm necessitated a huge number of spinners and carders. These were usually women and they worked in their own homes, in the weaver's house, or in a rented room. Though they also were badly paid, many women preferred the independence of such labor to the dependent status, though with greater security, of being a domestic servant. In the late sixteenth century the Augsburg city council became worried and irritated about this "as the women have complete freedom as to when they work and when not, and freedom to walk around with young journeymen all during the week." It forbade all unmarried women to live on their own, though it is doubtful if this prohibition was regularly enforced.[12]

Master craftsmen also hired pieceworkers to work in their shops alongside apprentices and journeymen. These workers were usually limited to packing, finishing, polishing, or similarly unskilled tasks. Nevertheless, journeymen often complained that masters were using pieceworkers to do work that was rightfully theirs.[13] These objections became particularly bitter in the late sixteenth century when many journeymen could no longer hope to become masters but could look forward only to a life not much different from that of a pieceworker, being always employed in another master's shop. It is at this point that journeymen began to oppose all female labor in the shop. They were attempting to save a shred of their old position and honor by sharply differentiating their work from that of pieceworkers, who often were women.

Several other options were open exclusively for young women. Usually those options were chosen only as a last resort. Until the middle of the sixteenth century most cities ran municipal brothels, which were ordered to accept only foreigners and non-virgins. How the latter were determined is never explained.[14] Fear of syphilis combined with Reformation and Counter-Reformation morality caused the brothels to be closed in most cities by 1560, but illicit prostitution still thrived.[15] Public baths also hired women to perform

[11]Bothe, *Frankfurts wirtz.-soz. Entwicklung*, 212-13.

[12]Quoted in Claus Peter Clasen, *Die Augsburger Weber: Leistung und Krisen des Textilgewerbes um 1600* (Augsburg: Hieronymus Mühlberger, 1981), 132-33.

[13]Frankfurt Z, Posamentierer, II, Nos. 56 and 62; Nuremberg, Staatsarchiv, Ratsbücher (hereafter RB), 1519; Memmingen, Stadtarchiv, 441, no. 3 (1632); Munich, GA, Film 1020, no. 74.

[14]Strasbourg S., vol. 2, fol. 72; Memmingen, Stadtdenkbuch; Nuremberg RB 24, fol. 128 (1548), RB 26, fol. 354 (1553); Iwan Bloch, *Die Prostitution* (Berlin: Louis Marcus, 1912) 1: 740.

[15]E.g., Strasbourg S, vol. 29, fol. 154.

a variety of services. They helped patrons coming to undress, or held their clothes for them; they rubbed them, beat them with switches or scratched them with their fingernails to increase circulation; they shaved them, washed their hair, dried them, and oiled their bodies. In all cases they handled both male and female customers.[16] Hospitals during times of epidemics needed extra workers and extra pesthouses were opened. In these establishments, both women and men cooked, changed linen, bathed the patients, and buried the dead.[17]

A large share of the working poor were older, however, and could not have been hired by baths or brothels nor could have worked as agricultural laborers. They often turned to things which they could do in their own homes. Older women took in orphans when the municipal orphanage grew too crowded, or taught a few young children basic reading and writing.[18] They took care of the mentally ill or elderly, either in the home of the patient or in their own homes, and were paid a few pennies by the city or by the family.[19] Older couples or widows operated "sleeping houses," providing places for out-of-town visitors to stay at a lower rate than that charged by normal inns.[20]

The most common expedient was to make and sell small, simple items which were not in the province of any specific guild. These ranged from baked goods, such as pretzels, small rolls, sweet buns or cookies, to candles, sausages and tripe, vinegar, yeast, wooden spoons and bowls, and brandy.[21] These were either peddled house to house, or sold from small stands at various places throughout the city. One received permission to do this by making a special supplication to the city council. These supplications provide us with a glimpse into the life of the working poor. Responses to them give an idea of how the poor were viewed by the city councils and the guilds.

In 1632, for example, a woman appealed to the Strasbourg city council for permission to bake "Ayerwecken" (egg pretzels). She and her husband had been driven out of the Palatinate and then he had ridden off to fight in the bat-

---

[16]Luise Hess, *Die deutschen Frauenberufe des Mittelalters*, Beiträge zur Volkstumforschung 6 (Munich: Neuer Filser, 1940): 135; Karl Bücher, *Die Berufe der Stadt Frankfurt im Mittelalter* (Leipzig: Teubner, 1914); Munich, RSP, 1609, fol. 77. Women are actually identified in tax lists as "clothing-holder" or "rubber."

[17]Nuremberg ASB, No. 101, fol. 160; Memmingen, Ratsprotokollbücher (hereafter RPB), Feb. 9, 1588; Augsburg, Stadtarchiv, Collegium Medicum, Fasc. 5.

[18]Bücher, *Berufe*; Hess, *Frauenberufe*, 127; Stuttgart, Stadtarchiv, Findbuch, 1563 and 1581; Strasbourg S 1616, fol. 140; Frankfurt BMB 1505, fol. 106b.

[19]Memmingen, RPB, May 10, 1529; Frankfurt, BMB, 1545, fol. 89b; Munich, Steuerbücher, 1560-1640.

[20]Strasbourg, Akten der XV (hereafter XV), 1613, fol. 220a; 1620, fol. 168a; 1628, fols. 51 and 57; 1640, fols. 75 and 98; 1665, fols. 115a; Nuremberg, RB 23, fol. 80b (1545).

[21]Memmingen, RPB, March 20, 1618; Frankfurt: Bedebücher, 1346-1500; Munich, RPB 1601, fol. 82; Steuerbücher 1532, 1610; GA, Küchelbäcker, no. 6 (1625); GA, no. 2866; Strasbourg XV, 1623, fol. 106b.

tle of White Mountain and had "remained there along the way." Despite objections by the bakers that there were already too many people making pretzels and selling them without the proper taxes, the city allowed her to bake.[22] (Two years later it granted permission to several others as well "because all of the supplicants are poor people that are particularly hard-pressed in these difficult times."[23]) This case is typical for a number of reasons. She was a widow, driven far from her original home and into the city by a combination of religious and economic forces. The bakers felt threatened by her activities, but argued their side in terms of taxes which were being lost to the city. The council allowed her (and several others) to work despite the objections because of the emergency stiuation, but did not make a blanket statement opening pretzel baking to all.

In many other supplications the same attitudes emerge. The supplicants first stressed their desperate situations, i. e., "because as a poor widow I have nothing but what I earn with trials and work in sour sweat . . . as I already have one foot in the grave and few days left to live." Then they confessed total dependence on the city council's decision, i.e.,"I would see your permission as such great generosity that I would constantly and fervently pray to God for your health and salvation."[24] They often pointed out that weakness, age, or ill health made it impossible for them to do anything else, and frequently are described as "Anna with the one foot" or "the old man who hears badly" or something similar.[25]

If they were clever, the petitioners added a note about the consequences of not granting them permission, e.g., "If the meager piece of bread is taken out of our mouths, I and my five children will then be forced to turn to begging or to the municipal welfare fund."[26] They also frequently played on conflicts and jealousies between guilds by selling something which two different guilds felt they had the sole right to sell. Or they played a guild against the council, arguing that a guild had illegally prohibited them doing something, thus usurping the council's power in the matter. As a last resort they used pleas of their own helplessness or incompetence, arguing that their trade was so minimal they couldn't possibly be hurting anyone by it.[27]

The concerned guilds would answer the supplicants point by point. He or she wasn't that old or infirm, nor were there that many small children: "He is not really sick, but spends his day drinking and dicing and could use the eldest of his two daughters to make lace."[28] Or the sorry stiuation was actually the

[22]Strasbourg XV, 1632.

[23]Strasbourg XV, 1634, fols. 29 and 34.

[24]Memmingen, 441 (Strumpfstricker) 441 no. 3 (1662).

[25]Munich, GA, passim.

[26]Frankfurt Z, Metzgern, no. 65 (1648).

[27]Strasbourg XV, 1607, fol. 147.

[28]Strasbourg XV, 1639, fol. 117.

fault of the supplicant: "Her husband is a lazy louse, and it is her fault that she has attached herself to someone like that."[29] They would hint that he or she actually had some capital, so should live off that or invest it.[30] The guild often would take the somewhat curious tack that this person had been or would be too successful, thus driving regular master craftsmen out of business. Because of the supplicant's success, real or potential, the council should not feel any pity nor find that the person was "truly needy."[31]

The city councils weighed each of these supplications separately, usually granting permission if they felt this was the only way to keep someone off the municipal welfare rolls. They also recognized that the city possibly could profit from the activities of these people. During the Thirty Years' War, the council in Strasbourg allowed more than 40 people to sell brandy, justifying this with the comment "in consideration of the present hard times which all will recognize [this will allow them] not only to support themselves better and live through this, but we hope also to bring in more taxes from those who are drinking."[32] War brought refugees flocking into the city, but it also created opportunities, as these people had to be fed, clothed and housed. In addition, the market for used pistols, swords and armor improved.[33]

Occasionally the council refused permission even in desperate cases, if it felt a bad precedent would be set and too many people would apply.[34] Then it grudgingly allowed the applicant "a penny from the general welfare fund because she complains so loudly about her poverty."[35]

Thus the city council saw the working poor in two different lights. One showed them as a means to solve short-term needs for labor in the city. And so the council would allow them to enter into domestic service, work in guild shops, or sell small items whenever it perceived these measures were necessary. The other illumined for the council a way it could demonstrate its benevolence, generosity, and Christian charity without any threat to its own economic and political power. By allowing people to work for a few pennies to support themselves and their families, the council provided an acceptable alternative to begging and showed support for whatever kind of refugee that particular city attracted.

[29]Strasbourg XV, 1615, fol. 124.

[30]Strasbourg XV, 1674, fols. 130, 140, 175.

[31]Frankfurt Z, Ugb. D25, no. 2 (1692); C59 Cc (1639); Strasbourg XV, 1607 fols. 43, 54, 58, 84, 98, 103, 119. This is also a sixteenth-century phrase.

[32]Strasbourg XV, 1636, fol. 167b.

[33]Strasbourg XV, 1633, fols. 88, 177, 230; August Jegel, *Ernährungsfürsorge des Altnürnberger Rats* (Nuremberg: Sonderdruck des Nürnberger Stadtarchivs, 1937), 169.

[34] Nuremberg, RB 68, fol. 239 (1610); Munich, GA, Küchelbäcker no. 2307 (1660); Strasbourg XV, 1616, fols. 101 and 168; 1665, fol. 121; Frankfurt, BMB, 1495, fol. 21a; Memmingen RPB, Sept. 25, 1580.

[35]Nuremberg, RB, 62, fol. 4 (1603).

The guilds and crafts, on the other hand, felt that their status and economic security were threatened by these working poor. Whether it was journeymen objecting to pieceworkers in the shops, or innkeepers complaining of people running sleeping houses, the opposition always was led by those who were just above the working poor on the economic scale. Here, too, the issue was not solely an economic one but also involved the pride and group identity of the others. As their economic status declined, journeymen especially were forced to differentiate themselves in other ways from those who were not guild members. Simple supplications often became a battleground in the litigation war involving council, guilds, and later, journeymen over control of economic life in the city. Thus they acquired a symbolic importance much greater than is apparent at first glance. This explains why a widow's pleas to be allowed to make chemises should result in months of argument and calls for expert and foreign opinions on both sides.[36] The issue was not chemises, but control.

The poor themselves, however, were not simply silent pawns in this war. Though often smothered in secretarial prose, their voices come through in many of the supplications and court cases. A few examples are cited below.

A woman running a small sleeping house charged two out-of-town guests with failure to pay their bills. Not only had she sent someone to collect, finally she had gone herself "and stood at their door for three hours demanding payment, as she was an honest person who would be brought to ruin if they didn't pay." On the order of the court the guests finally paid more than they had owed originally, as she demanded compensation "for all of her time and trouble."[37]

Anna Weylandin, nicknamed the "Lumpenweiblin," was called before the Strasbourg Fifteen, the body handling internal affairs, on more than ten different occasions, charged with illegally selling herring, candles and imported cheese, among other infractions. She appeared only once, answering the other demands for her appearance with the comment, "No matter what in God's name kind of orders they give, I will not follow them."[38] Another Strasbourg woman appeared before the same body for calling a local nobleman "du Schelmen" because he had knocked over her rag stand. The phrase had a range of possible meanings, from "you stinking, putrified carcass" to "you vile and obscene wretch."[39]

An old man baking small rolls in Strasbourg answered the bakers guild's complaint: "Can I help it if my wares are good and tasty so that people prefer

[36]Memmingen, 471 (Schneidern), 4 and 5 (1641).
[37]Munich, Stadtgericht 867, 1602, vol. 10.
[38]Strasbourg XV, 1574, fol. 136b.
[39]Strasbourg XV, 1588, fol. 104.

them to yours?"[40] Another replied to the innkeepers guild: "Can I throw people out who feel comfortable in my house?"[41] Guilds often were accused of being motivated by "bitter jealousy, hatred, envy, and pettiness" rather than a legitimate desire to potect the quality of their products; their ability to meet the demand for certain items was also questioned.[42]

The spinners in Augsburg who worked on their own, not in a master weaver's house, defended their right to do so with the comment that "spinning is a fine and honorable occupation" and added that the money they made helped them to support their elderly parents, which they could not do if forced to move into a weaver's house.[43] The firewood sellers in Frankfurt defended their rights even more vigorously, brandishing sticks or grabbing wood out of competitors' hands.[44]

A woman asking to take in orphaned children strengthened her request with the statement, "I have asked God for his grace and help with such work."[45] Another, charged with practicing medicine illegally, gave God an even more active role: "God in heaven gave me my life and soul and gifts of healing, so I have no choice but to treat people."[46]

We should remember that these were people who often had neither family nor occupational group for a means of identity or a source of support in times of emergency. Despite this, as the examples indicate, they were willing to stand up to city councils, courts, and guilds to defend their right to work, their right to an existence not dependent on the charity of others. This was often a miserable existence, as shown by the agricultural wage charts, but it was still an independent one.

Thus we find in the working poor an autonomous sense of identity rather than one coming from membership in some corporate body such as a family, city, or guild. We have long seen the Renaissance as the time when, for some people, the sense of self shifted from the collective to the individual; usually we have noted this in artists and humanists, some merchants, and a few theologians. To these we must perhaps add the working poor who, out of necessity rather than intellectual choice, were forced to turn inward for their source of strength.

[40]Strasbourg XV, 1616, fols. 101 and 168.

[41]Strasbourg XV, 1585, fols. 77b and 79b.

[42]E.g., Frankfurt Z Wollenweber, Ugb. C32 R no. 1 (1663); Ugb. C59 Spengler, Aa no. 4 (1676); Strasbourg XV, 1633, fols. 88, 177, 178, 230, 232.

[43]1561, quoted in Clasen, *Augsburger Weber*, 132.

[44]Frankfurt, Verordnungen, no. 73 (1610).

[45]Frankfurt, Court Cases no. 56 (1677).

[46]Memmingen, 405 (Barbieren), no. 12 (1602).

Visitations and Popular Religious Culture: Further Reports from Strasbourg

James M. Kittelson
The Ohio State University

A DECADE OR SO AGO, SOCIAL HISTORIANS of the late middle ages and the Reformation typically limited their studies to the competing interests of the classes or estates that composed sixteenth-century society. Now they are also keenly interested in the actual religious beliefs and practices of these groups.[1] Commonly, the fundamental issue in this work is the correlation, or lack thereof, between what may be called the official religion of the *experti* and the actual religion of more ordinary people. As a consequence, it is no surprise that most studies conclude that there existed a remarkable tension between these two religious cultures and often see in them an expression of wider conflicts between the upper and lower classes or between those who governed and "the common person." Thus official religion, the most common object of traditional Reformation studies, is frequently seen now as but one more effort of cities and the bourgeoisie to dominate the countryside, lord, and peasant in early modern times.[2]

The study of popular religious culture has also become one way of charting the development of modern civilization, and rightly so. Yet, two fundamental uncertainties underlie the findings and general conclusions in this field. The first concerns the presence of what modern scholars define as magic or superstition in the religious beliefs and practices of ordinary people. It is almost universally assumed that the existence of these elements—the casting of sign, spells, or hexes, and the like—is sure evidence of vibrant lower class religious values that were held tenaciously in opposition to the upper classes' attempts to reform them.[3]

But embarrassing anomalies remain. In just this regard, it must never be forgotten that Philip Melanchthon was an avid follower of astrological predictions (for which Luther delighted in chiding him), that Giordano Bruno believed in astral magic (for which the Inquisition burned him), and that sign was regularly cast at many European courts. Modernity thus becomes a very

[1] See the discussion of recent literature in Natalie Zemon Davis, "From 'Popular Religion' to Religious Cultures," in Steven Ozment, ed., *Reformation Europe: A Guide to Research* (St. Louis: Center for Reformation Research, 1982), 321-341.

[2] A point of view expressed in, for example, Thomas A. Brady, Jr., "Social History," in *Reformation Europe*, 161 ff. The notion of "the common man" comes from Peter Blickle, *Die Revolution von 1525*, 2d ed. (Munich: Oldenbourg, 1981; Baltimore: Johns Hopkins University Press, 1982).

[3] The point of view of Gerald Strauss, *Luther's House of Learning. Indoctrination of the Young in the German Reformation* (Baltimore: Johns Hopkins University Press, 1978). For a dissent, see Thomas N. Tentler, *Sin and Confession on the Eve of the Reformation* (Princeton: Princeton University Press, 1977).

difficult thing to identify, for within the traditional categories of social history, surely Melanchthon and Luther, Bruno and the Inquisition, as well as the crowned heads of Europe were part of the elite.

It must be expected that learned professors (whose own intellectual parentage dates from the Enlightenment) would regard magic and superstition as the essence of popular religious culture. Nonetheless, there is a second reason that this assumption may be misleading the attempt to track the development of modern civilization.[4] Here, one may even put aside the thorny question of who exactly were "the common people" and, therefore the corollary question of who else's religion was "official." It is enough to note that there is little scholarly consensus on the extent to which orthodoxy, however defined, did indeed penetrate the minds and consciousness of common people, and if it did, when, to say nothing of how. It is certainly correct to insist in principle that "a religious culture should be seen in two-way communication with the structures of authority around it."[5] At the very least, this assertion has the virtue of neatly sidestepping the issue of what beliefs were appropriate to which rungs on the social ladder. But what are students of the development of modern civilization to conclude when specialists on popular religious culture disagree fundamentally over what exactly the evidence says with respect to the content of the religion of ordinary people?

The case in point is a recent debate[6] regarding the success or failure of Germany's Protestant reformers in imposing religious orthodoxy on the countryside through sermons, catechisms, visitations, and exhortations. One scholar took all Germany as his subject and concluded that the reformers failed to meet their objectives unless they had recourse to the coercive authority of their secular governments. Another, in seeking to replicate these findings, chose the city of Strasbourg and its villages as a case study. The disappointing result was that the case study flatly contradicted the more general treatment. Additionally, Strasbourg was one of the bases for the conclusions of the larger study. Consequently, those not intimately acquainted with the sources for each of these two studies are left with no solid grounds for deciding whom to believe with respect to what the sources do and do not say. Therewith the entire attempt to track the genesis of modernity with the signs of popular religious culture founders at its first step.

This exchange concluded with three suggestions for reconstituting the history of German popular religious culture during the sixteenth century:

---

[4]See the critique of H. C. Erik Midlefort, "Witchcraft, Magic, and the Occult," in *Reformation Europe*, 183-209. The standard point of departure is Keith Thomas, *Religion and the Decline of Magic* (London: Weidenfeld and Nicolson, 1971).

[5]Davis, "Religious Cultures," *Reformation Europe*, 324.

[6]Strauss, *Luther's House*, esp. the section on visitations, 249-308, and James M. Kittelson, "Successes and Failures in the German Reformation: The Report from Strasbourg," *Archive for Reformation History* 73 (1982), 171-72.

1. The exact objectives and methods of the reformers must be defined as they defined them and as they sought to meet them; scholars must not accord their more ambitious aspiration that, for example, all enter the kingdom of God or that all lead a respectable life, more than the status of a "wish-list" that no one expected to realize in the here and now.

2. Discovering whether pastors, i. e., representatives of the governors rather than the governed, achieved their objectives must be accomplished on the basis of parish-by-parish and year-to-year data wherever and whenever possible; sampling techniques merely open the door to false impressions.

3. Very local and even temporary circumstances must be taken into account for the simple reason that life in early modern Europe was lived in very local and narrowly temporal ways.

In sum, the debate is such that any general interpretations of popular religious culture before, during, and as a consequence of the Reformation are so premature as to be little more than exercises in metahistory. Indeed, exact time and place are absolutely crucial to understanding any period in which circumstance ruled with an iron fist.

These suggestions came from a close study of the visitation reports from Strasbourg's rural parishes. There it became clear that by the early 1560s the city's peasants were exhibiting more or less the religious beliefs and behavior that their civil and ecclesiastical overlords desired. But one difficulty remained, and it is the central issue in this discussion. Simply put, evidence from the end of the century suggests that within a generation the religion of the common people may have reverted as a norm to its previous condition. Obviously, it was necessary to account for this abrupt return. A finger was pointed at the Bishop's War of the 1590s and the consequent disruption of normal civil and ecclesiastical procedures. It was then suggested that once the war ended and the authorities were able to carry on their work, popular religious culture returned to its pre-war status. Specifically, people began once again to come to church in time to hear the sermon, children began again to learn the catechism, and extravagant celebrations of baptisms and marriages were again brought under control. Or so it was suggested.

Everything would be much neater if it were possible to report that further research denies to the Bishop's War any role in the evolution of popular religious culture in the environs of Strasbourg. It would therefore no longer be necessary to undertake the massive cooperative research efforts that this single stubborn reality seems to require. But, simply put, the case study continues to contradict the general study in all the ways noted above. The reports from the

end of the sixteenth and on into the seventeenth century reveal that the
Bishop's War was indeed but a temporary and highly debatable interlude in
Strasbourg's largely successful effort to force its citizens into religious ortho-
doxy of the Lutheran variety.

The report of the visitation of 1601 is the star witness in these
proceedings.[7] But before turning to it in particular, it is necessary to test the
dependability of all the evidence from the period in question. In particular, are
the reports reliable for the years after 1580 when Johann Pappus, rather than
Johann Marbach, was President of the Company of Pastors? Here it must be
added that the circumstances affecting religious life in the countryside, or contemporary scholars' impressions of it, include not just catastrophic events such
as wars, plagues and famine, but also more mundane factors such as changes in
personnel and the survival of records. To put the question more concretely,
did both Pappus and the city's government take the matter of the visitations
as seriously as did Marbach and the authorities earlier? Did they therefore produce, at least in principle, evidence of comparable reliability? Finally, did their
texts survive the ravages of time in sufficient number and continuity to allow
the same sort of analysis that is possible for the earlier generation?

With reservations, the answer to both questions is, "Yes." There can be
no doubt that both Pappus and Strasbourg's regime after 1580 were very intent
on carrying out the visitations to the extent that other circumstances allowed.
They sought therefore to supervise and control religious life in the city's fourteen rural parishes as closely as possible. The best evidence for these high intentions comes from deliberations regarding Marbach's successor during the
several months that elapsed between his death and Pappus's appointment to
succeed him.[8] Due in part to controversies between Marbach and Johann
Sturm, the rector of the academy, in the 1570s and then between Pappus and
Sturm beginning in 1580, the civil authorities took the occasion of Marbach's
death to reconsider carefully the exact character of the church's leadership.
The debate's point of departure was the deceased's habit of calling himself the
"superintendent" of the church while the church order of 1534 knew only the
title *Praesident des Kirchenconvents*, rendered here as "President of the Company
of Pastors." Indeed, the Senate and XXI, Strasbourg's chief governing body,
bluntly informed Marbach during his struggles with Sturm that "there is no
superintendent" of the church in Strasbourg except the government. And they

---

[7]In addition, Strauss, *Luther's House*, 298, quotes the reports of 1586 and 1598 to the
effect that catechism was poorly attended. In fact, in 1586 this statement was made only for
older children and not at all in 1598, for which only a fragment survives. Further, his nn.
250 and 251 must be in error. They are drawn from Archivum S.Thomae 45 (Archives
municipales de Strasbourg), cited henceforth as AST. The reports in AST 45 (see nn. 9-10
below) end in 1580.

[8]The sources for much of the following are the Procés verbaux de Senat et des XXI
(Archives municipales de Strasbourg), specifically the proceedings for the following dates:
April 15, July 7, July 19, July 29, September 27, November 11, November 22, November
29, 1581.

repeated this injunction when they appointed Pappus and spelled out his duties.

Nonetheless, even in the midst of this process of defining and redefining the authority and duties of the head of its church, Strasbourg's regime never questioned his responsibility to carry out the annual visitation in the country-side. Indeed, one clue that Pappus would be their choice is that the Senate and XXI chose him to conduct the visitation during the vacancy that followed Marbach's final illness. In addition to adherence to the Augsburg Confession, the visitation was thus one unquestioned aspect of official religious life in Strasbourg during the last half of the sixteenth century. Pappus and his assis-tants can thus be relied upon to have produced good evidence for religious life in the countryside during his term as President of the Company of Pastors.

But what of the surviving reports themselves?[9] For whatever reasons, are they as full and complete as for Marbach's years? Here the answer must be, "Not quite." To summarize, seventeen reports survive for the twenty-eight years between 1580 and 1607, that is to say, a little more than 60%. In addi-tion, their particular pattern of discontinuity allows but a series of still-lifes, as it were, of rural religious culture but do not make it possible to trace its year-to-year evolution in the manner that would be preferable. Specifically, reports are available for the following years: 1580-1584, 1586, 1588, 1590-1591, 1596, 1598, 1600-1602, 1604-1605, 1607. Still, these reports should provide enough evidence for a reasonable determination of whether the generally pos-itive results of Marbach's tenure in office continued under Pappus.

One more *caveat* is necessary. For Marbach's years the final reports are available in little quarto gatherings, that is to say, in the form in which Mar-bach actually presented them to the civil authorities. What remains from Pappus's years is a little more puzzling. Prior to 1600 the reports are found in a single folio volume in which they appear, year after year, in seriatim fashion, rather like a personal diary. These may, then, be notes for Pappus's oral presen-tations to the Senate and XXI and probably should be regarded as summaries of the transcripts that were generated from each parish but which do not sur-vive. Yet even a more detailed report, that for 1600, provides difficulties with respect to its reliability. This report is broken down on the preferable parish-by-parish basis with the dates noted for each visit. It includes both praisewor-thy and deplorable conditions. But in the introduction to the report for the following year, the year in question, Pappus remarked that he had been or-dered to include only those matters that required corrective action. In 1602 he

<hr />

[9]They are located at AST 45 and 208. The individual reports have no numbering nor is the volume in which they are contained paginated. Hence, specific references can be made only by date and, sometimes, by the name of the particular parish being discussed. For the visitations in general, see Kittelson, "Successes and Failures," and Jean Rott, "Les visites pastorales de Strasbourg au XVI^c et XVII^c siècles," in *Sensibilité Religieuse et Discipline Ecclesiastique,* ed. Georges Livet (Strasbourg, 1975), 5-17.

returned to the fuller format of 1600, and then in 1604 and following back to the briefer version.

The reports themselves are thus not, strictly speaking, comparable. Therefore, the researcher who places great weight on those that reported only the negative will paint one picture while a quite different picture could be derived from using reports but a year earlier or later. In order to do one's very best to avoid giving false impressions, it is therefore absolutely essential to read all the reports over a number of years and to take strict account of the exact internal and external conditions under which they were generated.[10]

Doing so confirms the generally positive evaluation of the work of Strasbourg's rural pastors throughout the sixteenth century. Pappus's first report, of July 18, 1580, may be taken as an initial example.[11] He noted that the parsonage at Illwickersheim was badly in need of repair and passed on the complaint from Niederhausen that the village had been without a pastor for over a year with the predictable result that many people were falling back into their old ways due to the influence of nearby Catholic territories. But Pappus's only general complaint had to do with church administration in the countryside. The elders (*Kirchenpfleger*) in parish after parish complained that the local civil authorities (*Schultheissen*) were interfering with church matters and disrupting their work. But the contrary was also true. Some elders were obviously very zealous in the pursuit of what they took to be their duties, at least if complaints are to be believed that they had "taken upon themselves more matters than those over which the magistrates had given them authority." Yet other elders complained that they were overworked because, in addition to assisting the pastor with catechism and discipline, they must also care for the poor and the sick who moved about from village to village in search of yet another handout.

As a base line from which to begin an assessment of rural religious life in the environs of Strasbourg, two conclusions thus emerge from the report for 1580. Initially, it is obvious that both lay and clerical leaders were vigorously doing their duty as they saw it. Secondly, from what the report lacks—widespread evidence of religious dissidence, extravagant festivals, ignorance of the catechism, failure to attend church, to participate in the Lord's Supper, and the like—it is apparent that religious practices in the countryside

---

[10]Here it must be noted again that Strauss, *Luther's House*, 298-99, placed great weight upon the report for 1601 in arguing that Strasbourg fit the pattern of failure that he found for Lutheran Germany as a whole and that he did so with few references to other reports. For them, see n. 7 above. Here too there must be a typographical error. The note refers to the report of 1600 although the material quoted is from 1601.

[11]AST 208, 18-21 July 1580. The first half of this year's visitation was conducted a month earlier by Johann Fabri, the pastor at St. Thomas. He heard rumors of exorcisms at six parishes and in addition found one Anabaptist, one broken marriage, too much cavorting among the youth in one parish, and a vacant pastorate. All the pastors complained about their low salaries. AST 45, fol. 846-49v.

more or less met the expectations of Pappus and the other visitors. Put differently, the work that Marbach had begun in the 1550s was continuing, and successfully so, except in the one parish that had been without its own pastor for over a year.

The contrast between this report and the dismal situation that seems to have prevailed in 1601[12] is instructive at just this point. That year Pappus began by listing fourteen "failings and abuses that caused complaints at all or certainly the majority of villages." These included criticisms of the personal lives or conduct of office of some of the pastors, neglect of church services on weekdays, lavish celebrations at marriages, baptisms, and fairs, the failure of older children and adults to attend catechism, the barbarous behavior of youth in general, parental laxity, tendencies toward "papist idolatry," sorcery, exorcism, and the casting of sign, blasphemy and swearing, gluttony, drunkenness, and rampant gambling in the taverns. These charges are fairly typical for many areas in Protestant Germany and can certainly be used to argue that the Reformation was no more successful in the environs of Strasbourg on a long-term basis than it may have been in many other places.

There is, however, good evidence to suggest that Pappus's complaints ought not perhaps be taken too seriously. The first such comes from the parish-by-parish detailed reports in this very document. In sum, they do not support the general conclusions that Pappus put forth at its beginning. For example, in the fourteen parishes there was one report of a broken marriage, two named incidents of religious dissent (one Catholic and one Anabaptist), and two concrete examples of magic and superstition. But five incidents of such gross deviance are not many from fourteen parishes.

Three of these parishes illustrate in another way the dubious character of Pappus's general characterization of religious life in the countryside at the beginning of the sixteenth century.   At Illkirch and Graffenstaden he found "some" magic and soothsaying. These practices must not have been terribly widespread, for he then dismissed the whole matter by reporting that the parishioners "were shown from God's word what a terrible sin it is" to engage in them. For its part, the Ruprechtsau indicates how very difficult it is even to determine what the terms in the documents denote.   Pappus declared that "many people" there believed in signs, leaned toward "papism or other errant opinions," and therefore did not come to church or communion.[13] But what is intended by "many"? Is it possible that "magic," "sign," and "superstition" are simply code words for "papism"? Finally, should one take Pappus at his word, and if not always, then when? Obviously the documents must be read with great care. Sampling both within the total documentation and within any one document can very easily yield dubious impressions.

[12]AST 208, 28 April-19 June 1601, but see n. 10 above.
[13]AST 208, 28 April-19 June 1601.

This conclusion is further strengthened by comparing the other specific complaints from the visitation for 1601 with the much fuller report for the previous year. From Pappus's point of view, the problems in 1600 included the following: Niederhausen had now been without a pastor for fourteen years; at Almansweiler the pastor's salary was too small; in Dorlisheim the schoolmaster was lazy; in Boxweiler two new citizens rarely came to church and never to the Lord's Supper, and the parsonage was in disrepair; the church at Wasselheim was too small for the congregation; in Rommelsweiler one young man refused to attend catechism and was also a notorious blasphemer and womanizer; the people in Zehnacker went to nearby Catholic villages for fairs and celebrations "and on this account they learn much that is not good"; in the Ruprectsau there was a refugee schoolmaster, one Jacob Steller, who was on the public dole and should be found a post. In sum, the detailed report suggests only what must be taken as the minor problems that were endemic to early modern Europe. Evidence of rampant religious dissent is simply not forthcoming.

Even so, it is at least arguable that Pappus's general conclusions in 1601 should be given weight on the grounds that he regarded them as believable. The details would then be no more than details. Just here the context of the previous year's report becomes especially important in determining the actual status of popular religious culture in the countryside.

One fact is notable at the outset. Although much longer, the report for 1600[14] lists precisely the same sort of problems as that of 1601 with but one exception. In 1600 Pappus was especially exercised to examine and report on the clergy. He therefore went to great pains to identify each by name, note how long they had held their posts, and describe carefully how they conducted their ministries. One pastor was complimented for conducting catechism so well that women attended with their babes in arms. Another's manner was so forbidding that one parishioner who was ill asked him not to visit (the pastor was admonished to deal "with his listeners, both young and old, in a friendlier manner").[15] In sum, and if only by virtue of its omissions, the report for 1600 also flatly contradicts the general assessment for 1601.

It is therefore apparent that in these, as in more formal documents, the exact intentions of their author must determine the interpretation of their contents to a great degree. In just this regard there are two characteristics of the report for 1600 that bear directly upon how seriously the one for 1601 should be taken. In the first place, the one for 1600 has no section, either by way of introduction or conclusion, in which Pappus offered a general assessment of religious life in the countryside. Secondly, and as might be expected, the details about individual parishes varied little between 1600 and 1601.

[14]AST 208, 22 April-12 June 1600.

[15]Ibid., for Nonnenweiler, "alsbald der Pfarrer zu jnen kamme, So muessen Sie sterben."

Leaving aside such global judgments as that everyone in a particular village drank too much or preferred dancing to attending evening prayer, the record for 1600 shows the following: one woman, unnamed, who did incantations; two cases of religious dissent (one Catholic and one person who despised the eucharist—the same as for a year later?); and two troubled marriages, including one pastor whose wife was admittedly difficult but who was told that striking and swearing at her were unlikely to improve matters. In sum, the hard evidence for widespread public immorality, superstition, magic, and religious dissent is identical for 1600 and 1601.

What, it must be asked, happened between 1600 and 1601 to make the reports so different in terms of their general—but not their specific—findings? As Pappus noted in the preface to the report for 1601, he had been ordered that year to visit every village, whether it had a parish or not, and to report on both religious and civil matters. This is to say, having been told to do a general survey of public morals in Strasbourg's villages, he gave his superiors precisely what they asked for, and he did so even when the evidence he uncovered did not warrant the conclusions he drew from it.

The report of 1601 is in fact reminiscent of a change in the reports during Marbach's years when he was ordered to shorten them and to include only problems that required some action.[16] Interestingly, in 1602 Pappus returned to the format of 1600 only to be forced by the Senate and XXI to continue for the remainder of his tenure as President of the Company of Pastors just the sort of investigation that he undertook in 1601. The rest of his visitations therefore reported little more than problems.

The evident conflicts between specifics and generalization within the report for 1601 and between it and those around it suggest that the reports do reflect the desires of those who authorized them. In 1601 and then in 1602 the Senate and XXI got more or less the report that it wanted. Yet, the complications in actually using these documents do not end here, for, like any skilled bureaucrat, Pappus used the visitations to promote his own objectives by also giving his superiors the message he wanted them to hear. His accounting for why the general conclusions should be so dismal in 1601 is very revealing in just this regard. After listing the fourteen problems he found, he added, "Before the war there had been in most places specific ordinances [that governed public behavior]. . . . Because, however, these ordinances completely disappeared during the war, the local authorities and the elders did not carry out their tasks well, and the lawbreakers—even if they were brought to task—would not submit themselves to discipline."[17] The problems therefore

---

[16]The change occurred in 1563. See Kittelson, "Successes and Failures," 159.

[17]AST 208, 28 April-19 June 1601. "So sind doch vor dem krieg an den mehrertheilen auch Sondere Ordnungen gewesen. . . . Weil aber durch den Krieg die Ordnungen hinweg kommen woellen, weder die Schultheissen vnd Kirchenpfleger gern vugen, noch die Verbrecher, wenn Sie schon angefordert werden, die Strafen gern erlegen." The translation in the text is very loose.

were all the fault of the Senate and XXI which had insisted, against the advice of the pastors, upon fighting a useless war.

Here is precisely the cause that was suggested in an earlier study for the apparent decline in proper public religion toward the end of the century, namely, the Bishop's War.[18] The problem with this interpretation is that there is little ancillary evidence that the raw ravages of war all by themselves did much damage at all to the religion of the peasants. Here it should be noted that during the 1590s Pappus and the other pastors had vehemently opposed the city's continued prosecution of the war not only for humanitarian reasons but also because it disrupted the work of the church.[19] The Company of Pastors was perfectly correct on both counts, but the visitation of 1596—the first after the war—contains not a single comment about its direct destructiveness. In fact, the only such reference is from 1601, the report in question, and it is to a single church in one village and a parsonage in another that had been burned down and were now replaced.[20] The conclusion is obvious: in and of itself, the war may well have made no difference to the tenor of religious life in Strasbourg's rural parishes.

In just this regard it is interesting that Pappus himself, as quoted above, did not single out the simple fact of war as the cause for a decline in public piety. Rather, he pointed to the attendant breakdown in the work of both the civil and ecclesiastical authorities. He was probably right. The decade of the war saw only three scattered visitations of the rural parishes, one each in 1596, 1598, and 1600. If there was a reversion in popular religious culture—and this much has by no means been proven—then the suspension of visitations was a chief cause. The other side of the coin is equally true: the visitations themselves were an important force for religious change in the countryside.

The evidence nonetheless remains dubious on all sides. Should the report of 1601 be summarily dismissed as unreliable because it was so much the product of its authors' differing intentions? Or should students of popular religious culture simply throw up their hands in dismay at the possibility of learning anything reliable from any of these documents? Quite the contrary in both instances. Treating the reports and the subject they are supposed to illuminate with nothing more than common sense may make it impossible to reach the broader conclusions of, for example, cultural anthropologists, but it will make possible a reasonably accurate picture of religious culture in the countryside around Strasbourg, and perhaps elsewhere as well.

In the first place, having determined the civil and ecclesiastical authorities' exact objectives, the researcher needs to ask, "Were there any problems that recurred in nearly all the reports or nearly all the parishes that were visited?" In fact, there were nearly always reports of disrupted marriages, chil-

---

[18]Kittelson, "Successes and Failures," 173-74, nn. 68, 69.

[19]Series AA, 733ª (Archives municipales de Strasbourg), fols. 83-88v; 89-97v; esp. 90v.

[20]AST 208, 19 May 1600 at Wasselheim and May 6, 1600 at Dorlisheim.

dren born out of wedlock, and even of one woman who was betrothed to two men and refused to marry either one of them because she was happily cohabiting with someone else (the village was scandalized). Every settlement appears to have had its village drunk and no-account, its youth who were feeling their oats, and its public house where immoral deeds were said to be committed. In addition, there were pastors who drank too much, quarreled with their wives, and became embroiled in power struggles with the local political authorities. Finally, those villages, like Zehnacker, that lay close to Catholic territories in the religious patch-quilt that was Alsace were more likely to exhibit vestiges of the old religion, such as coming to church late, than were those geographically at the center of Lutheran territories.

The report for 1582, one year after the visitation in question, illustrates just these patterns.[21] Here Pappus discussed first the pastors, then problems in general religious life, and finally public morality with emphasis upon marital matters. All the pastors received a good report in all respects, except for the new pastor at Allmansweiler, one Peter Leandrus. Some of his parishioners thought "his life too worldly and high-spirited," they disapproved of his providing lodging to "questionable foreigners," and they declared that he had "disagreeable children" (some things, it appears, never change). The pastor at Niederhausen, Johann Fabri, had died a few months earlier and his place had been taken by a local boy who had attended seminary for a time. The villagers naturally hoped that he would be given the post permanently. A school had been erected in Dettweiler through the assistance of the local political authorities, and the residents now requested a subsidy for it from the central government.

Pappus could be briefer on the last two points. Attendance at services and participation in the sacraments has "been improved through exhortations in so far as possible" but there were still problems in Kehl, just across the Rhine. In most places, the older children were not attending catechism with the consequence that "what the pastor brought forth in them with great effort, they are freely and suddenly forgetting." The pastor at Illkirch wished a seminarian to assist him on Sundays. Finally, there were a number of complaints about the villagers' public behavior, a few of which merited mention and action. One man in Niederhausen and another in Ittenheim had deserted their families; in Dorlisheim a man was accused of abducting two women (he denied it); a wedding had occurred in Wasselheim without the concurrence of the father of the bride; at Dosenheim a man's wife had left him three and one-half years earlier and now, rumor had it, she was being remarried in Vienna.

And so the reports continue with their fascinating glimpses into what must be called the humdrum of village life in sixteenth-century Alsace. Sometimes the accounts give pause. In 1583 Pappus wrote, "in the Barr exactly half

---

[21]AST 208, 21 July 1582, the date the report was written rather than the date of the visitations themselves.

the catechumens have died. Last year there were 430 children, in this visitation 215."[22] Yet, even horrors such as this suggest only that life was indeed tenuous in early modern times. For the purposes of this study, and coldly so, one thing is clear: in spite of everything, there is no compelling evidence for overwhelming public immorality, superstition, magic, and irreligion in the rural environs of Strasbourg during the second half of the sixteenth century.

What the reports of visitations do and do not say about the transition from premodern to modern religious culture among the lower classes therefore still depends very much upon the interpretation given to them. Still, two points in particular need emphasis: first, it must be asked whether the few concrete instances of deviant behavior and the rare general condemnations of peasant belief and action are to be given credence on the grounds that most people were taking the path of least resistance and simply cooperating with the civil and ecclesiastical authorities.

If not impossible, it is very difficult to answer that question with regard to a territory that expressly refused to investigate the private beliefs of its subjects so long as they conformed outwardly to what was expected of them by way of attending church, learning the catechism, and the like.[23]

A second consideration may nonetheless at least provide some perspective in trying to answer the question. But a glance at beliefs and practices now, 400 years later, might suggest that Marbach, Pappus, and their pastors went about as far as they could go by way of imposing respectable religious conformity upon the ordinary people of their time. One might even turn the tables upon the search for religious modernity and ask what is to be made of the popularity of astrology, parapsychology, faith healing, and the fascination with flying saucers that is so much a part of the late twentieth century? In fine, can it be proven that deviance from official values and prescribed behavior was any greater as a proportion of the total population in the sixteenth century than is the case now? At least for Strasbourg and its environs, it seems not.

One concluding point is both obvious and necessary. By the end of the century Protestant pastors were remarkably successful in creating precisely the religious culture they sought to create, at least in so far as it can be certainly documented. One aspect of this effort, and one that both supports and modifies Keith Thomas's findings,[24] is that Protestants did identify their Roman Catholic opponents not just as blasphemers (as did the earlier generation) but also as purveyors of magic and superstition. Nor were they entirely arbitrary

---

[22]AST 208, 1 August 1583. "Ist auch des Catechismi halben nirgend sonder mangel ohn das an merhrertheil orten die bessten Jugend mit todt abgangen. Achten aber die Pfarher Iren vleiss das sie die vbrig desto mehr anhalten. Zu Barr is gerad das halbe theil des Catechismi gestorben. Vor ein Jar waren Ir 430 kinder. In dieser Visitation 215." Pappus did not identify a cause for the devastation.

[23]For the origins of this policy, see James M. Kittelson, *Wolfgang Capito, From Humanist to Reformer*, (Leiden: Brill, 1975), 200 ff.

[24]Thomas, *Religion and Magic*, 146-47.

in doing so. It must be remembered that defenders of the old church by no means promoted only the "magic" of the mass; they also in fact reported wondrous signs, magical healings, and marvelous mysteries of all sorts. One Jesuit in the region of Alsace was so successful that Marbach felt compelled to reply to his claims in a very long book that bore the title, *On Portents and Miracles*, for none of which Marbach had any use on the grounds both of true religion and common sense.[25]

It may very well be true, then, that the separate theological paths of the confessions made very real and abiding differences in the territories over which they held sway. Whether the specifically Protestant way marks therefore the beginnings of distinctively modern religious culture is another matter. Perhaps, given the conceptual problems involved, it is fundamentally a matter of opinion.

[25]Johannes Marbach, *Von Mirackeln und Wunderzeichen . . .* (Orsel: Nicolaus Henricus, 1571).

Harold Grimm as a professor at The Ohio State University

Pamphlet Woodcuts in the Communication Process of Reformation Germany

Richard G. Cole
Luther College, Iowa

THE REFORMATION PAMPHLET WOODCUT played an important role in the communication process of the German Reformation. More than a continuation of visual traditions enhanced by the printing press, this type of woodcut was a mix of a number of variables creating a potent factor in the struggle to capture adherents to new religious doctrines. Recently, American, English, and German historians alike have been paying increased attention to the significance of the pamphlet medium during the Reformation. Nevertheless, they have continued to ignore the woodcut, an integral part of the medium.[1] Hundreds of thousands of Reformation pamphlets were printed in the early decades of the Reformation, most of them illustrated with woodcut emblems. Professor Carl Christensen's fine recent study, *Art and the Reformation in Germany,* alludes to woodcut illustrations in Luther's Bible but does nothing with pamphlet woodcuts as a Reformation art form.[2] Robert W. Scribner's *For the Sake of Simple Folk; Popular Propaganda for the German Reformation* presents a carefully collected body of illustrations and woodcut data. But Scribner underplays the richness of woodcut images by seeing them as primarily a continuation of medieval visual phenomena intended for a semi- or non-literate audience.[3]

Many centuries prior to the Reformation, Pope Gregory the Great stated that paintings of religious scenes were books for the illiterate. By the end of the fourteenth century the Christian image-world was rich. In the early decades of the sixteenth century a newly forming cultural milieu stimulated both the literate world and the non-literate. The Reformation woodcut, especially in the period from 1519 to about 1540, seems densely packed with imagery from the increased Renaissance awareness of classical authors, the revival of Hermetic ideas, the growth of interest in the Cabala, the rich ground of regional folklore, the continuation of medieval religious traditions, and the revival of astrology.

Peter Burke asserts that the cultural elite of Renaissance and Reformation Europe participated in the culture of the simple folk for a brief but significant

[1] See Hans-Jaochim Köhler, ed., *Flugschriften als Massenmedium der Reformationzeit* (Stuttgart: Ernst Klett Verlag, 1981).

[2] Carl C. Christenson, *Art and the Reformation in Germany* (Athens, OH: Ohio State University Press, and Detroit, MI: Wayne State University Press, 1979), 123.

[3] R. W. Scribner, *For the Sake of Simple Folk: Popular Propaganda for the German Reformation* (Cambridge: Cambridge University Press,1981), 3, 7.

moment.[4] Burke is supported by data in the Reformation woodcut. The hiatus between the high and the common culture later grew wide again under the influence of dialectically minded Calvinists and Methodists and the impact of the industrial revolution.[5] Burke's view of religion may be distorted, but his thoughts about this brief juncture of the *Kultur des Volkes* and the *Kultur der Gelehrten* help form the context in which to understand Reformation emblems. A similar conclusion is put another way by Frances Yates in *The Art of Memory*. In her view, modern scholars have neglected the fact that the rhetorical image, which had common appeal, was a part of the classical revival during the Renaissance.[6] Finally, I agree with Professor E. William Monter's statement in a recent issue of the *Archive for Reformation History* that it is time to get on with a study of ". . . exactly what was being printed during the 1500s, on what topics, in what languages, with what illustrations."[7]

The Reformation image, while closely connected with older traditions, took on new forms and was an important rhetoric in the communication process of the sixteenth century. The image, in Reformation times as well as today, is an efficient way of storing information that may defy verbal description—in such subjects as mechanical devices, astronomical orbits, and geometrical forms. Furthermore, pictures may help long-term memory since images may evoke powerful feelings in the viewer that will never be forgotten.[8] Nevertheless, several caveats are in order concerning the relative importance of the visual image. William Ivins, in his book, *Prints and Visual Communication*, was one of the first scholars to suggest that the technology of printing and its ability to produce an exactly repeatable pictorial statement may be more significant than the image itself.[9] Elizabeth Eisenstein has concluded that one can rarely be certain whether a subtle illustration was intended or not.[10] Even though images found on many pamphlet title pages were purely decorative, thousands of pamphlets in the sermon category alone were emblematically illustrated. The woodcuts of the Reformation pamphlet picture become for us what Bernd Moeller called "der reformatorischen Meinungsbildung."[11] It is

[4]Peter Burke, *Popular Culture in Early Modern Europe* (New York: Harper & Row, 1978), 24-25.

[5]Ibid., 239, 270.

[6]Frances A. Yates, *The Art of Memory* (Chicago: University of Chicago Press, 1966).

[7]E. William Monter, "Reformation History and Social History," *Archive for Reformation History* 72 (1981): 9.

[8]See John T. Richardson, *Mental Imagery and Human Memory* (New York: St. Martin's Press, 1980), 61, 63, 144.

[9]William M. Ivins, *Prints and Visual Communication* (Cambridge: Harvard University Press, 1953), 3.

[10]Elizabeth Eisenstein, *The Printing Press as an Agent of Change*, 2 vols. (New York: Cambridge University Press, 1979) 1: 260. See 255-272 for a discussion of scientific illustrations.

[11]Bernd Moeller, "Einige Bemerkungen zum Thema Predigten in Reformatorischen Flugschriften," in Köhler, ed., *Flugschriften*, 264.

well also to note that, practically speaking, the visual image is the only Reformation expression we have that does not require translation into some secondary linguistic symbolism.[12]

The fertile period of the printed woodcut illustration began about 1470 and continued well into the sixteenth century. A number of artists of high quality such as Albrecht Altdorfer, Hans Holbein, Hans Sebald Beham, Urs Graf, Hans Burgkmair the Elder, Lucas Cranach the Elder, and his son, Lucas Cranach the Younger, helped to form the visual world of the woodcut.[13]

Robert Scribner summarizes scholarship on the rhetoric of the image, that is, how the artist intended the image to work in the propaganda battles of the Reformation. He points to familiar idioms within which the illustrators worked: rampant anti-clericalism, socio-economic grievances, biblical images and proverbs, and cultural stereotypes.[14] Each image had, as in medieval times, an allegorical, anagogical, and tropological meaning; that is, a veiled, a mystical, and a figurative significance.[15] A dove for example may signal an image of Christ, hint of the Holy Spirit, and be a sign of purity. The image may work in several ways on the emotions of the viewer. It could create and ease simultaneously some kinds of tension, such as good versus evil; point to some negative force and suggest that it depart; exploit hostile forces in the culture, such as anti-clericalism; portray some ideological or theological assumption or indicate some eschatological meaning; culturally assimilate the viewer by identifying the German burgher or peasant with Christianity in general or with Anabaptism or Lutheranism; incite the viewer to action, if only to read further in the pamphlet.[16] Few Reformation images may seem as complex as the above analysis suggests, but there is evidence to indicate some real "visual speedup" in the Reformation woodcut.

How does one define and distinguish among the propagandistic woodcuts, emblematic woodcuts, printers' devices, and other species of Renaissance and Reformation illustrated symbolism? One of the most valuable tools for understanding visual emblems is a book written by Henri Estienne II (1528?-1598), a son in the famous sixteenth-century French family of printers. He wrote *L'art de faire les devices . . . (The Art of Making Devices)* while well aware

---

[12]Arthur M. Hind, *An Introduction to a History of Woodcut*, 2 vols. (New York: Houghton Mifflin Co., 1935) 1: 35-36.

[13]German Democratic Republic, *Theses Concerning Martin Luther* (Dresden: Grafischer Grossbetrieb Volkerfreundschaft, 1983), 23. One of the anonymous writers in this piece of obvious Marxist propaganda writes that the German woodcut artists such as Dürer, Lucas Cranach (*sic*), Peter Vischer, to name a few, "created a new vision of man which progressive forces could use as a model for their own development." Although the Marxist approach is frequently misleading, the awareness of something new in Reformation woodcuts is an interesting and probably correct idea.

[14]Scribner, *Simple Folk*, 58.

[15]Ian Siggins, *Luther and His Mother* (Philadelphia: Fortress Press, 1981), 60.

[16]Scribner, *Simple Folk*, 245-46.

of the work of the Florentine historian Paolo Giovio (1483-1552), demon-strating the maze of interconnections among European humanists. Their acquaintanceship was much like that of Erasmus with the emblematist Andrea Alciati (1492-1550), author of the famous *Liber Emblematica* which was first published in 1531.[17] Estienne wrote, "It is in these devices as in a mirror, where without large tomes of philosophy and history, we may in a short tract of time, and with much ease plainly behold and impart in our minds, all the rules of both morall and civell life. . . ."[18] He believed, as did many of the sixteenth-century image makers, that materials from both the New Testament and Egyptian heiroglyphics were useful to convey hidden meaning:

> We see the Holy Ghost denoted by the Pellican, both the Pellican and Christ shed their precious blood for their young or loved ones. God is also represented by the Sun, Rocks and Lilley . . . . How about Egyptian Hieroglyphicks for it is certain that in these veils lye hid some meaning and those who first formed these devices had no other idea than only that.[19]

The emblem, Estienne continued, was something that should appeal to many people[20] and ". . . instruct us by subjecting the figure to our view, the sense to our understanding. Therefore, [the emblems] must be something covert, sub-tle, pleasant, and significant. If the picture is too common it ought to have a mystical sense; if they be obscure, they must clearly inform us by the words provided. They must be analogick and correspondent."[21] Here, Estienne reite-rated Giovio's advice that the emblem motto, if there is one, must be relevant to the poetic picture.[22] These rules apply to pamphlet woodcuts whether the image is a coat of arms for a noble family or an illustration for a sermon by Martin Luther.

It is strange that Estienne's work has not been examined more fully by modern scholars since he seems to capture the visual world of the sixteenth century.[23] Most of the images we see in the Reformation woodcuts, from birds to mountains, are discussed by him.[24] Although he was a keen student and stal-

---

[17]Henri Stegemeir, "Problems in Emblem Literature," *Journal of English and German Philology* 44 (January 1946): 29. Concerning Alciati's relationship with Erasmus see Henry Green, *Andrea Alciati and his Book of Emblems* (London: Grübner & Co., 1872), 7.

[18]Henri Estienne, *The Art of Making Devices*, transl. Thomas Blount (London: R. Royston, 1648), 13. The full title of the original edition first published in French is: *L'art de faire les devises, où il est traicté des hieroglyphiques, symboles, emblemes, aenygmes, sentences, paraboles, reuers de medailles, armes, blasons, cimiers, chiffres & rebus.*

[19]Ibid., 17.   [20]Ibid., 33.   [21]Ibid., 7-8.

[22]Quoted in Robert J. Clements, *Picta Poesis: Literary and Humanistic Theory in Renais-sance Emblem Books* (Rome: Edizioni di storia e letteratura, 1960), 20.

[23]For example, neither Christensen nor Scribner mentions Estienne.

[24]Estienne, *Making Devices*, 21

wart champion of the image, he also exposed the nemesis of images for scholars. He believed that the visual drawing of the emblem served as the body which satisfied the eye while the mind is enriched by the soul of the emblem, the printed motto or words. Language was to enrich the mind while the visual image aroused only sensual or tactile satisfaction.[25] Estienne forces the conclusion that people of the Reformation period likely viewed the emblem as a mystical medley of pictures and words, with meanings that were not always altogether obvious.

The last quarter of the fifteenth century and the first half of the sixteenth century were rich in these silent and visual parables called emblems. Part of this is the work of Andrea Alciati, whose name was a "household word" in much of western Europe during the Reformation.[26] Alciati's work was becoming widely known when Martin Luther wrote to Lazarus Spengler (July 8, 1530) explaining his own emblem (see Illustration 1) which had first appeared in a simpler form in 1519:

> The heart suggests that when one believes from the heart, then comes justification; the cross is a sign of life and vitality, not death; the whiteness of the rose gives and is the color of spirits and angels; the blue field is a heavenly sign; the golden ring suggests that heaven lasts forever.[27]

In one sense Martin Luther used his personal emblem as a teaching device,[28] which was exactly what Alciati had in mind when he dedicated the French edition of his book of emblems to the "princely son of the noble Jacque Duc de Chastelle Heraut."[29] Books of emblems were used in the seventeenth century not only for moral edification but for teaching rhetoric.[30] Alciati's influence as well as Luther's may be seen in the work of the famous Lutheran educator Comenius (1592-1670) who was noted especially for his pictorial method of teaching Latin with his emblem textbook, *Orbis sensualium pictus* of 1654 (*Visible World*).[31]

[25]Ibid.   [26]Clements, *Picta Poesis*, 17.

[27]*Luther's Works: American Edition*, ed. Jaroslav Pelikan and Helmut T. Lehmann, 55 vols. (St. Louis: Concordia Publishing House and Philadelphia: Fortress Press, 1955-1976), vol. 49: *Letters II*, ed. Gottfried G. Krodel (Philadelphia: Fortress Press, 1972), 358-59. Henceforth cited *LW*.

[28]An example is in Karl Kaulfuss-Diesch, *Das Buch der Reformation* (Leipzig: Voightländer Verlag, 1917), 163.

[29][Andrea] D'Alciat, *Emblemes* (Lyons, 1563), 3. French editions of Alciati's work are more readily available than the German first edition of 1531. The edition used here is in the rare book room of the Wilson Library, University of Minnesota-Minneapolis.

[30]Clements, *Picta Poesis*, 65.

[31]See Johan Amos Comenius, *Orbis sensualium pictus* (1654), transl. Charles Hoole (London, 1777).

Illustration 1. Illustration of Luther which was originally printed in Leipzig by Wolfgang Stöckel in 1519. Reprinted in: Karl Kaulfuss-Diesch, *Das Buch der Reformation* (Leipzig: Voightländer-Verlag, 1917), 163. The figure in lower half is Martin Luther's emblem in the 1530s.

Much of the early Reformation was Luther's movement; thus his attitude toward the use of images is important. He was sympathetic to images from the religious tradition of the medieval church and the popular secular tradition as well. Sharing the commonplace view that images incited higher piety than

just listening to sermons, Luther believed in using art to enhance ethical aspects of life and to teach content.[32] He did not hold images in churches, even
including religious scenes painted on altars, to be contrary to the word of
God.[33] About visual art he said, typically, "Here we must admit that we may
have images and make images, but we must not worship them. . . ."[34] He further stated, "Images or pictures taken from the scriptures, however, I consider
very useful yet indifferent and optional. I have no sympathy with the
iconoclasts."[35] Luther accused the German iconoclasts of inconsistency because even though they opposed religious images they were "glad to have images on gulden, groschen, rings, and ornaments. . . ."[36] Finally, Luther wrote
in his well-known pamphlet, *Wider die hymelischen propheten von den Bildern und
Sacrament . . .* (1525) (*Against the Heavenly Prophets in the Matter of Images and
Sacraments*), "Yes, would to God that I could persuade the rich and the mighty
that they would permit the whole Bible to be painted on houses, so that all can
see it. That would be a Christian work."[37]

Luther took his own advice when publishing his New Testament in the
September and December editions of 1522.[38] He undoubtedly was familiar
with earlier illustrated vernacular Bibles such as the *Kobergerbibel*[39] appearing
in Nürnberg in 1483 and the *Biblia pauperum* originating in Bamberg before
1500.[40] The biblical illustrations in both were closely related to drawings from
medieval manuscripts. In the *Biblia pauperum* the illustratons are cluttered,
crude, and may even have been visual hindrances. Eisenstein argues that Bible
illustration in general was low in quality and poorly printed in early popular
editions.[41] Lucas Cranach the Elder, with whom Luther worked closely, maintained the thematic relationships of earlier editions but his work was far superior to that of his predecessors. He tailored his work to specific and easily
recognizable scenes in German cities. (See Illustration 2.)

[32]Christensen, *Art and Reformation,* 15

[33]*LW 36: Word and Sacrament II*, ed. Abdel Ross Wentz (Philadelphia: Fortress Press,
1959): 258-260.

[34]*LW 51: Sermons I*, ed. John W. Doberstein (Philadelphia: Fortress Press, 1959): 82.

[35]*LW 37: Word and Sacrament III*, ed. Robert H. Fischer (Philadelphia: Fortress Press,
1961): 371.

[36]*LW 46: The Christian in Society III*, ed. Robert C. Schultz (Philadelphia: Fortress
Press, 1967): 183.

[37]*LW 40: Church and Ministry II*, ed. Conrad Bergendoff (Philadelphia: Fortress
Press): 99.

[38]Alfred Götze, *Die hochdeutschen Drucker der Reformationzeit* (Berlin: Walter de
Gruyter & Co., 1963), 54.

[39]Phillip Schmidt, *Die Illustration der Lutherbibel* (Basel: Friedrich Reinhardt, 1962),
66.

[40]See Ludovici Hain, *Repertorium Bibliographicum* 2 vols. (Berlin: Josef Altman, 1925)
1: 435.

[41]Eisenstein, *Printing as Change* 1: 108, 258.

[42]Schmidt, *Lutherbibel*, 210, 215.

Illustration 2. Upper woodcut accompanies Chapter 11 and lower one illustrated Chapter 18 of the Book of Revelation in D. Martin Luther, *Biblia / da ist / die gantze Heilige Schrift Deudsch* (Wittenberg: Hans Lufft, 1534), CXCI, CXCVI.

Within the complex visual world perceived by sixteenth-century artists, three major strands join together to form the Reformation woodcut. One important source of this imagery was the interests and discoveries of Renaissance humanists. Many were familiar with Plutarch's *Moralia*, which is filled with explanations of Greek and Egyptian imagery drawn from astrological, plant, and animal observation. For example, in his essay on "The Cleverness of Animals," Plutarch recounts Euripides' belief that birds were "heralds of the gods" and Socrates' statement that he considered himself a "fellow slave of swans."[43] One common image in pamphlet woodcuts is a feathery messenger from God. Luther himself took the swan as a symbol of his ministry.

Complementing Plutarch was the recovery in 1419 of a Greek copy of the *Hieroglyphica* of Hor Apollo, a legendary priest of Egypt. *Quattrocento* humanists like Ficino worked from manuscript copies of the *Hieroglyphica* while in the early decades of the sixteenth century a number of printed editions and translations followed the first by Aldus Manutius in Venice in 1505.[44] The most recent reprinting of the *Hieroglyphica* was in 1967 by Henkel and Schöne as an appendix to their massive *Emblemata*. Here one may learn the significance for the ancients of a multitude of images, such as the snail, hawk, or pissing ape.[45] An additional Renaissance revival was thirteenth- and fourteenth-century Christian interest in Jewish Cabalism, complicating even further the strange tissue of symbolism permeating the sixteenth century.[46]

A second strand in the makeup of the visual world of the Reformation period derives from the organization of thousands of emblems in the *Emblemata* by Henkel and Schöne. The first section deals with the world of nature, which includes the macrocosmos; the four basic elements of earth, water, fire, and air; the plant world; and the animal world divided by land and water. The second section considers the world of man and includes people, human anatomy, social classes from king to peasants, historical persons, buildings, jewels, games, hieroglyphic symbols, clothing, furniture, tools, and war implements. The third section is dedicated to the world of spirit and deity, including personification and mythology, the ancient gods, and Christ and Christian symbols.

A third source of inspiration for woodcut artists was the incredibly rich and fertile production of printed materials in the first half-century of printing. Certainly the Bibles printed by Koberger and, perhaps even more importantly,

[43]Plutarch *Moralia* 12: 413, transl. Edwin L. Mindar, Jr. (Cambridge: Harvard University Press, 1961). Luther liked to cite Plutarch's imagery. See *LW* 1: 68-69 and cf. Plutarch *Moralia* 5: 129.

[44]Don Cameron Allen, *Mysteriously Meant* (Baltimore: Johns Hopkins University Press, 1970), 112. Also see Marian Harmon, "Classical Elements in Early Printer's Marks," *Classical Studies in Honor of William Abbott Oldfather* (Urbana: University of Illinois Press, 1943), 67.

[45]Arthur Henkel and Albrecht Schöne, eds. *Emblemata* (Stuttgart: J. B. Metzersche Verlagsbuchhandlung, 1967), 2097-2110.

[46]Harold Bayley, *A New Light on the Renaissance* (London: J. M. Dent & Co., 1925), 90.

his publication of Hartman Schedel's *Weltchronik* in 1493, were useful to later illustrators. Further, there were thousands of one-page items known as *Einblattholzschnitte*. Max Geisberg has collected and classified many of these into six categories: Science and Technology, Political Biography, Turks, Popular Culture, Women, Emblems and/or Pictorial Devices.[47] Clearly the pictorial world was rich in Luther's day; it is not strange that so many in the great flood of Reformation pamphlets were copiously illustrated.[48] These illustrations were part of the sixteenth-century cultural milieu, not just simple devices for the illiterate.

Illustrations 3 through 9 were chosen to portray a small but representative sample of the Reformation woodcut. Illustration 3 was printed in Leipzig in 1519.[49] The popular image of the Wild Man is juxtaposed with a title in Latin referring to the Reformation event of the Leipzig Debate. The Wild Man image was first recorded in the fourth century B.C. by a Greek historian, Callisthenes, who accompanied Alexander the Great on his Asian expedition. Callisthenes described a number of wild and monstrous races living in Asia, accounts which passed into medieval European folklore.[50] In the sixteenth century, writer and printer Henri Estienne noted a German tendency to use Wild Man images.[51]

Interpreting these images is not easy, but there are several possibilities. Peter Burke suggests that the Wild Man is a symbol of sexuality.[52] Others have argued that Wild Man and Forest Woman belong to the category of nature spirits who signify power and goodness on many different levels.[53] Wild Man imagery also fits into what a number of scholars call the "reversible world" in popular iconography. This means that nothing associated with the Wild Man would be normal. In such a case a satiric reference is made from the popular culture to the Reformation. The image in Illustration 3 thus suggests something as powerful as Luther's statements at Leipzig and points to a perception that something since the beginning of the Reformation has been proceeding counter to the normal everyday world of sin and corruption. The Saxon heraldry, the Wild Man image, the Latin title referring to the Leipzig Debate,

[47]See Max Geisberg, *The German Single-Leaf Woodcut: 1500-1550*, 4 vols. (New York: Hacker Art Book, 1974); reprint of *Der Deutsche Einblatt-Holzschnitt* (Munich, 1923).

[48]Richard G. Cole, "The Reformation Pamphlet and Communication Processes," in Köhler, *Flugschriften*, 139-61.

[49]A copy is in the rare book room of Luther College, Decorah, Iowa. The classic study exploring the problem of ape lore and Wild Men is Richard Bernheimer, *Wild Men in the Middle Ages* (Cambridge, MA: Harvard University Press, 1952).

[50]It was common for sixteenth-century authors of travel literature to use Wild Man folklore imagery. See Richard G. Cole, "Sixteenth-Century Travel Books as a Source of European Attitudes Toward Non-White and Non-Western Culture," in *Proceedings of the American Philosophical Society*, vol. 116, no. 1 (February 1972), 59-67.

[51]Estienne, *Making Devices*, 68.

[52]Burke, *Popular Culture*, 187. The other themes are food and violence.

[53]*The German Legends of the Brothers Grimm*, ed. and trans., Donald Ward, 2 vols. (London: Davidson Publishing, 1981) 1: 360.

Resolutiones Lutheriane super pro positionibus suis Lipsiae disputatis.

C Lipsiae ex Aedibus Wuolffgangi monacensis . 1 5 1 9 .

Illustration 3. Resolutiones Lutheriane super pro positionibus suis Lipsiae disputatis (Lipsiae: Wuolffgangimonacensis, 1519). This pamphlet which is located in the Rare Book Room of Luther College Library, Decorah, Iowa is published with permission.

could arouse much interest by offering visual as well as verbal food to a wide range of German viewers.

A more specific example of a reversible world depiction is Illustration 4, a woodcut appearing early in the Reformation. The image exhibits a large group of people, identifiable as monastics by their garb, carrying spears and other weapons. Hoisting a battle standard embroidered with the crucified Christ, they rush into battle against an invading Turkish horde.[55] The cartoonist played on anti-monastic sentiments to create an absurd image. Irrespective of their vows and withdrawal, monks did little if anything in normal life; they certainly would never do battle.

Another pamphlet title page offering the possibility of interpretation at several levels is shown in Illustration 5, drawn from the diverse woodcuts used by the printers of Urbanus Rhegius, a prolific pamphleteer and important Lutheran reformer. For the literate, an intriguing title claims to inform how to recognize false prophets. The wolf is a powerful image in European folklore and may indicate a variety of signals. Frances Yates suggests that a wolf image of the type shown here might suggest to the viewer the idea of virtue.[56] Virtue is quite the opposite of what is depicted in this disgusting and virtueless scene. The image of two clerical wolves (Canonicus and Monadius) devouring a sheep needs little interpretation. Early in the Reformation, illustrations by Lucas Cranach the Elder in Luther's *Septembertestament* of 1522,[57] and later in the full Bible of 1534, suggest that a sheep is a powerful symbol of the 144,000 chosen in Revelation 14. Moreover, wool was sometimes an image for Christ since the equation of fleece and special treasure (Christ) was current in the visual world of the sixteenth century.[58] The Bible verse from Jeremiah 10:21, a slight variant of Luther's 1534 Bible, is a powerful statement of what happens when clerics narrow their hearts and God is forgotten. Finally, viewing the image in Illustration 5 should enable one to remember the name of Urbanus Rhegius, so boldly printed, and to reinforce visually the verse from the Bible.

Illustration 6 shows the title page of a sixteenth-century German pamphlet purporting to be a translation from Latin and Arabic of a letter dated about 1350 from Rabbi Samuel to Rabbi Isaac. It is related to Reformation-era

[54]David Kunzle, "World Upside Down: The Iconography of a European Broadsheet Type," in Barbara A. Babcock, ed., *The Reversible World* (Ithaca: Cornell University Press, 1978), 76. Also see Natalie Z. Davis, *Society and Culture in Early Modern Europe* (Stanford: Stanford University Press, 1975), chap. 5.

[55]*Anzeigung zu eroberen die Türcky/un erlösung der Christenheit* (n.p., 1523). The type fonts appear to be the same as those from the press of P. Gengenbach of Basel. See Götze, *Drucker*, no. 17. Gegenbach was one of the chief printers of the early works of Johann Eberlin von Günzburg. There is some internal evidence which indicates, in my opinion, that the pamphlet is the work of Eberlin.

[56]Yates, *Memory*, 63.

[57]Schmidt, *Lutherbibel*, 106.

[58]Henkel and Schöne, *Emblemata*, 1634.

Illustration 4. Illustration taken from (Johann Eberlin?), *Anzeigung ze eroberen die Türcky /
unerlösing der Christenheit* (n.p., 1523). Copy is located in Bayerische Staatbibliothek,
Munich.

Illustration 5. Urbanus Rhegius, *Wie man die falschen Propheten erkennen / ja greiffen mag / Ein predig zu Mynden inn Westphalen gethan* (Wittenberg: Hans Frischmut, 1539). Illustration is from a copy held by the Stadt- und Universitätsbibliothek, Frankfurt am Main. Listed in Paul Hohenemser, *Flugschriften-Sammlung Gustav Freytag* (Hildesheim: Georg Olms Verlagsbuchhandlung, 1966 reprint), no. 3468.

Illustration 6. Illustration is from: Rabbi Samuel, *Ain beweisung / das der war Messias kommen sey / des die Juden noch on ursach zukünfftig sein / warten* (Augsburg: Silvan Otmar, 1524). Listed in Hohenemser, no. 3183. A copy is in the Stadt- und Universitätsbibliothek, Frankfurt am Main.

interest in Jewish Cabalism and is significant here as an example of bird and animal symbolism. The woodcut is a virtual aviary of storks, pelicans, swans, pheasants, doves, and even butterflies—all creatures of the air with some divine significance.[59] The snail, although a dirty and slow creature, carries a figure mounted on an orb and may signify a patient, divine and/or powerful king.[60] The two dogs in the left-hand corner present images of loyalty and sagacity;[61] the trumpeter riding on a bear is a sure sign of a prophet. Positive bird images in Illustration 6 are fairly common in the woodcut genre; negative images suggested by ravens and crows are also frequent. A simpler illustration is exhibited on a pamphlet by Johann Eberlin von Günzburg, a leading South German reformer. Illustration 7 contains an image of Christ as a pelican shedding its own blood, a jester, and the rear view of a human excreting. Anal views of monkeys or humans occur relatively frequently in pamphlet woodcuts. Excrement is not necessarily vulgar or shocking but may be sending a signal that a transmutation of values may be in order, which is the message of the pamphlet. The viewers would understand that manure is a transmuted substance and thus would stand as a symbol of change.[62] The omnipresent Bible verse recalls the multifold manner in which Luther's biblical translations reached the public mind.

Yet another method of teaching the Gospel message is seen in Illustration 8. Known as *Bilderbogen* (sheet of pictures), images of this type frequently served as title pages for Bibles printed in the 1530s and 1540s.[63] This particular example was a pamphlet title page for a sermon by Urbanus Rhegius. The woodcut is split by a tree with leaves on the right side and bare branches on the left. This portrays the hope and newness of the Gospel versus the barebones Law of the Old Testament, a dichotomy used often during the Reformation.[64] Beginning at the upper right-hand corner and moving clockwise, we note the Holy Spirit pictured as a dove, the Annunciation, the crucifixion of Christ, the hope of the chosen represented by a sheep, the resurrected Christ spearing death. Along the bottom of the woodcut a naked sinner is being chased by a devil with horns and at the same time is offered hope both by the old Law of Moses and Christ. In the left center is the omnipresent image of Adam and Eve sitting under God who gives Moses the commandments. These images were common prior to the Reformation, but not in widely distributed printed form. As the images stress the biblical centrality of Christ and

[59]Bird symbolism was common in the ancient world. See Plutarch *Moralia* 5: 173.

[60]Henkel and Schöne, *Emblemata*, 1277, 2100. Useful in determining the meaning of symbols for the early modern period of history is J. Edwards Cirlot, *Dictionary of Symbols* (New York: Philosophical Library, 1962).

[61]Plutarch *Moralia* 12: 379.

[62]Cirlot, *Dictionary*, 64.

[63]James Strachan, *Early Bible Illustrations* (Cambridge: Cambridge University Press, 1957), 81.

[64]Scribner, *Simple Folk*, 216.

Illustration 7. Illustration from Johann Eberlin, *Ein getrewe warnung an die Christen / in der Burgawischen marck / sich auch fürohin zu hüten von aufrur / unnd vor falschen predigernn* (n. p., 1526). Listed in Hohenemser, no. 3299. A copy is in the Stadt- und Universitätsbibliothek, Frankfurt am Main.

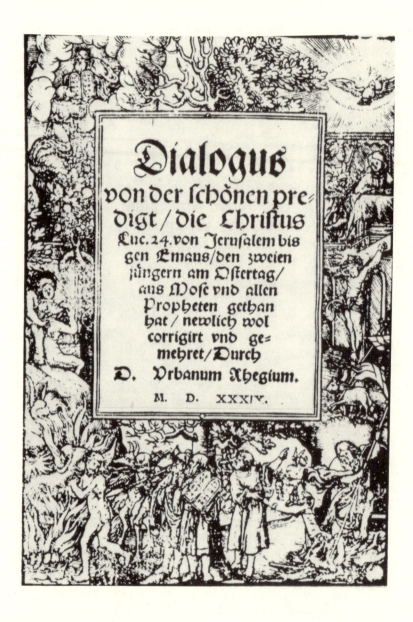

Illustration 8. Illustration is from: Urbanus Rhegius, *Dialogus von der schönen predigt / die Christus Luc. 24. von Jerusalem bis gen Emaus / den zweien jüngern am Ostertag / aus Mose und allen Propheten gethan hat / newlich wol corrigirt und gemehret* (Wittenberg: Joseph Klug, 1539. Listed in Hohenemser, no. 4010. A copy is in the Stadt- und Universitätsbibliothek, Frankfurt am Main.

his divine fulfillment of the Law through the Gospel, they convey the main elements of Reformation theology, especially that of Luther and his well-known friend, Urbanus Rhegius. Thus, the *Bilderbogen* became a major vehicle for the illustration of Reformation doctrine.

The last example used from this rich world of Reformation imagery was done by Lucas Cranach the Elder (1472-1553). Illustration 9 was printed by George Rhaw in Wittenberg and was used several times by Rhegius and other polemicists in their attack on religious radicals in Westphalia. Note the mountains in the background; mountains were usually a clue that the pamphlet originated in or was to be identified with Wittenberg, a play on the name and not on geography.[65] Young David, who looks much like Martin Luther, has knocked Goliath unconscious with his slingshot and is about to administer the final blow. Luther's friends look on from the background. Again, barren branches on the tree's left side and rich growth adjacent to the right hint of the Law-Gospel antithesis.

Much work still needs to be done to determine the significance of Reformation woodcut emblems as special weapons in the pamphlet exchanges of doctrine, dogma, and polemic in Reformation Germany. The illustrations sampled here reveal at least a small part of the secular and religious traditions stemming from earlier times which were reshaped into something new by the Reformation printing press. When the entire realm of Reformation woodcuts is considered, it is worthwhile to modify considerably Robert Scribner's constricting assessment that the "visual propaganda of the half century of Reformation was overwhelmingly Lutheran."[66] The woodcut drew upon much more than just religious controversy, just as did the Reformation movement itself. Reformation meaning is found in images filled with animals, birds, wild people, mountains, plants and trees, none of which is specifically Lutheran. This illustrates that the Reformation woodcut is another factor in the complex rhetoric of sixteenth-century communication processes. Unsophisticated by standards of either the Italian Renaissance or the twentieth century, the woodcuts were clever, pleasing, emblematic, enigmatic, and instructive. The pictorial symbols of the Reformation pamphlet give us further evidence with which to unlock the consciousness of Reformation times, not only of the "common man" but all members of Reformation society.

[65]Maria Grossman, "Wittenberg Printing, Early Sixteenth Century," *Sixteenth-Century Essays and Studies*, ed. Carl S. Meyer, 1 (1970): 65.

[66]Scribner, *Simple Folk*, 249.

Illustration 9. Illustration is from: Urbanus Rhegius, *Widderlegung der Münsterischen newen Valentinianer und Donatisten bekentuns / an die Christen zu Osnaburgk / inn Westfalen* (Wittenberg: Georg Rhaw, 1535). Listed in Hohenemser, no. 2626. A copy is in the Stadt- und Universitätsbibliothek, Frankfurt am Main.

Luther In Music and Verse

Kyle C. Sessions
Illinois State University

MUCH HAS BEEN SPOKEN AND WRITTEN over the centuries about the associations of Martin Luther with music. His love of music and awareness of his musical times are common knowledge. His sayings and writings are accentuated repeatedly with assertions of the value and utility of music, which he held second only to the Holy Spirit in order of gifts from God to man.[1] The impact of Luther's hymns upon the course of Western music through Heinrich Schütz, J. S. Bach, and many others is virtually legend.[2] Scholars in the Reformation revival of the nineteenth century and since have studied copiously and meticulously his music, musical compositions, melodies, and publication.[3] One volume of the American Edition of his works is devoted entirely to his liturgy and hymns. Regrettably long out of print is Paul Nettl's engaging popular-scholarly study, *Luther and Music*.

Luther on music, Luther as musician, Luther's uses of music—what more is there to be said? The effort of this study is to examine Luther in music, that is, Luther's doctrine in musical settings. The premise is that Luther's teachings were expressed in musical form at the level of popular culture.

[1]See Walter E. Buszin, "Luther on Music," *Musical Quarterly* 32 (1946): 80-93; Theodore Hoelty-Nickel, "Luther and Music," *Luther and Culture*, Luther Lectures 4 (Decorah, IA: Luther College Press, 1960): 145-211; D. Jehle, "Luther und die Musik," *Neue Kirchliche Zeitschrift* 28 (1918): 868-98. Among fullscale works, see Karl Anton, *Luther und die Musik*, 3d ed. (Zwickau: Johannes Herrman, 1928); Paul Nettl, *Luther and Music*, trans. Frieda Best (Philadelphia: Muhlenberg Press, 1948).

[2]Friedrich Spitta, "Luther und Schütz," *Monatschrift für Gottesdienst und Kirchliche Kunst* 22 (1917): 317-19; Leo Schrade, "Heinrich Schütz and Johann Sebastian Bach in the Protestant Liturgy," *The Musical Heritage of the Lutheran Church* 4, ed. Theodore Hoelty-Nickel, Valparaiso University Church Music Seminar (St. Louis: Concordia Publishing House, 1954): 46-63.

[3]Walter Blankenburg, "Geschichte der Melodien des evangelischen Kirchengesangbuchs"; and Paul Gabriel, "Geschichte des Kirchenliedes," vol. 2, pt. 2 of *Handbuch zum evangelischen Kirchengesangbuch*, 4 vols. (Göttingen: Vandenhoeck und Ruprecht, 1953 ff.); Friedrich Blume, *Die evangelische Kirchenmusik* (Potsdam: Athenaion, 1934); rev., exp., trans., *Protestant Church Music, A History* (New York: W. W. Norton & Co., 1974); Paul Gabriel, *Das deutsche evangelische Kirchenlied von Martin Luther bis zur Gegenwart*, 3d ed. (Berlin: Evangelische Verlagsanstalt, 1956); Johannes Klein, *Geschichte der deutschen Lyrik von Luther bis zum Ausgang des Zweiten Weltkrieges* (Wiesbaden: Franz Steiner, 1960); Hans Joachim Moser, *Die evangelische Kirchenmusik in Deutschland* (Berlin: C. Merseberger, 1954); Wilhelm Nelle, *Geschichte des deutschen evangelischen Kirchenliedes*, 4th ed., photo. repro. (Hildesheim: Georg Olms, 1962); Carl von Winterfeld, *Der evangelische Kirchengesang . . .* (Leipzig: Breitkopf und Härtel, 1843); Philipp Wackernagel, *Bibliographie zur Geschichte des deutschen Kirchenliedes im XVI. Jahrhundert*, unaltered photomechanical reprint of ed. Frankfurt am Main 1885 (Hildesheim: Georg Olms, 1961).

This inquiry focuses first on Luther's own music, especially the hymns he wrote, to examine them for doctrinal content expressed in subject matter, idioms, and images appealing to common minds. Luther's first hymn was written in 1523, inspired by report of the martyrdom of two fellow Augustinian brothers in Brussels on July 1, 1523, for professing his teachings. "A New Song Here Shall Be Begun," ("Ein neues Lied wir heben an")[4] is a ballad in form and structure and combines a balladeer's account of the event with an evangelical gloss celebrating the courage and steadfastness with which the martyrs gained their "true priesthood . . . and enter[ed] Christ's own order."[5] In composing a ballad, Luther chose a universally popular form of song, one which was used repeatedly in all levels of culture to spread news, to express thought and feeling, and to propagandize. "Folk ballads told the stories of kings and villains, of treason and heroism, of battles and banditry."[6]

Luther's new song became popular immediately and revealed to himself his considerable musical and poetic powers. Twenty-four of his thirty-seven hymns were composed in the next several months of 1523 and 1524.

The exact order of succession of his compositions is not perfectly established, but probably his second effort was "Dear Christians, Let Us Now Rejoice" ("Nun freut euch, lieben Christen gmein").[7] Likewise balladic in form, this hymn does not, however, narrate an inspiring incident. Rather, it recounts Luther's inmost experience, personalizing the grace of God toward man through Christ:

> v. 2: Forlorn and lost in death I lay
>   A captive to the devil . . .
> v. 3: My good works they were worthless quite,
>   My will hated God's judging light. . . .
> v. 4: Then God was sorry on his throne . . .
>   His good help he would send me. . . .
> v. 5: To his dear Son he said: "Go down.". . .
> v. 6: The son he heard obediently. . . .
> v. 7: He said to me: "Hold thou by me,
>   Thy matters I will settle;
>   I gave myself all up for thee.". . .[8]

---

[4]*Luther's Works: American Edition*, ed. Jaroslav Pelikan and Helmut T. Lehmann, 55 vols. (St. Louis: Concordia Publishing House, and Philadelphia: Muhlenberg Press, 1955-77), vol. 53: *Liturgy and Hymns*, ed. Ulrich S. Leupold (1965), 211-16. Henceforth cited *LW:AE* 53. Also *D. Martin Luthers Werke: Kritische Gesamtausgabe*, 100 vols. (Weimar: Hermann Böhlhaus Nachfolger, 1888-1966) 35: 91-97, 411-15, 487-88. Henceforth cited *WA* for Weimar Ausgabe.

[5]V. 6. ll. 2-4 in *LW:AE* 53: 215; *WA* 35: 413.

[6]*LW:AE* 53: 212.

[7]Ibid., 217-20; *WA* 35: 133-35, 422-25, 493-95.

[8]*LW:AE* 53: 219-20; *WA* 35: 423-24.

Drawing upon the music of the Bible, Luther took from Psalm 12 the theme
for an assault on those who restrict the Gospel in "Ah, God, from Heaven
Look Down" ("Ach Gott vom Himmel sieh darein"):

> v. 1: Ah, God, from Heaven look down and view;
>   Let it thy pity weaken;
>   Behold thy saints how very few;
>   We wretches are forsaken.
>   Thy word they will not grant it right,
>   And faith is thus extinguished quite. . . .
> v. 2: They teach a cunning false and fine
>   In their own wits they found it;
> v. 3: God will out root the teachers all
>   Whose false appearance teach us. . . .[9]

In both of these instances, Luther set the verses to an already existing sacred
folk song.[10]

Luther in music touched the people as worshippers through his liturgical
writings. In terms of exposure and familiarization, this music probably
reached the greatest numbers. His liturgical writings include a Latin Mass,
German Mass, orders for some of the occasional services (especially Baptism),
collects, liturgical chants, the Agnus Dei, Latin and German liturgies, Te
Deum, Magnificat, Communio, and Gloria. Yet Luther did not compose or
synthesize a Luther liturgy. He wrote this music mostly in response to a need
or on the occasion of a request from a friend. Thus the spread of Luther in
music to where his liturgies became normative for Lutheran worship was
through choice and preference.[11]

Luther's music became disseminated—or made available—through print.
All of his liturgical writings, with the exception of a formula for ordination,
appeared in print, usually comprising a segment of a hymnal. Hymnals were
the most copious means for spreading Luther in music, though not the first.
The earliest printed versions of Luther in music were his hymns and the earliest printed hymn was in the broadsheet format.[12] The practice of broadsheet
dissemination was initiated with "A New Song" and was continued with three

---

[9]*LW:AE*: 225-28; *WA* 35: 109-20, 415-17, 488-89.

[10]Ibid., 208.

[11]Ibid., xiii-xvii.

[12]Ibid., 212. Prof. Roger Chartier, Paris, strongly emphasizes the role of the
broadsheet as a format that brought print intimately into the common life of the non-literate
popular world, in the homes, churches, shops, confraternities, squares and marketplaces;
"Seminar on Popular Print Cultures in Early Modern Europe," Newberry Library Center
for Renaissance Studies, Chicago IL, April 4, 1985.

more early compositions: "From Trouble Deep I Cry to Thee," ("Aus tiefer Not Schrei ich zu dir"), "Would That the Lord Would Grant us Grace," ("Es wollt uns Gott ganädig sein"), and "Dear Christians, Let Us Now Rejoice" ("Nun freut euch, Lieben Christen Gmein").[13]

In 1524 appeared a pamphlet-like collection of four Luther hymns and four more by other authors. Known as the *Achtliederbuch*, it marks the first appearance of Luther's music in a printed book. Demand for the *Achtliederbuch* prompted immediate re-edition twice by the printer, Jobst Gutknecht in Nuremberg, although he claimed Wittenberg on the cover. A pirate edition by Melchior Kamminger in Augsburg also appeared, presumably in response to demand.[14]

This reaction to his compositions set Luther immediately about the preparation of an authorized collection. Printed by Joseph Klug of Wittenberg, it contained all of Luther's twenty-four hymns composed by him up to that point, approximately Pentecost of 1524, plus about the same number of hymns from other sources. Its familiar title, *Waltersches Gesangbuchlein*, is a reference to the musical collaborator on the work, Johann Walther. He was bass and later Kantor (music director) at the court of elector Frederick; subsequently he worked with Luther on the plainsong of the German Mass (1525) and was Luther's lifelong friend and musical associate.

By 1526, the *Waltersches Gesangbuchlein* was issued in an "enchiridion" format also, that is, with only a single melody line. The work had appeared originally as part books for choir. This transition initiates the entry of Luther in music as hymnals into availability in the home, the school, and private life.

From these beginnings, a multitude of hymnal publications containing Luther's religious songs followed. The most authoritative bibliographic assessment of this vast realm of hymnals, *Das deutsche Kirchenlied/DKL* (1975) lists at least twelve publications in the year 1524 alone that contain Luther hymns.[16] Wittenberg was the place of publication of most of these but that location quickly gave way to the major printing centers of Germany. Nuremberg emerged early as a principal city for printing hymnals. Thus this city's atmosphere became charged with Luther's teaching in music.[17]

---

[13]*LW:AE* 53: 191-232.

[14]Kyle C. Sessions, "Luther's Hymns in the Spread of the Reformation," (Ph.D. diss., Ohio State University, 1963), 185-88.

[15]Ibid., 169-70.

[16]*Das Deutsche Kirchenlied DKL, Kritische Gesamtausgabe der Melodien*, ed. Konrad Ameln, Markus Jeny, and Walther Lipphardt, vol. 1, pt. 1: *Verzeichnis der Drucke von den Anfängen bis 1800* (Kassel: Bärenreiter, 1975); published as *Répertoire International des Sources Musicales RISM* B/VIII/1, 3-6.

[17]Kyle C. Sessions, "The Reformation in Print: German Hymns and Hymnals," American Historical Association, December 29, 1973. For a discussion of hymnals directly involving Luther as editor, see *WA* 35: 315-34.

Nuremberg was inclined toward the Lutheran Reformation early in the 1520s.[18] One person who gave voice in his poetry to Luther's doctrines was the prolific Nuremberg poet, Hans Sachs. Sachs was also a master cobbler, an early adherent of Luther, and a *Meistersinger*. The *Meistersinger* created music and verse under strict and complex rules of composition. They are, in fact, a prime example of the extraordinary levels of skill and technique often required of amateurs in transmission media of the popular culture. Membership in the *Meistersinger* was drawn from the ranks of common craftsmen, such as shoemakers.[19]

Among Sachs' six thousand poems stands a 1523 work entitled *Die wittembergisch nachtigall, die man ietzt höret uberall*.[20] Analysis of it will reveal how basic Luther doctrines became versified commonplaces of expression and understanding.

At the outset of the poem, morning is dawning and a wondrous nightingale is singing. The false and maddening light of the moon had led the flock astray. They followed the roar of a lion, which attacked them from its lair. A marauding pack of wolves attacks; many other beasts and dangers assault the lost sheep. At the call of the nightingale as day breaks, wolves, lions, and other beasts are rendered harmless. The flock is led by the nightingale toward the bright new day.[21]

In the event the parable has not been grasped, Sachs reveals that the nightingale is Martin Luther. Then he launches into an extended tirade against the depredations suffered by the flock while misled in the deceptive moonlight. This catalogue of abuses rounds in turn upon monks, nuns, priests, habits, tonsures, offices of worship, endless prayers, kneeling, bowing, bending, bells, organs, smoke, candles, lanterns, wax, salt, holy water, fees for any and all services, pilgrimages, shrines, relics, fasting, feasting, genuflecting, confraternities, indulgences, processions, the Kiss of Peace, signs of grace, endowed masses, monies for new churches, costly altars, precious vessels and instruments, rents, and interest.[22]

All this is called the pope's worship and the papacy comes now under Sachs' scrutiny. This is the lion, i.e., Leo X, and his tyranny is the law. He orders and forbids things that God never did, such as fasts, interdicts, celibacy,

---

[18]See Harold J. Grimm, *Lazarus Spengler, A Lay Leader of the Reformation* (Columbus: Ohio State University Press, 1978).

[19]*The New Schaaf-Herzog Encyclopedia of Religious Knowledge*, 1911 ed., s.v. "Sachs, Hans," by G. Holz; Peter Burke, *Popular Culture in Early Modern Europe* (London: Temple Smith, 1978), chap. 4, esp. p. 103.

[20]Adelbert von Keller and E. Goetze, eds., *Hans Sachs*, 26 vols. (Tübingen: Literarisches Verein, 1870-1908; rpt. ed. Hildesheim: G. Olms Verlagsbuchhandlung, 1964) 6: 368-86. Subsequent references to page and line will omit ibid.

[21]Pp. 368-70. The similarity of these images to the opening canto of Dante's *Inferno* is unmistakable. However, the lion and wolf are traditional symbols for pride, lust, and violence.

[22]Pp. 371-72.

and the ban. The prophecy in 1 Timothy 4 is fulfilled that the church in latter days would follow practices inspired by the devil.[23] Worse yet is to come with the ravages of the wolf pack, that is, the priests, monks, nuns, bishops, and abbots: "I mean, the sheep are really shorn."[24]

Next in Sachs' indictments is the multitude of money-sucking endeavors of the church, especially, of course, indulgences: "As the coin in the coffer rings / A soul upward to heaven springs."[25]

The bishops and their costly courts teeming with scribes and notaries are blasted, and finally the "sophists" and theologians—"the learned ones in the long gowns"—get their due.[26]

The peroration sums it up so far: everything is for sale; salvation is for money. Christ's teachings have been completely lost.[27]

Steven Ozment has drawn pointed attention to the immense personal burden that religion prior to the Reformation called upon the worshipper to bear. Hans Sachs, in this exposition of church practices, seems to be crying out against that crushing load.[28]

But Luther's clear call has exposed these misdeeds and revealed again the Word of God, the Holy Scriptures. Now the author commences a reinterpretation of the parable according to the teachings of Luther. Into the darkness comes the light of day, the Gospel, which shows us Christ:

> The inborn Son of God
> Who does all things for us,
> Fulfills the law with his own power,
> The curse redeems, the sin repays.
> Eternal death is defeated,
> Hell is wrecked, the devil bound
> And God to us rewards grace.[29]

The person who believes on that and trusts the words in his heart comes to know without a doubt that he is reborn. The new Christian does Christian works. "But note here very carefully / These things have nothing to do with blessedness. / Blessedness one already has / Through faith in Christ."[30]

---

[23]Pp. 372-73.

[24]P. 373, l. 37.

[25]P. 374, ll. 33-34.

[26]P. 375, ll. 37-38

[27]P. 376.

[28]Steven E. Ozment, *The Reformation in the Cities: The Appeal of Protestantism to Sixteenth-Century Germany and Switzerland* (New Haven and London: Yale University Press, 1975), chap. 1: "Lay Religious Attitudes on the Eve of the Reformation."

[29]Keller, *Sachs*, 376-77, ll. 30-36.

[30]Pp. 378; 379, ll. 21-24.

As this poem moves toward conclusion, it is not difficult to perceive the commonplaces of Luther's teaching that Sachs has voiced, principally *sola scriptura*, justification by faith, and the irrelevance of works. These have been set in a broad polemic against the whole corrupt system of works. From that point, Sachs concludes with a universalized appeal:

> Turn back from the popish desert
> To our Shepherd, Jesus Christ,
> Who is a Good Shepherd.
> He has tasted death
> To which we all are lost.
> He is our only chance
> And our only hope,
> Justification and salvation.
> All who believe on his name
> And that desire, say "Amen."[31]

A second work of popular verse to be examined here involves the parable of the Prodigal Son. The image of the chastened and repentant son returning to his loving father is a popular motif in Reformation iconography. The subject received frequent treatment by artists portraying visually the concept that only the son's faith in his father's mercy and love can gain for him the forgiveness and grace which, according to Luther, all Christians must seek in God.[32]

The work at hand is a verse drama written in 1527 by Burckhard Waldis. The title page identifies it as a *Fastnachtspiel*, a carnival play composed especially for the season of festivities preceding Lent, or specifically for Shrove Tuesday. Carnival prior to Lent was a primary outlet for expression in the popular culture of early modern Europe. Burckhard Waldis' play, *Der verlorne Sohn*, thus is centered in a mainstream of popular culture.[33] Written in rhymed

---

[31]P. 386, ll. 5-15.

[32]See Carl Christensen, "Reformation and Art," in *Reformation Europe: A Guide to Research*, ed. Steven E. Ozment (St. Louis: Center for Reformation Research, 1982). Hans Sachs wrote a large number of *Fastnachtspiele*; e.g., *Drei Fastnachtspiele* (Leipzig: Insel, 193?); *Fastnachtspiele*, ed. Theo Schumacher (Tübingen: M. Niemeyer, 1959).

[33]Burkard Waldis, *Der verlorene Sohn* (1527), ed. and intro. by Gustav Milchsack, in Neudrucke Deutscher Litteraturwerke des XVI. und XVII. Jahrhunderts, No. 30 (Halle a/S: Max Niemeyer, 1881), i-x, 1-67. Waldis (b. ca. 1490) was the son of a comfortably and honorably ancient family in Hesse near Allendorf on the Werra river. After education he entered the Franciscan order, which sent him by 1522 to Riga. That capital city and principal port of Livonia (Latvia), ruled by the Teutonic Knights, was in the throes of reformation. In the aftermath of an iconoclastic outburst the city fathers and the archbishop sent Waldis and three companions to seek help from emperor and pope. This journey in 1523-1524 apparently was Waldis' conversion experience. Imprisoned briefly upon return to Riga, he was released upon converting, left the order, took up the trade of tinsmith and commenced a literary career mostly in Protestant propaganda. Imprisoned by the Knights in 1536 in an intrigue to secularize the order, he was freed in 1540 through intervention by his brothers,

couplets of iambic meter, basically quadrameter, its language is Low German. The author was a recognized poet and craftsman in Riga, the main port and capital city of present-day Latvia, then Livonia and part of the domains of the Teutonic Knights. Its intended audience probably was the German commercial community in Riga.

The Parable of the Prodigal Son, by Burckhard Waldis, opens with an "Actor" who recites an extended eulogy on the antithesis of man's sin and Christ's redemption. The device is repeated with the Devil who sent Anti-Christ and God who sent the Word.[34] This ended, a Child rises and recites the parable of the Prodigal Son in Luke 15:11-32. The whole Preface concludes with the Luther hymn of supplication, "Now Let Us Pray to the Holy Ghost" (1524).[35]

The first act opens with Prodigal Son commencing to question his station in his father's house. His older brother, he learns, is fully obedient and serves to please their father and earn his share. An argument ensues as the elder insists the father will cast out a lazy servant and the younger retorts that he is a son, not a servant, and entitled to half. Seeking out their father, he declares:

> I am your son:
> That gives me a name.
> Now give me the inheritance
> That rightly is mine.
> I wish to have it now,
> . . . .
> That I might see the world.
> This is what I demand.[36]

The father, greatly upset, tries to reason with the boy, but finally concedes:

Landgrave Phillip of Hesse, and the Riga magistrates. He returned to the family seat in Hesse, studied one semester at Wittenberg, entered the Protestant ministry and contributed polemical verse to the Schmalkaldic Wars. He died in 1566, leaving a modest literary legacy of which the *Fastnachtspiel* is the best and among the best of German sixteenth-century drama, a psalter, and an extensive collection of heavily autobiographical fables. See Karl Goedeke, *Burchard Waldis* (Hannover: n.p., 1852); Gustav Milchsack, *Burkard Waldis; Nebst einem Anhange: Ein Lobspruch der Alten Deutschen von Burkard Waldis*, Ergänzungsheft zu: Neudrucke Deutscher Litteraturwerke des XVI. und XVII. Jahrhunderts, No. 30 (Halle a/S: Max Niemeyer, 1881); "Burchard Waldis," in Karl Goedeke, *Grundrisz zur Geschichte der deutschen Dichtung*, 2d ed., 2 vols. (Dresden: L.S. Ehlermann, 1886), 2: *Das Reformationszeitalter*, 447-53; *Allgemeine Deutsche Biographie*, 1875-1912 ed., s. v. "Waldis, Burckhard," by Waldemar Kamerau.

[34]Waldis, *Der verlorene Sohn*, ll. 87-134. Subsequent references will omit ibid.

[35]*LW:AE* 53: 263-264, a contrafact of a popular *Leise*. Waldis would have been familiar with the hymn from the Erfurt Enchridion of 1524 and subsequent editions.

[36]Waldis, *Der verlorene Sohn*, ll. 339-43, 348-49.

Your part I give you complete.
See that you protect it well
And that you exercise caution with it
That you do not turn to shame.
See, there it is, full and all,
Complete to the last penny.
That should make you happy.[37]

Prodigal Son departs—"Ade, ade, ick far dar hynn"—and the scene
shifts to a bawdy house as Rogue enters and greets Bawd, the brothel keeper,
with anticipation of food, wine, gambling, and women. But times are hard,
says the keeper:

My troubles are so oppressive
That day or night I get no rest.
And I tell you, you better hear it:
That Luther is responsible.
For what he's been writing and teaching
Has turned the world upsidedown.
If that monk had spared his hand and mouth
And stayed by his mass and vespers,
Many of the things would still be going
That make the world go 'round.
The monks have come out of the cloister;
Even peasant wives disobey their priests.
But the worst I tell you yet:
Unchastity is judged and damned.
. . . .
His idea is to destroy all the brothels.
How are so many poor girls to earn a living
Who never learned sewing and spinning?[38]

He laments that he, too, is out of a profession and knows no other. But
the rogue promises better times:

A little bird has brought good tidings:
A rich man has a son
Who will come to no good.
He carouses and pays no mind,
His heart is ruled by pleasure.
I anticipate much by him.[39]

[37]Ll. 437-43.
[38]Ll. 464-78, 483-85.
[39]Ll. 514-19.

These two do a little plotting and hand rubbing. But it seems the boy doesn't
need much encouragement:

> Let's go! I've got money enough.
> . . . .
> I'm young in years, not old,
> Healthy in life and well formed.[40]

The rogue buddies up with Prodigal Son, promising to make sure he
has everything he wants; he knows this little place that serves good wine and
good women. Off they go to the brothel, where Rogue cues Bawd this is the
special guest he had promised. For openers the boy calls for wine and the
keeper replies:

> Young man, many have I:
> *Vino amabile* from Corsica,
> A Malmsey from Candia,
> A Muscatel from *Monte Flascon,*
> And from Florence a Trebiann.
> A noble wine from Rhodes
> . . . wine of Lesbos . . .
> Alsatian, Rhine . . .
> French . . . Austrian.
> So drink whatever you want.
> And if you aren't satisfied with the girl
> I'll let you have the wife.
> What more do you want that I should be doing?
> Sit down at my table!
> I'll bring you wild game, fish,
> Goose, hen: whatever your heart desires.[41]

Musicians are called and Else the whore comes in, accompanied by
Gretel, and—well, there's no need to go much farther with this. They feast
and carouse.

> *Prodigal Son:*
> Three dice and a card
> Is my coat of arms;
> Six tart and pretty maids,
> Three on each side.[42]

[40]Ll. 547-54.
[41]Ll. 620-38.
[42]Ll. 727-30

But shortly things turn nasty. They drink and eat up his money and the brothel keeper gets the rest at dice. The Prodigal Son is upset:

> That game should happen to the devil.
> . . . .
> You haven't been fair with me.
>
> *Bawd:*
> What a sorehead you are.
> When you had money
> . . . .
> You had no cares.
>
> *Rogue:*
> The Devil is in you.
> What do you mean, scum,
> That the host is unfair?
> He won your money fairly.
> You've got no beef.
> Sit still and quit bawling.[43]

The two conspirators now really unload on the young fool. They take away his dagger for safekeeping. The Host takes his fine cloak for payment, the Rogue takes his trousers and vest. The young man is coming to realize his friends are false. The Rogue is especially ruthless:

> You can save your words.
> I'll slap you until
> You can stand up only behind a door.[44]

The Prodigal Son turns for help to Else; she turns him down. He turns to Gretel; she turns tables on him:

> I wasn't good enough for you before;
> Now you aren't my problem.
> Back when you were the big man
> I was cruelly betrayed by you.
> You had no thought then
> That you'd be back at my door.[45]

[43]Ll. 786, 789, 790-91, 793-99.
[44]Ll. 852-54.
[45]Ll. 901-906.

And so, Prodigal Son finds himself on the street, naked, hungry, and alone. Here he encounters the rich citizen, whom he implores to hire him, promising complete and faithful obedience. The rich man doesn't need any more servants but his overseer can use someone to tend the pigs. A quick shift of scene:

> *Overseer to Prodigal Son:*
> All right, if you want your wages
> There's plenty to do. . . .
> Clean the pens, put out the food.
> Be quick, they're hungry.
> See to it they do well under you.[46]

Even so, the young man is not promised any food and he laments long about hunger stabbing at his heart.

At this point the Actor reappears and proceeds (for 225 lines) to explain the message of everything up to this point:

1. In the father's house are two kinds, the faithful and the unfaithful. He loves them both.[47]

2. The unfaithful son has gone to live in a far land where the Devil is strong and men live in sin and self-indulgence. Nothing can protect him. He has turned away from the father and toward sin. His reward is hunger and thirst.[48]

3. The young sinner can't do anything to assist his own condition. His struggle to fill his bag with the filth of the pigs is only obedience to his overseer, i.e., his priest.[49]

4. Christ came to earth, through the mercy of God, to comfort all sufferers. God pities our eternal misery; to help us he sent us Christ on earth.[50]

Act One concludes with the singing of Psalm 13 (Ps. 14, Protestant): "The impious fool says in his heart, 'There is no God.'"

The second act opens with Prodigal Son:

[46]Ll. 1018-23.
[47]Ll. 1050-88.
[48]Ll. 1089-1174.
[49]Ll. 1175-1268.
[50]Ll. 1269-76.

> I see on earth no comfort
> Which might save me.
> Wherever I turn or wander
> There is grief on all sides.[51]

Finding no hope on earth, the son decides in his utter misery to throw himself on his father's mercy. Change of scene to:

> *Father:*
> Dat ys myn Szohn, den ick dar seh.[52]

And he rushes to meet the boy:

> Welcome, my beloved son!
> I see your grievous need.
> Forward, I want to comfort you.
> Come to my arms,
> Let me embrace you.
> You will have all my grace,
> So I declare from the heart.[53]

> *Prodigal Son kneels before Father:*
> I see well I have found grace.
> Oh, my father, I am thine.
> I will now follow thy will.
>
> . . . .
>
> I acknowledge before you all my sins!
> I pray father, bless me.
> . . . .

> *Father:*
> A son you will be, think no more.
> What has happened is past.[54]

The father orders the best clothes be brought and the fatted calf killed, because his son who was dead has returned. At this point everyone joins in singing a hymn, Luther's "Jesus Christ, Our Savior True" (1524).[55]

[51]Ll. 1278-91 paraphrase.
[52]L. 1303.
[53]Ll. 1312-18.
[54]Ll. 1319-21, 1340-41, 1343-44.
[55]*LW:AE* 53: 258-59.

But now the oldest son comes out of the fields:

What is going on around here?[56]

Well, the servant tells him that his young brother has returned and the father has ordered a feast because he is at home again and without sin.

> *Oldest Son:*
> This thing is not right.
> I have the work and the trouble,
> Another has the grace and reward.[57]

The oldest son refuses to join the feast. The father entreats him to come in and be joyous, but he is bitter because he has worked for years without complaining or reward ("Not even a kid to celebrate with my friends," ll. 1418-1419, Luke 15:29) while the other has wasted his inheritance and now has the place of honor.

Am I supposed to like this?

> *Father:*
> My son, now please calm yourself.
> You have been with me always.
> All I have is yours;
> You rule over all my goods.
> Therefore you should have a good attitude
> And be joyous with me.
> Your own brother,
> Who had sunk to death in sin,
> Is now alive again.[58]

But the oldest son is not reconciled and, vowing to go away, leaves his father's presence. Then, in a lengthy monologue (ll. 1497-1541), he comes to perceive what has taken place: his good works are not a matter of his salvation. He is assured a place among the best places in the many dwellings in his father's house. He reviews a vast catalog of scriptural demonstrations that works done in love and mercy are most cherished by God. In concluding his conversion, he declares he "will bring to my father a holy life without an order."[59]

[56]Waldis, *Der verlorene Sohn*, l. 1376.
[57]Ll. 1401-3.
[58]Ll. 1426-35.
[59]Ll. 1536-37.

Once again the Actor appears, to explain the meaning of the second act:

1. God grants his grace with no regard for the works of man; it is out of his sheer mercy.[60]

2. The Prodigal Son has acknowledged his sins and returned to his father's grace. The father cannot wait to cloak the sins of the son with the finest clothes.[61]

3. The oldest son realizes that a father who forgives the meanest and weakest will not forget the strong.[62]

He concludes:

His approval and eternal life
He will give us in love.
So we may all come to him.
So help us Jesus Christ, Amen.[63]

Now comes the resolution of the drama, through clarification of the several symbols contained in the parable. Some already have been revealed, as the fine cloak that is symbolic of God's grace that cloaks man's sinful nature. The overseer represents the manmade authority of the church. The fatted calf stands for the sacrifice of Christ.

Here at the conclusion the brothel keeper, a symbol for the sinful world, confesses his trust in the Lord, repents his abuse of the Prodigal Son, acknowledges his wretched life and begs for God's forgiveness.

The Actor replies that grace and holiness are already given us through Jesus Christ. Then Actor embarks on a long exposition of the scriptures on the mercy of God.[65] At the end of all this they sing Luther's hymn, "From Trouble Deep I Cry Unto Thee" (1523).[66]

Oldest Son reappears in the guise of a hermit suppliant before the Cross. He cries out in thankfulness for the Father's grace and for his total life of obedience, his total avoidance of sin. His curious but consistent behavior joins his newly acquired awareness probably to symbolize the conversion of the faithful

[60]Ll. 1542-70.
[61]Ll. 1571-1667.
[62]Ll. 1712-15.
[63]Ll. 1810-13.
[64]Ll. 1835-60, 1926-1934.
[65]Ll. 1861-1925.
[66]*LW:AE* 53: 221-24; based on Ps. 130.

church to Luther's unique teachings on justification and works, in which the latter are of no consideration in the former but follow from it.[67]

Finally, the Actor repeats the whole message: Joyful forgiveness awaits all who humbly repent. Christ's redemption is for all.[68]

The Benediction and Close follow, performed by the Child who started all this, concluding:

> Through Christ's bitter dying and death
> May we gain eternal life. Amen.[69]

The *Fastnachtspiel* has been recognized as an important medium of expression in popular culture. Usually the plays are exceedingly satirical and abusive toward the Roman church. They legitimize for a moment popular high jinks and larking, play acting and games playing, and general blowing off steam. In this they reinforce by inversion several levels of official authority and control.[70]

But the carnival play also serves functions that look toward change. It offers an alternative form of mass communication, exposing the official world and undermining its dignity. In this it propagandizes the Reformation world view. Furthermore, the carnival play, like the entire carnival revelry, is a form of ritual desacralization. It reduces the spiritual and ideal to material reality and then offers a restructuring of a system that has lost its dignity and support. "The restructuring of this world is . . . most effectively carried out with the removal of the old religious order and the establishment of a new."[71]

This play thus may be understood for its function as an expression of popular culture. It fits the structural characteristics of popular drama as it obeys the rule of two and the rule of antithesis. That is, most of its narrative is dialogue and its dramatic tension is found in opposites: faithful and unfaithful, rich and poor, sin and repentance, pride and humility, loss and return.[72] For good measure it also celebrates the three principal themes of carnival: food, sex, and violence.[73]

In addition to the central Lutheran doctrine of the all-embracing mercy and love of God the Father, the play expounds a number of themes entirely Lutheran in their teaching. The Prodigal Son in the depths of his sin is hungry physically and in spirit. The cloak placed by the father over the son covers his

---

[67]Waldis, *Der verlorene Sohn*, ll. 1935-76.

[68]Ll. 1987-2024.

[69]Ll. 2035-36.

[70]Burke, *Popular Culture*, 185; Robert Scribner, "Reformation, Carnival and the World Turned Upside Down," *Social History* 3 (1978): 314-22.

[71]Scribner, "Reformation, Carnival," 322-24, 325.

[72]Burke, *Popular Culture*, 137.   [73]Ibid., 187.

sins, as we have seen, but does not remove or dismiss them. The soul remains fallen, but forgiven. This forgiveness is real, made real in the calf, the sacrifice of Christ. The only means to the father's forgiveness, mercy, and grace is faith in Him and return to Him. The oldest son, the faithful son, symbolizing perhaps the church, rejoices in his salvation irrespective of his obedience and works. Finally the whoremaster—that is, the world—repents and is assured forgiveness.

In its theme, structure, composition, and message, this play conforms to expression of Luther's doctrine in verse in the popular culture. The whole world is turned upsidedown—one function of carnival is to turn the world upsidedown—and an alternative meaning and structure for the world is clearly offered. Hans Sachs, in *The Wittenberg Nightingale*, has desacralized the official order and offered an alternative. Luther's hymns repeatedly stress God's mercy and man's justification by faith through the Word. The case to be made in this article may be rested.

But none of these musical media help much in the great problem of the history of popular culture. They are cultural artifacts created for the popular masses, not created by them. These may be musical expressions of Luther's teachings in popular culture, but they don't necessarily reveal for us the popular mentality. Rather, they are projections by the elite of what the popular mind should be. As Carlo Ginzburg reveals brilliantly in his work, *The Cheese and the Worms*, popular mentality in a real sense doesn't exist.[75]

[74]Waldis, *Der verlorene Sohn*, l. 470; Scribner, "Reformation, Carnival," 326.

[68]Carlo Ginzburg, *The Cheese and The Worms: The Cosmos of a Sixteenth-Century Miller*, trans. John and Anne Tedeschi (New York: Penguin Books, 1982), xi-xxvi.

140

Harold Grimm in 1975 at The Ohio State University

We Must Have the Dear Ladies:
Martin Luther and Women

Jonathan W. Zophy
Carthage College

ACCORDING TO LUTHER, WOMEN ARE faint-hearted, flighty, haughty, weak in spirit, gossipy, vain, incapable of profound thought, and not up to the demands of public responsibility. Yet Luther had a deep love for his wife and his daughters and was kind to many other women. He also defended women publicly from their numerous detractors, advocated something close to partnership in marriage, and worked to increase educational opportunities for girls. While a number of scholars have noticed these ambivalent attitudes, explaining them has been more difficult.[1] While I cannot claim to be able to resolve these seemingly contradictory attitudes exhibited by Luther, I would like in this essay to offer a few speculations on some of the factors which may account for his mixed messages about women.

At first I would like to venture into the problematic area of Luther's early years in relationship with women. Given the sketchiness of our evidence about his childhood, one should hesitate to draw too many inferences about the influence of his formative years upon his adult thinking. Moreover, recent research by Ian Siggins and others has raised questions about Eriksonian notions that Luther suffered unduly from an unhappy childhood and that he may have had some sort of Oedipus complex.[2] While the miner's son surely had a hard upbringing, he seems to have felt a deep affection for both of his parents. In this regard his last surviving letter to his mother is particularly instructive. He wrote:

[1] They include Joyce Irwin, "Society and the Sexes," in *Reformation Europe: A Guide to Research* (St. Louis: Center for Reformation Research, 1982), 350; Susan Karant-Nunn, "Martin Luther: Advocate of Change or Continuity in the Status of Women?," unpublished paper, January, 1973; Ingetraut Ludolphy, "Die Frau in der Sicht Martin Luthers," *Vierhundert-Jahre lutherische Reformation, 1517-1967: Festschrift für Franz Lau zum 60. Geburtstag*, ed. Helmar Junghans, Ingetraut Ludolphy, and Kurt Meier (Göttingen: Vandenhoeck & Ruprecht, 1967), 204-21; George Tavard, *Women in Christian Tradition* (Notre Dame, IN: University of Notre Dame Press, 1973), 172-74; and Sherrin Marshall Wyntjes, "Women in the Reformation Era," in Renate Bridenthal and Claudia Koonz, eds. *Becoming Visible: Women in European History* (Boston: Houghton Mifflin, 1977), 173-74. Thanks to Professors Donald Michie of Carthage College and Angela Howard Zophy of the University of Wisconsin-Parkside for their constructive criticisms of this paper and to Professors Susan Karant-Nunn and Merry Wiesner for sending me several of their papers on Luther and women.

[2] Ian D. K. Siggins, *Luther and His Mother* (Philadelphia: Fortress Press, 1981). See also Erik H. Erikson, *Young Man Luther: A Study in Psychoanalysis and History* (New York: Norton, 1958), esp. 71, 73, and 257; and the critiques by Roland Bainton and Lewis Spitz in Roger Johnson, ed., *Psychohistory and History: The Case of Young Man Luther* (Philadelphia: Fortress Press, 1977). See the more balanced interpretation in Martin Brecht, *Martin Luther, Sein Weg zur Reformation, 1483-1521* (Stuttgart: Calwer, 1981).

My deeply beloved Mother! I have received my brother James's letter concerning your illness. Of course this grieves me deeply, especially because I cannot be with you in person as I certainly would like to be.[3]

It has been noted by Bainton and others that Luther's regard for his mother also may have been shown in his naming of one of his beloved daughters in honor of Margaret Luder.[4] Luther himself grew up in a household with a large female presence. He had four sisters, one of whom died in 1520, while the other three married and lived apparently traditional lives as housewives.[5] This is about all we know of them, but it is enough to at least suggest that Luther was accustomed to the company of women and girls in the small and intimate world in which he grew up. As an older brother of four sisters, might Luther have accustomed himself to the role of protector of girls and women?

From an early age, living in small and crowded homes, Luther must have become aware of many of the joys and sorrows of family life including sexual intimacy between adults, the pain and difficulty of childbirth, and how hard women of his mother's circumstances had to work. One of his most vivid remembrances of his childhood was an image of his mother carrying firewood on her back.[6]

What Luther did not see about women in his patriarchal world of mines, farms, shops, homes, and schools is also significant. He did not encounter female classmates with whom he might have compared his cleverness in school. He may have met some women shopkeepers, weavers, peddlers, barmaids, and prostitutes, but he did not meet women lawyers, doctors, or even professors, for his Erfurt, unlike medieval Bologna, had no tradition of women on its faculty.[7]

As Luther grew to young manhood, much of his time was spent in the predominantly masculine world of school, the university, and later the cloister.

---

[3]*D. Martin Luthers Werke: Kritische Gesamtausgabe*, 100 vols. (Weimar: Hermann Böhlaus Nachfolger, 1888-1966), *Briefwechsel* 6:103-106. Hereafter cited *WA* for Weimare Ausgabe.

[4]Bainton in Johnson, *Psychohistory*, 31.

[5]Alfred Läpple, *Martin Luther, Leben, Bilder, Dokumente* (Munich: Delphin, 1982), 35.

[6]*Luther's Works: American Edition*, ed. Jaroslav Pelikan and Helmut T. Lehman, 55 vols. (St. Louis: Concordia Publishing and Philadelphia: Muhlenberg Press, 1955-1977), vol. 54, *Table Talk*, ed. Theodore G. Tappert (Philadelphia: Fortress Press,1967), 78. Henceforth cited *LW:AE*.

[7]On working women in the period see Claus-Peter Clasen, *Die Augsburger Weber, Leistungen und Krisen des Textilgewerbes um 1600* (Augsburg: Hieronymus Mühlberger, 1981); and Merry Wiesner, "Paltry Peddlers or Essential Merchants? Women in the Distributive Trades in Early Modern Nuremberg," *The Sixteenth Century Journal* 12, 2 (1981): 3-14.

Indeed, it must have had some impact upon him that his peak sexual years, by the usual physiological standards, were spent in environments where women were viewed as "occasions for sin." The Augustinians, as Heiko Oberman has observed, had become especially strict about prohibiting *Umgang* (intimate acquaintance) between their members and women.[8]

Luther claimed, according to the *Table Talks*, that when he was a monk he "did not feel much desire," but he admits that he had "nocturnal pollutions in response to bodily necessity."[9] Why was it that he "didn't even look at the women when they made their confessions. . . ."? He was quite aware of this avoidance of women. "In Erfurt I heard the confession of no woman, in Wittenberg of only three women."[10] Was he aware of why he avoided women? Did he know that he was suppressing normal human desires to serve mother church and was he aware of the psychological price he may have been paying in that service?

Life in the all-male environment of the monastery has been designed to be difficult. One finds oneself "leaping over shadows" as one priest has eloquently expressed it. More recently, ex-seminarian Paul Hendrickson has written of monastic life:

> Too often, I think we were given to understand our sexuality as the enemy of chastity—if we were given to understand it at all. . . . I have the image now of a fierce, humming sensuality among us, a blooded presence, while up above, where we wore our smiles, there were only our piety and comraderie.[11]

While Luther may not have been quite as "in touch with his feelings" as some moderns, it is interesting to note that after leaving the celibate world Luther fathered six children from his forty-second to his fifty-first years and openly proclaimed his sexuality. "I go to bed each night with a beautiful woman and that is my Katie," he boasted.[12]

Luther as a member of the medieval church came to know fully its misogynistic traditions. These are so familiar and well documented that we need not comment on them at length here. A few samples of medieval thinking about women should suffice to illustrate the mindset and conditioning that

[8]Heiko Oberman, *Luther, Mensch zwischen Gott und Teufel* (Berlin: Severin and Siedler, 1982), 139.

[9]*LW:AE* 54: 15.

[10]Ibid.

[11]Interview with Rev. Frank Lane of Columbus, Ohio on his life in a monastery in Innsbruck, Austria, July 1979. Paul Hendrickson "Fear of Faggotry: Growing up in the Seminary," *Playboy* 29, 10 (October 1982): 140.

[12]*Ich, Martin Luther: Starke Sprüche über Weiber, Fürsten, Pfaffen undsoweiter*, compiled by Arnulf Zitelmann (Frankfurt a. M.: Eichborn, 1982), 12.

Luther later rebelled against. As Charles Wood has written, "Misogyny permeates the assumptions of most medieval writers."[13] Among those most frequently quoted by modern writers is Tertullian, who defined woman as "a temple built over a sewer." He wrote of Eve:

> You are the gateway of the devil. You persuaded him whom the devil dare not attack directly. Because of you the Son of God had to die. You should always go dressed in mourning and rags.[14]

Even though many Christian theologians were not as virulent in their anti-femaleness as Tertullian, many agreed with St. Augustine of Hippo that it was "good for a man not to touch a woman" and with St. Thomas Aquinas that women were "defective and misbegotten."[15] Given the reverence of the medieval mind for authority, such statements were extremely influential in forming the received tradition and conventional wisdom about women.

A summary of much of the worst in Western thought about women is provided by the German Dominicans Heinrich Kramer and Jakob Sprenger in their *Malleus Maleficarum* of 1486:

> [Woman] is more carnal than a man. . . . She always deceives. . . . What else is woman but a foe to friendship, an inescapable punishment, a necessary evil, a natural temptation, a desirable calamity, a domestic danger, a delectable detriment, an evil of nature, painted with fair colors. . . . To conclude, all witchcraft comes from carnal lust, which in women is insatiable.[16]

While Eve was the great symbol of the sinful woman, the ideal woman for many in the Middle Ages was the Virgin Mary, who was hailed as the "Queen of Heaven" and whose human sexuality was often vehemently denied. According to Kramer and Sprenger, "The whole sin of Eve was taken away by the benediction of Mary."[17]

---

[13]Charles T. Wood, "The Doctor's Dilemma: Sin, Salvation and the Menstrual Cycle in Medieval Thought," *Speculum* 56 (October 1981): 712.

[14]Quoted by Simone de Beauvoir, *The Second Sex*, trans. and ed. H. M. Parshley (New York: Alfred Knopf, 1978), 167. On Tertullian see also Tavard, *Women*, 58-63.

[15]St. Augustine, *Confessions*, trans. W. Watts (Cambridge, MA: Harvard University Press, 1946), 69. See also Rosemary Radford Ruether, "Misogynism and the Virginal Feminism in the Fathers of the Church," in her *Religion and Sexism: Images of Woman in the Jewish and Christian Traditions* (New York: Simon and Schuster, 1974), esp. 156-66. Convenient reference is provided by Rosemary Agonito, *History of Ideas on Women: A Source Book* (New York: G. P. Putnam's, 1977).

[16]*Malleus Maleficarum*, ed. and trans. by Montague Summers (London: Hogarth Press, 1928), 41-48. See also Vern Bullough and James Brundage, *Sexual Practices and the Medieval Church* (Buffalo, NY: Prometheus Books, 1982), 152.

[17]Ibid., 44.

Luther, too, had a soft spot in his heart for Mary, although as a biblically based reformer he denied her most of her medieval titles. He accepted the tradition of Mary as an ideal of woman and motherhood and did special honor to her as the mother of Jesus. As Lewis Spitz has pointed out, throughout his life Luther kept an icon of the Blessed Virgin in his study. He also wrote a commentary on the *Magnificat*.[18]

Luther is less traditional in his frequent defenses of women, even that oft-maligned primal sinner Eve. In 1535 he called Eve "the mother of us all . . . full of faith and love . . . a heroic woman."[19] More sarcastically, he wondered why, since "the pope's church has invented such a vast swarm of saints, it is indeed amazing that it did not give a place on the list to Eve, who was full of faith, love, and endless crosses."[20] As Luther reviewed the implications of the Eve story, it appears that he began to expand the focus of his sympathies from Eve to the plight of women in general. He wrote in his commentary on Genesis, "The female sex has been greatly humbled and afflicted, and it bears a far severer and harsher punishment than the men. For what is there of such things that a man suffers in his own body?"[21]

Indeed, Luther took it upon himself to become a champion of women in his later years. This is particularly interesting because, even at Luther's Wittenberg University, ridiculing women as worthless was highly fashionable, as Maria Grossmann has shown.[22] On numerous occasions Luther publicly denounced those who despised and reviled women. "A man who speaks ill of woman has no inkling of what his mother did," is a fairly typical utterance from Luther in this period.[23] He attributed much of the calumny against women to the evils of "ungodly celibacy."[24]

In defending women Luther had the pleasure of being able to criticize some of the intellectual giants of the Western tradition. For example he took on Aristotle and, by extension, many scholastics, such as Thomas Aquinas, when he wrote:

> This tale fits Aristotle's designation of woman as 'maimed man'; others declare that she is a monster. But let them themselves be monsters and sons of monsters—these men who make malicious statements and ridicule a creature of God in which God Himself

[18]L. W. Spitz, Jr., "Psychohistory and Luther: the Case of Young Man Luther," in Johnson, *Psychohistory*, 76. *LW:AE* 21: 297-358.

[19]*LW:AE* 1: 115, 137, 219.

[20]Ibid., 325.

[21]Ibid., 200.

[22]Maria Grossmann, *Humanism in Wittenberg 1485-1517* (Nieuwkoop: B. DeGraff, 1975), 59.

[23]*WA* 10/2: 293, 8-10; *LW:AE* 1: 118.

[24]*LW:AE* 1: 118.

took delight as in a most excellent work, moreover, one which we
see created by a special counsel of God.[25]

Women to some degree reaped benefits from Luther's general theological
quarrel with the medieval church.

By the time Luther wrote some of his most forthright defenses of the
female sex, he had been happily married for almost a decade and had been seriously at odds with the old church for almost fifteen years. He attributed much
of his change in attitude toward women to his own new understanding of
marriage.

> When I was a boy, the wicked and impure practice of celibacy had
> made marriage so disreputable that I believed that I could not even
> think about the life of married people without sinning. Everybody
> was fully persuaded that anyone who intended to lead a holy life
> acceptable to God could not get married but had to live as a celibate
> and take a vow of celibacy. . . . By the grace of God now everyone
> declares that it is something good and holy to live with one's wife
> in harmony and peace.[26]

Doubtless Luther's understanding of marriage and women had been furthered
by his own experience of ten years of connubial bliss with that extraordinary
woman, Katherine von Bora.

Perhaps the most striking and attractive feature of Luther's newly raised
consciousness about women was his conception of something approaching
partnership in marriage. In his later discussions of marriage Luther emphasized the cooperation and mutual respect that husband and wife must have for
each other in order to be good parents. The role he assigned to the mother of
the child conforms to convention: She must live and care for the child, suckle
it, rock and bathe it—without neglecting her "wifely duties" to her husband.
However, Luther also made it clear that parenting should be a form of
partnership and assigned a great deal of importance to the role of the father in
caring for a child. He recognized that not everyone shared this idea:

> Now you tell me, when a father goes ahead and washes diapers or
> performs some other menial task for his child, and someone ridi-
> cules him as an effeminate fool—though the father is acting in the
> spirit just described and in Christian faith—my dear fellow, you
> tell me, which of the two is most keenly ridiculing the other?[27]

[25]Ibid., 70.

[26]Ibid., 135.

[27]*LW:AE* 12: 45. See the discussion in Karen Hensel's senior seminar paper,
"Luther's Attitudes toward Women," Carthage College, 1978, 8-10. Also useful is Steven
Ozment, *When Fathers Ruled: Family Life in Reformation Europe* (Cambridge, MA: Harvard
University Press, 1983).

By advocating that a man, as well as a woman, has a role in caring for and nurturing a child, Luther demonstrated an innate compassion for all human beings as feeling and caring individuals, regardless of sex. Luther also elevated the status of "women's work" by having the paterfamilias participate in it, even if Luther thought women were naturally better at it than men.[28] Luther's general concept of vocation raised the status of all forms of work, including that traditionally assigned to women

In his commentary on Genesis, the reformer further elaborated his conception of partnership in marriage. He wrote:

> Whatever the husband has, this the wife has and possesses in its entirety. Their partnership involves not only their means but children, food, bed, and dwelling; their purposes, too, are the same. The result is that the husband differs from the wife in no respect other than in sex; otherwise the woman is altogether a man.[29]

Obviously Luther's sexism comes shining through here, for the highest compliment he can pay a woman is that in some respects she is like a man. It should also be noted that if Luther advocated a form of partnership in marriage it was not an equal partnership. For Luther, man's rule was supreme in the home as it was in the world.[30]

Luther also helped open the door of educational opportunity for women by advocating the rights of young girls to obtain at least a modicum of education. As early as 1520, in his famous *Address to the German Nobility*, he had sighed:

> Would to God that each town had also a girls' school, in which girls might be taught the Gospel. . . . Should not every Christian be expected by his ninth or tenth year to know all the holy Gospels, containing as they do his very name and life?[31]

This call was repeated in 1524 in his letter, *To the Councilmen of All Cities in Germany That They Establish and Maintain Christian Schools*. Action eventually followed word, for in 1533 Luther helped establish the Wittenberg *Mädchenschule* in which the town girls had a chance to learn the rudiments of reading, writing, music, simple mathematics, prayers, Bible verses, Psalms, and Luther's own *Short Catechism*. As Susan Karant-Nunn has demonstrated, this

[28]*LW:AE* 1: 202; *WA* 42: 151.

[29]*WA* 42: 137.

[30]*LW:AE* 1: 202; *LW:AE* 15: 130. See also the discussion in Barbara Beuys, *Familienleben in Deutschland: Neue Bilder aus der deut. Vergangenheit* (Reinbek bei Hamburg: Rowohlt, 1980), 221-23.

[31]Martin Luther, *Three Treatises* (Philadelphia: Fortress Press, 1970), 98-99.

modest academy served as a model for similar institutions organized after 1533 in at least the larger towns in Lutheran territories.[32]

Luther had no intention of expanding women's sphere through education. The purpose of the schooling for girls was to make them better able to function as subordinates and Christians in the home. It was not intended to open windows on the larger world. Luther insisted that the training of young girls be accomplished in an hour a day and not interfere with their household duties.[33] The emphasis was on training and indoctrination in proper moral values and not on independent thinking. As Susan Karant-Nunn has written of the Lutheran girls' school in Zwickau:

> The women refined their pupils and inculcated prevailing standards of modesty, decency, and chastity upon them. The intellectual content of their lessons was not paramount: the moral content was.[34]

Despite their limitations, the Lutheran girls' schools were an advance over the almost total absence of similar schools for girls in Catholic Germany. By urging the hiring of women to instruct the young girls, Luther also helped to open up the teaching profession to women. While he had no intention of changing their traditional role as wife and mother by encouraging women to read, he unwittingly helped set in motion the larger movement toward woman's equality. Might not women learn from the Scriptures a different lesson about their assigned spheres in life than Luther intended?

Indeed, how did he handle those portions of Scripture that seemed to suggest that women might have a different place in society than he was willing to give them? Luther conceded that, while "in Christ there is no distinction between women and men," in the "outward sphere . . . distinctions and inequalities among Christians appear."[35] According to Luther, equality between the sexes existed on this earth only in Paradise; had there been no sin, woman might have been the equal of man. For Luther, women were more than just "necessary evils" and "antidotes to sin." "Woman is needed not only to secure increase but also for companionship and for protection. The management of the household must have the ministrations of the dear ladies."[36]

Luther loved the "humbled sex" so much that he could not bear to think of a world without women, such as he had formerly known among the Augustinians. He wrote:

[32]Karant-Nunn, "Martin Luther," 11; *LW:AE* 45: 368.

[33]*LW:AE* 45: 370.

[34]In her "Continuity and Change: Some Effects of the Reformation on the Women of Zwickau," *The Sixteenth Century Journal* 13, 2 (1982): 19.

[35]*LW:AE* 1: 38, 203.

[36]Ibid., 116; *LW:AE* 45: 36.

Imagine what it would be like without this sex. The home, cities, economic life, and government would virtually disappear. Men can't do without women. Even if it were possible for men to beget and bear children, they still couldn't do without women.[37]

Yet if the "dear ladies" are really so important to the fabric of civilization, why can't they be allowed to function in positions outside the home? Again, according to Luther, original sin is to blame. Because of original sin, "the rule remains with the husband and the wife is compelled to obey by God's command."

He rules the home and the state, wages wars, defends his possessions, tills the soil, builds, plants, etc. The woman on the other hand, is like a nail driven into the wall. She sits at home.[38]

Her sitting is greatly assisted by those "broad hips" as Luther once observed.[39]

When on occasion a woman is put in the place of a king, "she always has a counsel of leading men, by whose counsel everything should be administered," according to Dr. Luther's selective interpretation of history.[40] For Luther the reason for this natural dependence on men is that women's minds just aren't good enough for serious and important matters. "For the longer they [women] deliberate about important and difficult matters, the more they complicate and obstruct the business."[41]

Not only should women stay out of politics, for Luther they should play a lesser role in religious affairs as well. While reluctantly recognizing a number of Old Testament examples of "how women have prophesied and thereby attained rule over men, land, and people," Luther suggested that it would be better "not to be concerned about the right of these women of the Old Testament to teach and rule." Instead, we should turn to the New Testament, where "the Holy Spirit, speaking through Paul, ordained that women should be silent in churches and assemblies."[42]

It is revealing that Luther overlooked the full implications of Joel's prophecy (2:28) that your sons and *your daughters* shall prophesy. He also glossed over the significance of the examples of Deborah's "rule in Israel"; the prophetess Hulda; and Sarah, "who directed her husband and lord, Abraham, to cast out Ishmael and his mother, and God commanded Abraham to obey

[37]*LW:AE* 54: 160-161.
[38]*LW:AE* 1: 202.
[39]Ibid., 8.
[40]*LW:AE* 15: 130-131; *WA* 20: 149.
[41]*LW:AE* 6: 60.
[42]*LW:AE* 40: 388-390.

her."[43] Furthermore, in turning to the New Testament, Luther ignored the example of the egalitarian manner in which Jesus treated women, finding refuge in the sexist dictums attributed to Paul, Luther's great hero.[44]

Why was Luther so uncomfortable with the idea of sharing power with women? Certainly some of his ambivalence comes from ambivalences in the Christian tradition regarding women. Another factor is Luther's social conservatism and fear of change. He was clearly a conservative revolutionary, for if women should take men's roles, "there would be disturbance and a confusion of all social standing and of everything," said Luther.[45]

Luther's attitudes toward women had been expanded by the experience of his marriage and family life. Yet while that experience had given him different insights into parenting and woman's worth than he had encountered as a monk, it still reinforced his notions of woman's traditional roles. After Luther became a public figure as a reformer, his acquaintance with women from a variety of social classes increased dramatically. He was, after all, in contact with women such as Mary, queen of Hungary; Margaret, duchess of Brunswick; Duchess Elizabeth of Saxony; Elizabeth of Brandenburg; Duchess Sibylla of Saxony; and that influential reformer of Strasbourg, Katherine Zell; plus a score of other less well-known women. He treated them all in a friendly and respectful fashion, but the contacts were not enough to overcome his limited notion of women's abilities.[46]

Luther loved women enough to treat them kindly and to defend them from the more misogynistic attacks of his fellow theologians. Yet he could not bring himself to love women as more than lesser beings even if they were equal in Christ. He failed to recognize the implications of much in the Scriptures which suggested that women can play a much larger role in society than had been traditionally assigned to them.

[43]Ibid.

[44]See for example Luke 10:38-42.

[45]*LW:AE* 26: 356.

[46]A small collection of Luther's letters to women have been gathered in Mary Cooper Williams and E. F. Keever, eds., *Luther's Letters to Women* (Chicago: Wartburg, 1930) and more recently in Reinmar Zeller, ed., *Luther wie ihn keiner kennt* (Freiburg im. Br.: Herder, 1982), 13-27.

Martin Luther and the City of Zwickau

Susan C. Karant-Nunn
Portland State University

THE CITY OF ZWICKAU, located in the present-day German Democratic Republic, has recently enjoyed a revival of interest in its late medieval history. There are three reasons for this. The first pertains to the search for Thomas Müntzer, the central figure in the Marxist historiography of Soviet and East German Reformation scholars. Müntzer sojourned and preached in Zwickau and sharply aroused public opinion. This makes it desirable to discover what forces were at work to make Müntzer so attractive to one part of the populace in that town of more that 7,000, and so repellent to another part. The second, related to the Müntzer phenomenon, is the Zwickau Prophets. These men obviously got their title from the city (one was not a native). When the three radicals, Niclas Storch, Thomas Drechsel, and Marcus Stübner, left town rather than face interrogation by the pastor and the city council, they gained everlasting fame by going to Wittenberg and presenting their views to the young, impressionable Philip Melanchthon. Melanchthon admired Stübner.[1] The third reason lies in urban and social history. Historians of our generation have vigorously taken on the study of cities and villages all over the world. In Reformation studies, the work of Bernd Moeller has had great heuristic value.[2] The study of Zwickau has had to wait until relations between East Germany and the West became sufficiently stable to allow Western scholars access to unreexamined urban archives. Robert Scribner's distinguished doctoral dissertation on Erfurt is one of the earliest results of this political relaxation.[3]

Two scholars previously described the relationship between Martin Luther and Zwickau. The first was Ernst Fabian, whose article, "Der Streit Luthers mit dem Zwickauer Rate im Jahre 1531," appeared in 1905.[4] This is a narrative work, concentrating specifically on Luther's battle against the city council in 1531 over the matter of firing the preacher in St. Catherine's Church, Lorenz Soranus, without the knowledge or consent of the pastor, Nicolaus Hausmann, who was Luther's personal friend and confidant. The other account of this struggle is very recent, the work of Dr. Helmut Bräuer, formerly chief archivist in Karl-Marx-Stadt (Chemnitz), now *Oberassistent* in

---

[1] *Philippi Melanchthonis opera quae supersunt omnia*, ed. Karl Gottlieb Bretschneider, 28 vols. (Halle: C. A. Schwetschke, 1843-1860) 1: 182. Nicolaus Müller, ed., *Die Wittenberger Bewegung 1521 und 1522*, 2nd ed. (Leipzig: M. Heinsius Nachfolger, 1911), 139.

[2] See his article and responses to it in *The Urban Classes, the Nobility and the Reformation*, ed. Wolfgang J. Mommsen (Stuttgart: Klett-Cotta, 1979).

[3] "Reformation, Society and Humanism in Erfurt, c. 1450-1530," (Ph.D. dissertation, University of London, 1972).

[4] *Mitteilungen des Altertumsvereins für Zwickau und Umgegend* 8 (1905): 71-176. Hereafter cited as *MAZU*.

the History Department at Karl Marx University in Leipzig. His study is enti-tled *Zwickau und Martinus Luther*[5] Bräuer's research on the subject is factually thorough and reliable. He attempts to place the confrontation between Luther and Zwickau's ruling fathers in a socio-economic perspective. This is a worth-while enterprise, one at which he achieves much success. I have reservations, however, about his methodology, which forces the population of Zwickau into two neatly separated ideological camps corresponding too closely to eco-nomic status. The result is, obviously, Reformation as class war.

I propose in this study not to focus exclusively on the quarrels of 1531, nor even on the immediately preliminary bouts. I will go back to the beginning of any perceptible relationship between Martin Luther and Zwickau to try to un-derstand the nature of their interaction at the time Lutheranism was being es-tablished in the city. This will shed additional light on the events of 1531, but to do so is incidental to the principal purpose.

From the earliest sixteenth century Zwickau had ties to Wittenberg, and many Zwickauers were informed of major events there. Wittenberg was one of the electoral residential cities, which kept the traffic of government flowing in and out. The presence of one of the three regional universities there from 1502 attracted sons of Zwickau, though before Luther's ascendance, Leipzig, being closer, was more frequently visited.[6] Stephan Roth, who became Zwickau's secretary and councillor, while studying in Wittenberg reported on events there, and he later married Ursula Kruger, sister-in-law of George Rhaw, the distinguished Wittenberg printer. Thus Zwickau's educated and governing class, its "scribal" society, had continuing reason to know what was going on in Wittenberg and was more susceptible than the common people were to influences from it and other urban centers. They formed a small and elite group. Judging by the frequency and intensity with which the guilds pe-titioned the city council for public scribes and reckoners, we have to conclude that the portion of society with direct access to the written word was distinctly in the minority.

But as Robert Scribner has pointed out in his book, *For the Sake of Simple Folk: Popular Propaganda for the German Reformation*, pictures too were printed and disseminated among the masses.[7] In addition, preachers and other literate persons conveyed the message of the printed word to analphabetic popula-

---

[5]Subtitled *Die gesellschaftlichen Auseinandersetzungen um die städtische Kirchenpolitik in Zwickau (1527-1531)* (Karl-Marx-Stadt: n.p., 1983).

[6]Between 1502 and 1521, 53 Zwickauers enrolled in Wittenberg and 88 in Leipzig. Between 1522 and 1546, 55 enrolled in Wittenberg and 17 in Leipzig. See Carl Eduard Förstemann, ed., *Album Academiae Vitebergensis ab A. Ch. MDII usque ad A. MDLX*, vol. 1 (Leipzig: Karl Tauchnit, 1841); Georg Erler, ed., *Die Matrikel der Universität Leipzig*, in 2d main part of *Codex diplomaticus Saxoniae Regiae*, vols. 16-18 (Leipzig: Giesecke und Devrient, 1895-1902).

[7](Cambridge: Cambridge University Press, 1981).

tions. Hence, Luther and the Wittenberg theologians did make themselves heard in Zwickau by means of agents formal and informal.

When in 1520 Luther dedicated his treatise, *On the Freedom of a Christian Man*, to Zwickau's burgomaster, Hermann (Luther misnames him Hieronymus) Mühlpfort, the two men were not actually acquainted. Luther wrote in his letter of dedication that the Zwickau preacher, Johannes Egranus, had praised Mühlpfort to him as a lover of the Holy Scripture. Mühlpfort came from an influential and well-to-do Zwickau family. An uncle, Heinrich, served on the city council for years, last appearing on the list in 1515-1516. He was a pious and literate man, who, at his death, left manuscripts including a work called "The Thorn of Truth and Righteousness."[8] Hermann Mühlpfort, whose own father died when he was very young, may have come to his interest in religion through this paternal relative. Hermann was inclined toward Luther's earliest teachings.

Mühlpfort was not the only civic leader receptive to Luther at this early date. There was also Laurentius Bärensprung, holder of a Master of Arts degree from the University of Paris and burgomaster in alternate years from 1510 to his death in 1533. More than any others, these two individuals were responsible for the establishment of Lutheranism as the official creed by 1525.

The first reference to Luther in the city council minutes dates from March 12, 1519.[9] The councillors resolved to write to "Doctorj Martino lutter. . . again" about obtaining a member of his order to preach for six months or so in St. Catherine's Church until a permanent preacher could be found. The city fathers were loyal to the Church and considered Luther to be so too, but they respected his forthright opposition to abuses. His utterances struck a sympathetic chord in Zwickau, where the council and Egranus had moved, each in his respective sphere, to criticize and contain the Church. Egranus was very attracted to humanism, particularly humanist biblicism. From his studies he came to object to the myth of the three marriages of St. Anne, the mother of the Virgin. The legend was popular in Zwickau and was inscribed on the Wohlgemuth Altar in St. Mary's Church. The local Franciscans became incensed and castigated Egranus in turn, but the councillors generally sided with their preacher. They appreciated his humanism, his persuasive delivery, his rational appeal to Scripture, his seriousness about his duties, and his upright life. They also wished, along with many non-patricians, to narrow the influence of the mighty Franciscans in parish affairs. As the conflict between Egranus and the Franciscans raged from 1517 to 1520, councillors and preachers alike saw themselves as Catholic. They struggled as Catholics for local control of their church and for the elimination of ecclesiastical abuses.

The council's efforts to find new clerical personnel through Martin Luther concluded ironically as Luther introduced Egranus to Thomas Münt-

---

[8]Zwickauer Stadtarchiv, Reg. III[d], no. 6a, 1504-1506. Hereafter cited as ZSA.

[9]Ratsprotokolle, 1516-1519 at 1519, fol. 19. Hereafter cited as R. P.

zer at the Leipzig Disputation. Possibly through the mediation of Egranus, the council allowed Müntzer to substitute while Egranus was on leave. Müntzer took up his temporary position in May of 1520 and, as is well known, turned the city on its ear.

Or so we have been wont to think. In reality the city already seethed with unrest that had not the slightest connection with the Reformation. During 1516 and 1517, the entire artisan population had risen up in a protest that threatened to shed blood and destroy property. Object of the protest was the city council's arrogation since early in the century of greater and greater authority over more and more aspects of civic life. Whereas in the fifteenth century the citizenry had functioned in quite a collective fashion, with frequent consultation between the councils and guild leaders, such cooperation had become increasingly perfunctory and noticeably superficial in the sixteenth. The last straw for the craftsmen came in 1509-1510 with the imposition of severe restrictions on the brewing of beer, which rivaled bread as the staff of life among the common people. The council intended through licensing fees to raise revenue and bring the entire process of brewing under the direction of its officials. The guildsmen and other ordinary folk were furious, fumed for years, went on strike in September of 1516, and finally agreed to present a formal list of grievances to the council. They protested changes in their right to brew, and they vented their collective spleen at the council's other recent acts of hauteur, including the imposition of steep fines or corporal punishment for minor transgressions.[10] The Saxon elector, John the Constant, stepped in and secured the triumph of the council. The people were forced to submit and to accept further encroachment on their traditional rights of assembly and consultation. Defeat obliged them to conceal their lasting ill will toward the councillors.

Thus, when the Reformation arrived, it entered an atmosphere already charged with unrest. Thomas Müntzer sensed the air immediately and thrived in it. Müntzer's contentious nature was already well known, even to Luther, who had written in his defense in 1519.[11] As long as Müntzer was content to criticize the Church, all was well and good. He raged against the Franciscans, as had been hoped and expected. But then he reviled Egranus himself, whom he found too cerebral and unprepared to break with Holy Mother Church. It turned out that he was more than ready to direct his homiletic skills against anyone prominent or in authority. He attacked the rich, including the councillors. At the same time he and Niclas Storch became acquainted, and they seem to have made common cause. The nature of the relationship between these social and religious radicals is not known exactly, but the city became increasingly cloven early in 1521. It was the Elector's official, however, the *Amthauptmann*, who forced the firing of Müntzer in April.

[10]ZSA, Aᵛ AII, no. 11.

[11]*D. Martin Luthers Werke: Kritische Gesamtausgabe*, 100 vols. (Weimar: Hermann Böhlau, 1888-1966), *Briefwechsel* 1: 392. Hereafter cited as WA for Weimar Ausgabe.

The council held none of this against Luther, whom it continued to consult any time a vacancy occurred among the city's clerical staff. After the Diet of Worms, Luther was taken out of circulation and placed in the Wartburg. The city fathers could not seek his advice now, but they had already taken his recommendation to employ as city pastor Luther's friend, Nicolaus Hausmann. Hausmann, a true devotee of the reformer, labored for the next decade to promote Luther's teachings in Zwickau.

Despite Müntzer's departure, the populace remained in turmoil. The Zwickau Prophets did their part until they were summoned to interrogation in mid-December, 1521, whereupon they left town. Unrest in Wittenberg held out to them the hope of a favorable reception by the citizenry. Luther was offended when he heard of Melanchthon's soft response to the prophets. He may have had both Zwickau and Wittenberg in mind when he wrote *A True Admonishment to All Christians to Avoid Riot and Revolt*, for a publication date of January 19, 1522, has been suggested for this pamphlet.[12] Luther had not the slightest insight into the unrest of Zwickau. Even if he had been told of the council's repeated infringement of the people's customary rights, he probably would have been as unmoved as he was shortly to be in the face of peasant revolt. Magistrates were magistrates, part of God's order; they should be obeyed. Furthermore, the magistrates in question were his apparent champions, a means of bringing God's truth to the ignorant urban masses.

In view of the developing closeness between council and reformer, it is not too surprising that the still alienated artisans, their disaffection recently renewed by the ouster of the popular Müntzer and the flight of Storch, did not unreservedly love Luther. The one strong bond between many craftsmen and the council was their mutual hatred of the friars and monks in their midst, that is, the Zwickau Franciscans, and also the Cistercians, whose local depot was called the Grünhainer Hof. The Dominicans were present in the city as well, and possibly also a few Carthusians, but these apparently made themselves scarce: popular diatribes do not refer to them.

The councillors and common people briefly made common and violent cause against the Cistercians at Carnival time in 1522. They stormed and vandalized the Grünhainer Hof on March 6. The councillors made it look as if they had had no part in the deed. So cathartic and satisfying an action was this that the council had its hands full preventing further rioting. When it learned that Luther was going to preach in Borna and Altenburg late in April, the council sent a messenger to beg him to include Zwickau in his tour. He agreed, arriving on April 29 and staying in Mühlpfort's home. He preached four sermons. Their subjects were as follows: (1) that good works flow from faith; (2) good works and marriage; (3) the true way (Christ) and the false way, and

---

[12]*Eine treue Vermahnung zu allen Christen, sich zu hüten vor Aufruhr und Empörung* (1522), WA 8: 676-687.

Christ's atonement for the sins of mankind; (4) faith and love, the duties of the priest (to preach and to pray), baptism, and prayers for the dead.[13]

Luther's naivete toward the divisions within Zwickau at this moment was manifested in his sermons, which had nothing whatever to do with unrest. Taken as a group, they were an introduction to Luther's teachings. One, delivered in the Franciscan friary, argued against the brothers' celibacy. A large number of people turned out, as many as 14,000 according to the chronicler Peter Schumann.[14] But Luther's visit probably did not calm the people as much as did the absence of a radical leader at the time. In November of the same year a man was arrested for composing a ditty against both Erasmus and Luther. Others were alleged to have aided him. He was banished for five years, a harsh penalty designed to set an example.[15]

For the next three years, until the Peasants' War, the relationship between the Zwickau councillors and Luther was cordial. Mühlpfort and Bärensprung worked closely with Pastor Hausmann in creating a Lutheran church, although the pastor was clearly subordinate to the council. He was required to seek the council's permission for any change he wished to make, and permission was not always forthcoming. Hausmann frequently sought Luther's advice; he wrote to him and he also travelled to Wittenberg. Devoted to Luther as he was, however, Hausmann was not merely his instrument. In some pragmatic situations, his vision was sharper than his mentor's. It was Hausmann who perceived the need to undertake a thorough visitation of all churches and who persuaded the princes to do so. He also convinced Luther of this need, helping the reformer become more finely attuned to the realities of life in town and countryside. During the early 1520s Hausmann gained more practical experience than Luther himself.

The first weakening of the bond between the city fathers and Luther came in the wake of the Peasant's War. Luther's notorious words in *Against the Murdering, Robbing Hordes of Peasants* startled and disillusioned even Zwickau's self-satisfied patricians.[16] The Zwickau council over the years had dealt repeatedly with the peasants of the area. The city had struggled constantly to gain jurisdiction over the rustics in neighboring villages. Even those more distant had to comply with Zwickau's economic monopoly within the *bannmeile*. But successive city councils also had sided with peasants in causes against certain noble abuses, such as herding sheep through their fields. In 1525 the council understood the peasants grievances. Muhlpfort testified to Roth on June 4, 1525, "Doctor Martin's reputation has fallen greatly among the common people and

---

[13]WA 10, 3: 103-12.

[14]Rudolf Falk, "Zwickau Chroniken aus dem 16. Jahrhundert," *Alt-Zwickau* 1 (1923): 4.

[15]R. P. 1522-1525 at 1522, fols. 15-16; R. P. 1522-1525 at 1523, fol. 29.

[16]WA 46: 49-55.

among the educated and uneducated."[17] A teacher at Zwickau's famous Latin school, Valentin Hertel, wrote to Roth, "It is amazing how bad the multitude feels toward him."[18]

Mühlpfort did not convey his disillusionment to the reformer, and on the surface there was no change in their friendly attitude toward one another. The pragmatic councillor realized that it would be unwise to alienate Luther. In March 1527, when he wrote to Roth, who was still studying in Wittenberg, he asked his friend to relay greetings to Luther and his wife.[19] Throughout the mid-1520s, Zwickau's rulers consistently approved the use of Luther's works for the Lutheran church, such as masses, other liturgies, and hymns. The city printing press, established in 1523, printed several of Luther's sermons and treatises.[20] Stephan Roth collected a cycle of Luther's sermons to extend through the entire ecclesiastical year and had these published.[21] Thus Luther was ever considered to be the highest authority on religious matters. However, intervention on his part in the practical governance of the church, direct or indirect, was most unwelcome.

Deterioration in the council's official relations with Luther came as a consequence of its growing unwillingness to do the bidding of Pastor Hausmann. In 1527 Elector John elevated a few leading urban pastors, geographically distributed throughout his lands, to the position of superintendent, to which pertained functions similar to those of the Catholic archdeacons. Hausmann was one who received this designation and was now formally responsible for a number of pastors in outlying rural parishes. His new powers, together with his instrumental role with the council in shaping Zwickau's Lutheran church, persuaded Hausmann of his superiority in religious matters. The council did not see things this way. It saw Hausmann's responsibilities as circumscribed and itself as the head of the city church. It had struggled long to eliminate rival Catholic corporations, including the Bishop of Naumburg and the local Franciscans and Cistercians. It had no intention of accepting a new contender for authority within the walls. This fundamental disagreement between Zwickau's magistrates and its pastor underlay all specific issues in the 1520s and, indeed, for the remainder of the Reformation era. From the start Luther sided with Hausmann.

There were many manifestations of this difference in perspective. A number of them antedate the famous conflict in 1531 over the council's dismissal

---

[17]Reprinted in Theodore Kolde, *Analecta Lutherana* (Gotha: 1883), 64-68. See Otto Clemen's interpretation in "Hermann Mühlpfort," Pt. 2, *Alt-Zwickau* 12 (1922): 46-48.

[18]Quoted by Ludwig Keller, "Ueber die Anfänge der Reformation in Zwickau," *Monatshefte der Comenius-Gesellschaft* 9 (1900): 176.

[19]WA, *Briefwechsel* 4: with no. 1091.

[20]Ernst Fabian, "Die Einführung des Buchdrucks in Zwickau 1523," *MAZU* 6 (1899): 41-128.

[21]*Sommerpostille.* . . (1526), WA 10, 1, 2: 211-441; *Festpostille.* . . (1527), WA 17, 2: 249-516; *Winterpostille.* . . (1528), WA 21: 1-194.

of the preacher in St. Catherine's Church, Lorenz Soranus. At the end of 1527 Hausmann and the council clashed on the subject of running the grammar school. Hausmann's position was that school personnel were lower level clergy and as such were subject only to his oversight. The council thought itself wholly responsible for governing the school, a point of view consistent with the history of that academy. To let Hausmann hire and fire or even reprimand teachers would be to relinquish one of the council's age-old privileges. The new community chest posed another problem that persisted until mid-century. The councillors had paid lip service since 1523 to the Lutheran ideal of the community chest as a mechanism for funding churches, schools, and charity. In practice they attempted to exploit this treasure to their own advantage. They tried to divert incomes and properties from endowments made by their forebears. They treated the chest as a source of loans for themselves and their relatives. Hausmann and his successor, Leonhard Beier, could hardly be uncritical of these practices.

In the autumn of 1528 Hausmann refused to wed a couple who had pledged their troth in secret, without their parents' consent. Disregarding Luther's published opposition to the practice (the Catholic Church had opposed it too), the council commanded Hausmann to wed the couple. Hausmann refused. The council sternly repeated its order to him to act.[22] He declined again because he held that the clergy rather than the council should decide marital and moral disputes. Finally the council had Adam Schuman, a deacon, perform the ceremony.[23] Hausmann did not easily accept this outcome, but Luther advised him to let the matter pass this one time.[24]

Hausmann and Paul Lindenau, preacher in St. Mary's Church, were strongly of the opinion that congregations had the right to hire and dismiss clergy. In this they followed Luther, who had published his views in 1523 under the title, *That a Christian Congregation or Community Has the Right and the Power to Judge All Doctrine and to Call, Install, and . . . Fire Teachers, Basis and Reason Taken from Scripture.*[25] Indeed, they went so far as to regard their own tenure as more legitimate than that of the preachers in St. Catherine's and St. John's churches inasmuch as the latter two had been called and appointed by the council unilaterally. The populace, aware of being excluded from government, sided with Hausmann and Lindenau. The visitation committee with jurisdiction over Zwickau was headed by Georg Spalatin, who wrote to Elector John on February 16, 1529, "that the other two preachers, at St. John's and St.

[22]R. P. 1528-1529 at 1528, fol. 16-17. See *Dass Eltern die Kinder zur Ehe nicht zwingen noch hindern, und die Kinder ohne der Eltern Willen sich nicht verloben sollen* (1524), WA 15: 163-69.

[23]R. P. 1528-1529 at 1528, fol. 17.

[24]WA, *Briefwechsel* 4: no. 1361, December 1, 1528.

[25]*Dass eine christliche Versammlung oder Gemeine Recht und Macht habe, alle Lehre zu urteilen und Lehrer zu berufen, ein- und. . .abzusetzen, Grund und Ursach aus der Schrift*, WA 9: 401-16.

Catherine's, are held in contempt and have almost no attendance at all [schier gar kein volck] because they were called by the council alone, and not also by the entire community as the pastor and Paul [Lindenau] were."[26]

In view of this background, it is hardly surprising that Paul Lindenau preached in an inflammatory manner against the council or that Nicolaus Hausmann did not reprimand him. Actually, Lindenau had launched his campaign of invective against the council as early as 1526. He made Hermann Mühlpfort his target on numerous occasions, as Mühlpfort graphically recounted to Stephan Roth in Wittenberg on March 15, 1527. On that very day, according to Mühlpfort, Lindenau had ranted against him from the pulpit, saying,

> Woe, woe, woe to you and all your children. You had foreign guests at your [son's] wedding and erected a shrine to Venus! Are you a patron of the Gospel? What a fine patron you are! You have advertised pleasure at your front gate! The word of God endures forever. Have that torn off and write: You have erected an altar to Venus, here it is in Zwickau! You whore, you lout, you proud wretch, you haughty boob, you high-falutin' donkey. You let yourself think that no one is more clever than you. . . . You hold council against me, you brought me here and want to drive me out again because I won't condone your airs, misdeeds, knavery, shitting around, thievery, and whoring! Note well, your power hangs by a thread, and when it is broken, your power will well and soon come to an end.[27]

Hausmann kept Luther informed of all these developments. More than once the reformer wrote personally to Lindenau, urging moderation. In a letter dated February 10, 1528, he stated, "I have begged you previously in letters, my Paul, to teach the word of God in peace and to refrain from [reference] to persons and to all those things that rouse the masses, which is usually without [positive] results."[28]

In January 1529 the ecclesiastical visitation committee was in Zwickau and found Lindenau in command of Lutheran teaching (*geschickt*) despite accusations to the contrary.[29] It likewise approved Lorenz Soranus, on whom the council was next to turn.[30]

[26]Weimarer Staatsarchiv, Reg. Ii 245, fol. 25. (Hereafter WSA)

[27]WA, *Briefwechsel* 4: 183   [28]Ibid., no. 1222.

[29]Georg Buchwald, "Die Protokolle der Kirchenvisitationen in den Aemtern: Zwickau, Crimmitschau und Werdau," *Allerlei aus drei Jahrhunderten* 1 (1888): 25.

[30]Ibid. Ironically, Soranus joined the effort to get rid of Lindenau, describing at length his colleague's misdeeds in a letter to the visitors dated February 22, 1529, WSA, Reg. Ii 245, fol. 61-64.

Hausmann was not himself disposed to employ Lindenau's polemic, but he would not, or could not, stop his preacher. He was at least partially in agreement with the content of Lindenau's attacks on authority, though not with his method. And even though Luther and Hausmann were in accord that vulgar diatribes from the pulpit did more harm than good, neither would concede to the council the right on its own to appoint or release a clergyman. In the end, Luther and the council could not agree on any definition of the spheres of church and state. In the heat of the battle Luther appealed to the Elector to intervene:

> Now Your Electoral Grace can well imagine that if this example should take root, [namely] that one would let a preacher be appointed or dismissed in opposition to the pastor, people could today or tomorrow hire a Müntzer or a Carlstadt depending on whether they were inclined or disinclined toward their pastor.[31]

Luther was singing a different tune than he had in 1523. He was no longer inclined to have congregations call their own clerics.

The council was not afflicted with any sense of wrongdoing. Having dismissed Lindenau, the gentlemen blithely wrote to Luther so informing him and requesting him to nominate a replacement. Throughout the subsequent fray, which the council seems not to have anticipated, the city fathers endeavored to stay on Luther's good side. When this proved impossible, they were surprised and chagrined. They saw themselves as acting for the wellbeing of the Christian community they ruled and as staying at all times within their rights. They sought reconciliation with Luther at the same time as they made decisions that were destined to antagonize him still further. They offered Luther a silver chain early in 1530, which he did not accept.[32] Shortly thereafter they fired Soranus, and they forbade Conrad Cordatus, sent by Luther to replace Lindenau, to preach; that was an act tantamount to firing him. In 1531 Hausmann left as well. Luther railed against Zwickau's representatives in Torgau in August, 1531, at the hearing ordered by the Elector. It was here that Luther "excommunicated" the governors of Zwickau.

This part of the story is well known. This brief exploration of the earlier relationship between Zwickau and Martin Luther reveals three things: (1) Luther had no grasp of nor interest in the deep divisions that existed within the citizenry before the Reformation began to bring the city and the reformer together. When Luther became a celebrity, popular opinion of him ran the gamut from very favorable to very unfavorable. (2) Early on, Zwickau's council linked itself to Lutheran teaching and determined to make it prevail.

[31]WA, *Briefwechsel* 6: no. 1790, March 4, 1531.

[32]WA, *Briefwechsel* 6: no. 1515.

Zwickau provides the example that Bernd Moeller searched for but could not find, of a city council that imposed its religious preferences on the entire citizenry.[33] (3) The councillors were not prepared at any time to sacrifice their newly won jurisdiction over religion within the city. On this point they unwittingly came into conflict with that very religious leader with whom they truly wished to be on good terms. Neither the council nor Luther was able to reconcile what must be termed the incompatible dimensions of church and state in the early sixteenth century. Luther understood the councillors' fears. At the peak of his battle with the Zwickau magistrates, he raged to Hausmann, "The villains are still spreading it around and accusing us to the Elector of wanting to capture their worldly dominion. . . ."[34] Who is to say that the obstacles between them might not have been surmounted if Luther had resided in Zwickau, as Zwingli did in Zurich and Calvin was to do in Geneva? In such a case, Luther might well have cooperated in the founding of what we term a magisterial reformation. But Zwickau and Luther were in a wholly different setting from that of the urban Reformation. They were in the rural East, and here the territorial prince was destined to triumph.

[33]*Imperial Cities and the Reformation*, trans. H. C. Erik Midelfort and Mark U. Edwards, Jr. (Philadelphia: Fortress Press, 1972), 60-61.

[34]WA, *Briefwechsel* 6: no. 1804.

Harold Grimm, passport photo and signature, undated.

Philip of Hesse's Vision of Protestant Unity and the Marburg Colloquy

William J. Wright
University of Tennessee at Chattanooga

THE EVENTS AT MARBURG IN EARLY OCTOBER, 1529 were an integral part of Philip the Magnanimous' attempt to realize his vision of Protestant unity. This involved the attainment of twin goals: first, the establishment of a pan-Protestant alliance and, secondly, the recognition of Christian brotherhood among all Protestants, with an end to the Sacramentarian controversy. Philip pursued his plan in competition with what may be called the confessional party, composed of Elector John of Saxony, Margrave George of Brandenburg-Ansbach (-Kulmbach) and the city of Nuremberg. The latter group preferred alliances among Germans which were in confessional agreement. Both groups used Luther's writings to rationalize their positions and attempted to enlist the personal support of the reformers. Philip called the Marburg Colloquy in an attempt to overcome some of the opposition of the confessional party, which in turn tried to sabotage the dialogue before it even began.[1] He sought to wrest Luther's authority from the confessional party at Marburg.

[1]Ekkehart Fabian, *Die Entstehung des Schmalkaldischen Bundes und seiner Verfassung, 1524/29-1531/35. Brück, Landgraf Philipp von Hessen und Jakob Sturm,* 2nd ed. (Tübingen: Osiander, 1962), 44-60; Michael Reu, *The Augsburg Confession: A Collection of Sources with an Historical Introduction,* trans. J. Bodensieck (Chicago: Wartburg Publishing House, 1930), 12-15; Walther Köhler, *Zwingli und Luther, Ihr Streit über das Abendmahl nach seinen politischen und religiösen Beziehungen,* 2 vols. (Leipzig: M. Heinsius, 1924-53) 2:35-36, 42-48; and René Hauswirth, *Landgraf Philipp von Hesse und Zwingli, 1526-1531,* vol. 35 of *Schriften zur Kirchen- und Rechtsgeschichte* (Tübingen: Osiander, 1968), 102-103.

Other good sources on the background of the Marburg Colloquy, and especially the leading role of the landgrave in the event include the following: *D. Martin Luthers Werke: Kritische Gesammtausgabe,* 100 vols., (Weimar: Hermann Böhlaus, 1888-1966) 30, 3: 93, hereafter cited *WA* (Weimar Ausgabe); Hans von Schubert, *Bekenntnisbildung und religionspolitik, 1529-30* (Gotha: Friedrich Andreas Perthes, 1910), 9-19; Hermann Sasse, *This Is My Body; Luther's Contention for the Real Presence in the Sacrament of the Altar* (Minneapolis: Augsburg Publishing House, 1959), 215-18, 266-67; Roland Bainton, "Luther and the Via Media at the Marburg Colloquy," *The Lutheran Quarterly* 1 (1949): 396-97; and *Corpus Reformatorum: Philippi Melanchthonis Opera omnia,* ed. Carolus Gottlieb Bretschneider (Halle: C. A. Schwetschke et Filium, 1834-64) 1: 1099-1102, nr. 637, hereafter cited as *CR.*

The term confessional party has been adopted solely to identify this group, not to take sides in the debate about John the Constant's motives regarding the Schwabach Articles and a Protestant alliance. Carl Christensen has recently elaborated three views of this problem. See Carl Christensen, "John of Saxony's Diplomacy, 1529-1530: Reformation or Realpolitik?" *The Sixteenth Century Journal* 15 (1984): 425. On the one hand, this writer agrees with Christensen that John's top priority was the political survival of Lutheranism and that he shared some of Luther's concern for doctrinal integrity. On the other hand,

The setting for this struggle among the Lutherans originated with the possibility that anti-Evangelical Catholics might attempt to use force to compel them to return to the Church; that is, to enforce the Edict of Worms. Philip never seemed to have had any doubts about either the likelihood of such action or how to respond thereto. He believed that the Evangelicals had to build an alliance that was ready to defend itself against all potential adversaries, either fellow princes or the Emperor Charles. All Protestants should be included in this alliance, "excluding none that adhere to the Gospel."[2] Also in the landgrave's vision of an alliance, all Protestant states should be included regardless of political form or growing national sentiments.

In 1524, the elector had joined with the landgrave in creating the Torgau League and then, in 1525, the Magdeburg League, which included the towns of Magdeburg and Bremen as well as several small principalities. Indeed, the elector had sometimes taken the leading role in these actions. These leagues were a response to the appearance of Catholic leagues at the time, but they had not as yet named potential foes. Then, the first Diet of Speyer (1526), with its attendant recess, relieved tensions for a while.

In mid-1529 came the hostile developments at the second Diet of Speyer. The security of the Protestants seemed gravely threatened again, by the emperor as well as by Catholic princes. Philip of Hesse now wished to develop another, even greater, alliance system but the elector balked at the idea. He was supported in this opposition by the margrave and by Nuremberg. In spite of the threatening situation, the confessional party wished first to pursue legal means to obtain security. It emphasized that one must trust God rather than alliances, a point made by Luther. The elector, nevertheless, wavered at the Diet of Speyer in April. Moreover, neither he nor the other confessionalists were so secure as to forego the alliance discussions of 1529 altogether.

A prevailing explanation of this divergence between Philip and the confessional party has been to view it as a response by the latter party to the aggressiveness and seeming recklessness of this restless young landgrave. Already he had almost plunged the electoral Saxons into a preventive war in 1528 in the

however, Thomas A. Brady's point that John played "a double game" in the second half of 1529 with the evangelical towns cannot be gainsaid. See Thomas A. Brady, Jr., "Jacob Sturm of Strasbourg and the Lutherans at the Diet of Augsburg," *Church History* 42 (1973): 183. This writer's contention is that both of these views fail to take cognizance of John's (and the confessional party's) political assumptions; namely, his view of the developing German monarchy. The confessional party did wish to drive the Swiss Zwinglians out of the picture, but not the Upper German towns. This contention is in keeping with what Christensen identifies as the thrid alternative understanding of the Schwabach articles, put forth by Walther Köhler: the articles were intended to wean Strasbourg and Ulm away from Zwingli into the Lutheran camp.

[2]*Politisches Archiv des Landgrafen Philipp des Grossmütigen von Hessen*, Hessisches Staatsarchiv, Marburg/Lahn, nr. 2544, 53r-53v; hereafter cited as *PA*.

This is from Philip's instructions to his representatives before the elector, October 29, 1529.

well-known Pack Affair.[3] But there was much more at issue. The two parties had fundamentally different views of the nature of the empire and the power of the emperor on the one hand, and the unity of Protestantism on the other.

Philip thought of the empire in its universal, medieval connotation, whereas the confessional party was influenced by a vision of the developing imperial monarchy. That German national movement had been first promoted by German humanists and had focused on the popular Emperor Maximilian. Then Luther's anti-papal demands, and especially his call for the reform of the Church by German authorities in the *Address to the Christian Nobility of the German Nation,* indeed for the creation of a German church with its own primate and national council, had furthered this national movement tremendously. But Philip saw something quite different in Luther's teaching and was not influenced by the national sentiments.

Philip and the confessional party likewise held different views of the office of the emperor. While the confessional party viewed the office in the Roman legal fashion as possessing supreme, irresistible authority (*imperium*) in the empire, Philip held to the Germanic tradition of an elective office. It is Philip's lack of concern for the developing imperial monarchy and his view of the office of the emperor that explain his leadership of the movement for a pan-Protestant alliance and his development of resistance theories in contrast to those of the confessional party.

Philip believed that his views and plans were strictly in keeping with Luther's teaching and, like the elector, wished to use Luther to lend authority to his policies. One can already see this, and his exasperation with Wittenberg, in his correspondence concerning the idea of preventive war in 1528, an issue closely related to alliance and resistance. "Doctor Martin has given us his opinion that we [princes] have authority and right to protect our subjects."[4] Wondering thus why the reformer had objections to his secular plans, the landgrave continued:

> Since I must protect my subjects . . . must I wait to protect them after they are dead; what good is that? Furthermore, if in temporal matters we were not to make use of human plans provided they are not contrary to the will of God, what need would we have for the universities where a great deal of reason is taught that is not contained in God's Word? Even Luther's own advice is not entirely without reason and worldly wisdom. He will say that we must trust God. That is true . . . but it is also written, "Thou shalt not tempt the Lord thy God."[5]

[3]Fabian, *Entstehung des Bundes*, 36 n. 129.

[4]*Luther's Correspondence and other Contemporary Letters*, ed. Preserved Smith and Charles M. Jacobs 2 (Philadelphia: Lutheran Publication Society, 1918): 439-40, nr. 794.

[5]Ibid.

Frustrated or not, the landgrave could not give up, for to establish a pan-Protestant alliance he must have the support of the supreme authority in Protestantism.

Philip and his advisers developed a theory of the right of the lesser Christian magistrate to resist the emperor and tried to convert Luther and the other princes to it in 1529. He argued that the emperor was a constitutional, elected figure whereas the territorial princes were hereditary and sovereign rulers. Moreover, Philip held that the emperor had sworn an oath by which he was bound to uphold the law of the empire.[6]

Typical of his exasperation in the campaign in 1529 to convert Wittenberg and the princes to his view was a letter to Luther in December. Philip was seeking to persuade the reformer to specific strategies of resistance, as well as to convince him of the rightness of the theory. Knowing Luther's most likely initial response, the landgrave indicated that he too had no doubt that almighty God would protect the Protestants: "And yet the ways and means that God has given us for this purpose are not to be despised."[7] (Luther's response was, "I trust in God, who boasts . . . that he makes naught the plans of Godless princes. . . ."[8]) The Hessian prince could not understand why Luther could not see that the making of alliances and the development of theories of resistance were temporal matters demanding the use of reason and worldly wisdom, obviously within the calling of secular rulers. Utterly exasperated with Luther (and with Melanchthon, who had once counselled him to play Jehoshophat), the landgrave ultimately commented, "We have no opinion [other] than that you will stand by your doctrine and will use all diligence to further whatever measures will serve to further and plant it."[9]

The landgrave's assessment of the Sacramentarian controversy, like his position on resistance, was very different from that of Wittenberg. The difference accounts to a considerable extent for his optimism concerning the value of a colloquy. He believed that the two sides in the dispute really held the same essential religious faith. At the Diet of Speyer in 1529 the landgrave stated his position: "No one wars against the flesh and blood of Christ."[10] In July 1529,

---

[6]Schubert, *Bekenntnisbildung*, 199-202. The originality of this constitutional argument with Philip and his advisors has recently been affirmed. See Quentin Skinner, *The Foundations of Modern Political Thought* 2 (Cambridge: Cambridge University Press, 1978): 127-129, 197-198, and 201-204; W. D. J. Cargill Thompson, "Luther and the Right of Resistance to the Emperor," in *Church Society and Politics*, ed. Derek Baker (Oxford: Basil Blackwell, 1975), 195 and 199-200; and W. D. J. Cargill Thompson, *Luther's Political Thought* (New Jersey: Barnes and Noble, 1984), 91 ff. Skinner maintains that the idea of a constitutional emperor figure owed much to humanist studies of Roman law but that the "federal theory" of empire was specifically original with these Hessians.

[7]*Luther's Correspondence* 2: 507-508, nr. 861.

[8]Ibid., 509, nr. 862.

[9]Ibid., 507-508, nr. 861.

[10]Köhler, *Zwingli und Luther* 2: 25-26.

he wrote to his representatives at a political meeting meant to expedite the alliance agreed upon at Speyer (the Particular Secret Agreement, discussed below), that Hesse would not be separated from Strasbourg, because their opinions in Strasbourg were good, not heretical: "They believe as well as we do, [that] Christ is in the Sacrament." [11] Nor did this prince's views narrow later. On June 11, 1530, he wrote to Melanchthon that he could not understand why the Saxons would not accept the uplanders—(i.e., in this context) upper Germans and Swiss—as brothers. "We are all of the same mind, all recognize Christ. . . ." All believe we must eat Christ for salvation in the sacrament, and none say that God is or is not able to do this or that, but that all things must be done "according to faith and Scripture."[12]

The same letter reveals that Philip also believed the two sides were in essential agreement on the nature of Christ's salutary presence in the Lord's Supper, in spite of the fact that the fifteenth article accepted at Marburg by the theologians specifically stated that they disagreed. Commenting on the dispute over whether the unbelieving would receive Christ in the Sacrament, Philip questioned, "How else can God be eaten than by the faithful and through faith, and since Christ has a perfected body, which does not feed the stomach, such opinions are not necessary."[13] This was Philip's understanding of a point argued by Luther at Marburg,[14] that Christ's presence is of his "glorified body," an idea that Luther took from William of Occam (*esse diffinitive*).[15]

This same letter to Melanchthon also clearly stated the landgrave's essential theology. He felt that the basic points, in addition to his view of the Sacrament, are belief in Christ, the idea that God is all powerful, justification by faith, and the authority of Scripture. Why he failed to mention the priesthood of all believers is not clear, but it is certain from other sources that he held this to be a fundamental premise. Philip understood these points of faith to be the basic premises of Protestantism as opposed to Catholicism. Those who held these basic premises should be accepted as Protestant brothers; other matters were adiaphora, if one may use a term Philip did not use here but which is a concept implied in his arguments.

If the landgrave believed that the sides really all held the same views, how did he explain the disputes over the Lord's Supper? Luther and Melanchthon believed the colloquy would be a waste of time because there were essential

[11] *PA*, nr. 240. 2.

[12] *CR* 2: 96-100, nrs. 718-720B.

[13] Ibid.

[14] Donald J. Ziegler, ed., *Great Debates of the Reformation* (New York: Random House, 1969), 88.

[15] Sasse, *This Is My Body*, 157-58.

differences between the sides, i.e., because the partisans were of different spirits. From Wittenberg prior to the colloquy they argued that everything had already been said. Why did the landgrave believe otherwise?

Philip's optimism was based on a different assessment of the controversy. He believed that the sides misunderstood one another. According to the Hessian, the theologians quarreled over words. "I have always thought," he wrote to Zwingli in January, 1531, that ". . . it was more a war of words between you [theologians] and not a matter of intention or belief."[16] In his correspondence with electoral Saxony in 1529, Philip wrote that one could not let theologians keep Protestants apart because they love to argue; if one gave them full reign, there would be new schisms every year, "indeed from day to day."[17] It is obvious why Philip believed he could win an agreement if he brought the partisans to Marburg, causing them to discuss the issues on an intimate basis, and under his influence. Events at Marburg in fact demonstrated the validity of his view concerning the theologians.

It is apparent that the confessional party, in contrast to Philip, was motivated by a fear that if the Lutherans embraced or even tolerated the Zwinglians, the hopes for reuniting Catholics and Lutherans would be endangered. It is this writer's contention that their fear resulted from a very basic view they held, consciously or unconsciously, of the empire and the office of the emperor, and not solely from religious concerns. They were influenced by the national movement for a German imperial monarchy. The concept of Germany was still vague regarding geographical boundaries, but it had accrued a historical and cultural mythology through the work of the humanists. It was capable of inspiring xenophobia and appealing to all German-speaking populations.[18] Most of all, however ironically or illogically, the office of the "universal" emperor was the main symbol and common element for the movement. The national appeal of the office had been boosted by Maximilian, who invented the title, "king of Germany," to accompany it.[19]

One must assume that national appeal in Luther's message to reform the German church strongly attracted the Lutheran princes and Nuremberg from the start. It is well known that many humanistic and rebellious knights, such

[16]*Huldreich Zwinglis Sämtliche Werke*, ed. Emil Egli, Walther Köhler, Georg Finseler, Oskar Farner, and Leonard von Muralt, vol. 2 (Leipzig: M. Heinsius, 1935), 322-24, nr. 1162.

[17]*PA*, nr. 2544, 51r.

[18]A. G. Dickens, *The German Nation and Martin Luther* (New York: Harper and Row, 1974), 40.

[19]William Stubbs, *Germany in the Later Middle Ages, 1200-1500*, ed. Arthur Hassal, reprint of 1908 edition (New York: Howard Fertig, 1969), 238-39. See also Lewis W. Spitz, *The Religious Renaissance of the German Humanists* (Cambridge, MA: Harvard University Press, 1963), 2, 116, 274; Hajo Holborn, *Ulrich von Hutten and the German Reformation*, trans. Roland Bainton, reprint of 1937 edition (Westport, CN: Greenwood Press, 1978), 40-41.

as Ulrich von Hutten, were moved by this aspect of Lutheranism. Emphasis on the concern of the princes for their "princely liberties" has obscured the strength of the national appeal for them.

It was because of national sentiments that the confessional party wanted German Lutherans and Catholics to bridge their differences, but without the pope. This explains the favor which Melanchthon's idea of including Catholics in the discussions at the colloquy enjoyed with Dr. Gregor Brück, the Saxon chancellor.[20] In concern for German unity, sacrificing the minority of German Zwinglians in the upland towns was a small price to pay. And good fortune it was that the major center of heresy, and Zwingli himself, lived outside of the developing monarchy, in the Swiss Confederation.

A consideration of the opposition of these same rulers to Philip's arguments for resisting the emperor, should he attack for religious reasons, supports the main contention. Because it could not support any theory of resistance to the emperor, Brandenburg-Ansbach never did join the Schmalkaldic League. Nuremberg followed the stance of Brandenburg-Ansbach. The special relationship which this great town enjoyed with the emperor, as well as her concern to stay in line with her powerful princely neighbor, explain her attachment to the national movement.[21] Margrave George's reverence for the office of the emperor was in keeping with the Hohenzollern principle of clinging to the imperial house to become great. Moreover, George could feel more an insider than the others because he had concluded successful dealings with Ferdinand (brother and regent of the emperor) and hoped to secure further legal and financial rewards from the Hapsburgs.[22]

Similarly enlightening is the curious refusal of Electoral Saxony to accept Philip's constitutional argument for resistance to the emperor. For several years after the founding of the Schmalkaldic League in 1531, electoral Saxony continued to offer the tortuous argument of its jurists to the effect that resistance could be offered to the emperor because they had an appeal to a general church council pending.[23] The elector and the other members of the confessional party had great difficulty accepting Philip's logical, effective theory of resistance because of the reverence they held for the office of the emperor. Electoral Saxony accepted Philip's argument only in 1536, and the Wittenberg reformers did so only when called upon by their elector. Brandenburg-Ansbach and Nuremberg never did accept Philip's view of resistance.

Even when Saxon Elector John did join the Schmalkaldic League, he always insisted that the League was directed against the house of Hapsburg

---

[21]Harold J. Grimm, *Lazarus Spengler: A Lay Leader of the Reformation* (Columbus: Ohio State University Press, 1978), 171-72.

[22]Karl Schornbaum, *Zur Politik des Markgrafen Georg von Brandenburg von Beginne seiner selbständigen Regierung bis zum Nürnberger Anstand, 1529-1532* (Munich: Theodor Ackermann, 1906), 12-13.

[23]Thompson, "Resistance to the Emperor," 187-92.

rather than against the office of the Emperor. The strength of his national sentiments is also seen in his continuing opposition to dealing with the Hungarian counter-king, John Zapolya, with whom Philip was ready to ally. John would not even support Zapolya financially.[24]

Also as a danger to their national imperial sentiments, the confessional party feared what they perceived as a spirit of revolution and radicalism present in the Zwinglian or Zwinglian-leaning towns. They knew well the words of Zwingli that the emperor and the empire were as much Roman offshoots as was the papacy. Precisely in this vein, Melanchthon wrote to Lazarus Spengler, prominent Nuremberg patrician-statesman and opponent of Philip's views of resistance, that there were dangers in Zwingli's teaching: "From these beginnings changes in the empire might follow."[25] Zwingli's view threatened the development of a German monarchy. Subsequently, Luther developed a rationale for resisting the Emperor based on the idea that if the emperor attacked the Protestants for religious reasons, he was really acting not by virtue of his office as emperor but as a servant of the pope, that is, ultimately as a minion of Satan.[26]

The demand for a common confession was what the confessional party held up publicly as their major reason for not cooperating in forming an alliance. That is, they claimed religious motives and believed their political views conformed to Luther's views. In fact, the Wittenberg reformers were opposed to the proposed alliance, too.

Certainly for Luther, religious issues were the basis for opposition to the Hessian plans for an alliance.[27] Earlier, Luther had been opposed to political arrangements for protecting the Gospel, as he had indicated in the midst of the Pack Affair of 1528, even though he did not doubt the authenticity of the plot at the time: "He who lives by the sword dies by the sword." In May 1529 he argued that God has always condemned such alliances in the Old Testament. But the most vexing problem with an alliance such as Philip was proposing, one without a common confession, was that it would necessitate allying with the enemies of God. Such an act, the reformer wrote, would grant these enemies of God aid to the detriment of souls and bring responsibility for the "Untugend und Lästerung."[28] Obviously, then, Luther had strong religious reasons for his opposition to Philip's alliance plans.

The great reformer also had more practical reservations. For one thing, he indicated that he did not see any need for such an alliance, for "the papal heap" was not ready or inclined to attack. In addition, he did not trust the landgrave.

[24]Höss and Klein, *Zeitalter des Humanismus*, 224.

[25]Reu, *Augsburg Confessions*, 15-16.

[26]Thompson, "Resistance to the Emperor," 192-193.

[27]Reu, *Augsburg Confessions*, 15-18.

[28]*WA: Briefe* 5: 75-78, nr. 1424; *Luther's Correspondence*, 435-38.

According to Luther, Philip was "a young, restless prince," who might use the alliance to do something foolish."[29] The Pack Affair and Philip's promotion of a preventive war were still much on the reformer's mind. These sentiments concerning the landgrave were shared by John; even years later, John Frederick continued to fear the landgrave.[30]

Why was Melanchthon opposed to a pan-Protestent agreement and what real influence did he possess? It is clear that Melanchthon held reservations that far surpassed the religious concerns of Luther. It is also clear that he was more involved in stopping Philip's plans. The humanist professor contacted the Nuremberg politicians in this matter, and we know that he was backed in these concerns and actions by the old Saxon chancellor, Gregor Brück.[31]

Melanchthon was opposed to any pan-Protestant alliance because it would undermine his great hope for a successful Lutheran-Catholic dialogue. Melanchthon developed the idea that Catholics should be invited to Marburg, claiming that he proposed it to Philip at Speyer in April. As he explained to the elector, the presence of some "learned and reasonable" papists was necessary, "otherwise there would be great talk about the Lutherans and Zwinglians coming together to make conspiracies, etc. . . ."[32]

Behind his demand for Lutheran-Catholic dialogue at this time lurked a fear in Melanchthon. Ekkehard Fabian, Walther Köhler, and Michael Reu have all noted that the humanist scholar seemed to have a profound fear that Philip's plans for a pan-Protestant alliance would endanger the universal church and empire. Indeed, Melanchthon became involved in developing the demand for confessional agreement as early as May 1529, precisely because he saw it as a means for preserving the universal church and the empire.[33]

For security, the confessional party preferred to court the favor of Emperor Charles, which they strongly believed they could win. It was for this reason that John called a meeting of the Lutheran states at Nuremberg in May 1529. There it was agreed to send a delegation to approach the emperor. The Protestation and Appelation, plus certain instructions drawn up by Lazarus Spengler of Nuremberg, were approved. Three delegates, none of them Hessian though Hesse had been represented at the meeting, were selected to approach the emperor with these documents. It was believed he would favor them, for it was assumed that Ferdinand, who had acted in his name at Speyer, had altered the intentions of Charles. These three left Nuremberg in July and

[29]*WA: Briefe* 5: 75-78; *Luther's Correspondence*, 488-489, nr. 841.

[30]Fabian, *Entstehung des Bundes*, 36 n. 129. John Frederick still showed distrust in 1547.

[31]Fabian, *Entstehung des Bundes*, 47-50; Reu, *Augsburg Confession*, 12-14.

[32]*Luther's Correspondence*, 477, nr. 830; *CR* 8, nr. 619; Sasse, *This Is My Body*, 213.

[33]Fabian, *Entstehung des Bundes*, 56.

finally got a first audience on September 14, at Piacenza[34] This was the beginning of the very embarrassing Piacenza Affair, which ended with the arrest of the delegates. Beyond the hope for imperial dialogue, the confessional party pursued other legal and peaceful arrangements, including agreements among estates at diets and clauses in customary inheritance alliances and friendship pacts. Moreover, they sought to place the authority for solving problems created by the Reformation in a general or national church council. This idea was proposed in 1520 by Luther in his *Address to the Christian Nobility* and Elector John still hoped that the terrible split (*Zwiespalt*) in the Christian religion could be settled by the Diet of Augsburg in 1530. Indeed, John spoke of the diet serving "in lieu of a council or national assembly."[35] Of course, John meant the split between Catholics and Protestants as opposed to the intra-Protestant division which concerned Philip when he spoke of *Zwiespalt*.

The concept of assigning the solution of the religious controversy raised by Luther to a general, or a national, church council was nebulous at best because there was a world of difference between a general and a national council. The Lutherans only clearly decided to favor the latter forum in 1537, when Pope Paul III really did call a general council. Like the term, "empire," "council" could be interpreted in two ways. Nebulous or not, it provided a legal justification for demanding a suspension of the Edict of Worms since the Diet of Speyer in 1526 had called for such a council. Thus the confessional party found additional security in favoring discussions between themselves and the Catholic party.

Finally, the confessional party also wanted to continue the purely political discussion between the German princes and towns, presumably to simply expand, if necessary, the Magdeburg alliance. Such a policy kept force open as a last alternative and kept the landgrave from becoming totally alienated.

What kind of alliance, if any, the confessional party would accept, and how they wished to proceed to form one, emerged from meetings at Schleiz and Schwabach in October 1529. In the first, the elector and the margrave met with Philip's representatives; in the later meeting, counsellors of the Protestant parties met. The confessionalists plainly wanted political meetings and did not want to be involved in pan-Protestant theological discussions. Meeting secretly at Schleiz, elector and margrave agreed to demand confessional agreement as a prerequisite to alliance in order specifically to bar the Swiss towns, which could not accept their confession. They then demanded of Hesse at Schleiz, and of all the participants at Schwabach, acceptance of their

---

[34]Grimm, *Lazarus Spengler*, 134. There was nothing curious about this, as Reu maintained. See Christensen, "John of Saxony's Diplomacy," 427. John wanted to trust the Emperor and was willing to do a great deal to promote the developing monarchy.

[35]*WA: Briefe* 5: 263-266, nr. 1538.

Schwabach Confession drawn up by and bearing the authority of Wittenberg.[36]

The Marburg Colloquy was a calculated attempt by the landgrave to gain the support of the Wittenberg theologians, especially Luther, for his policies. Philip sought at the least to wrest from the confessional party the authority of Luther being used by them to block his plans for a pan-Protestant alliance. If Philip could resolve the Sacramentarian controversy, Luther's religious objections to a pan-Protestant alliance would be overcome. Luther had argued that it was wrong to ally with those who did not hold the same religious views because it would make one guilty of their errors. This was the most important point for the opposing princes because it was Luther's strongest religious objection and, accordingly, they had based their demand for a confessional agreement on it.

The great reformer's other objections to alliances would not stand in the way once the Sacramentarian obstacle was removed. Philip little feared that the other princes would be moved by Luther's concern for using the sword. With regard to Luther's practical objection that the "papal heap" was not a real threat, he knew from past experience that both the Elector and Luther could be convinced otherwise. Had the results of the Piacenza Affair been known prior to the colloquy, Philip might have enjoyed more success than he did.

In his quest to win Luther to his side, Philip was emboldened by his own optimism, his faith in his ability to use face-to-face, small group meetings to bring agreement, his knowledge of how Luther reacted in such groups, and his assessment of the nature of the Sacramentarian controversy itself.

The Marburg Colloquy was not a spur of the moment idea and was not simply a response to the confessional party's refusal to carry through the Particular Secret Agreement. There is evidence that Philip first tried to assemble a colloquy in the summer of 1527.[37] In spite of the stormy atmosphere of 1528, he did manage to hold a preview or protocolloquy at the Diet of the Swabian League at Worms in December. The landgrave authorized a disputation between his court preacher, Erhard Schnepf, and the Worms preacher, Leonhard Brunner. From their pulpits the two preachers had raised the Sacramentarian controversy at Worms. In the course of the preview disputation the landgrave declared that he would assemble the followers of Luther and Oecolampadius (who had taken up Zwingli's cause) to settle the Eucharist controversy, "even if it costs 6,000 *gulden*."[38] Philip also undoubtedly called the Strasbourg politician Jacob Sturm to this meeting at Worms to discuss the idea of a colloquy and the possibility of political alliance.[39]

[36]Fabian, *Entstehung des Bundes*, 58-60.

[37]Schubert, *Bekenntnis*, 10-11.

[38]Ibid., 15-16, 18-19; Köhler, *Zwingli und Luther* 2: 25.

[39]Köhler, *Zwingli und Luther* 2: 25.

It was, however, developments at the second Diet of Speyer that made the need for unity a pressing issue and set the stage for the colloquy.[40] Philip's great hour of opportunity to assert his views arrived in April as Ferdinand and anti-Evangelical princes condemned and threatened the Evangelicals.[41] The result was the well-known protest after which the Evangelicals were called Protestants. More important to Philip was achievement of the Particular Secret Agreement on April 22, 1529, signed by electoral Saxony, Hesse, Nuremberg, Ulm, and Strasbourg. It was the first step toward a more detailed defensive alliance to be arranged at later meetings.[42]

The Particular Secret Agreement certainly was a great achievement for Philip and he had reason to be encouraged by his success. The parties agreed to meet again to conclude a definitive agreement based on mutual defense in the event of attack on account of religious differences. Unlike previous alliances, this one specifically named the Swabian League, the Imperial Cameral Tribunal, and the Imperial Regency Council as potential foes.[43] Moreover, he had succeeded in bringing electoral Saxony into the agreement in spite of the elector's and the Wittenberg reformers' disinclinations. With such a realistic achievement in hand, Philip had reason to think that he might convince the parties to recognize the emperor as a potential foe.

Immediately after the conclusion of the agreement, Philip began sending out invitations for what became the Marburg Colloquy. Basically he requested the presence of the theologians to hold a "friendly and good, genial discussion" about the "terrible split" in the Christian religion "concerning the flesh and blood of our Lord and Savior Jesus Christ." The purpose of the colloquy was the setting aside or settlement of that split.[44]

The landgrave was overly optimistic. For one thing, Margrave George still had not been brought into the discussions and still refused any discussion of alliances aimed at the emperor. More important, Philip probably did not know at the time that the elector had participated in the Agreement only out of extreme personal anxiety and in contradiction to principles he had already affirmed before April 22. The elector as is shown usually reacted stolidly to claims by Philip that the Protestant movement was in danger, especially if from the emperor and even when objectively evident. It is known that the electoral Saxon government had decided already, on April 19 and 20 (two days before the Agreement), that there could be no alliance without a common confession.[45]

---

[40]*Martin Bucers Deutsche Schriften*, vol. 4: *Zur Auswärtige Wirksamkeit, 1528-1533* (Gütersloh: Gerd Mohn, 1975), 323.

[41]Reu, *Augsburg Confession*, 10-11.

[42]Reu calls this Philip's great triumph, ibid., 11.

[43]Ibid., 10-11; Fabian, *Entstehung des Bundes*, 42-43.

[44]*PA*, nr. 245, fols. 1r-1v, 3r, and 4r. See also the clear statement in Philip's letter to Osiander, ibid., 9r-9v.

[45]Fabian, *Entstehung des Bundes*, 40-42.

It is difficult to say with any confidence why the elector acted on April 22 in contradiction to the principles established two days earlier. Outward causes for anxiety were the notorious recess of the Diet and the rejection of the protest by Ferdinand. The elector soon thought better of the Agreement, feeling more secure as he considered two other agreements reached at about the same time. One was the truce arranged among the majority of the estates in spite of the recess and their religious differences. The second was a non-agression pact concluded with the Elector of Mainz. Having re-thought the Agreement, Elector John secretly plotted and carried out with Margrave George the failure of several meetings of Protestant political representatives meant to fulfill the Agreement on May 22 at Rotach, at Nuremberg on May 23-27, at Saalfield on July 7-8, and at Schwabach on August 24.[46]

During the same time, the two princes called upon the Wittenberg theologians for a theological statement that could be used as a common confession, prerequisite to any political alliance. This was not a new idea, for both princes had suggested such a document late in 1528. The exact date of composition of this document is not certain, but it existed prior to the colloquy. It has come to be called the Schwabach Articles because it formed the basis for an important meeting in Schwabach in mid-October, after Marburg.[47] The confessional party was armed prior to the colloquy with a doctrinal statement carrying the authority of Wittenberg that would prevent Philip from achieving a pan-Protestant alliance and undermine his idea of Protestant brotherhood.

In addition to undermining Hesse's colloquy in this way, Brandenburg and Saxony also called for a meeting of the princes at Schleiz to begin on October 3, the same time that the colloquy was meeting in Marburg. This act undoubtedly was designed to emphasize their resistance to alliance with the southern Protestants, who were not invited to Schleiz, but also to keep Philip involved in political discussions with themselves. The Elector committed the ultimate act of sabotage, probably on September 15 or 16, by specifically instructing the Wittenberg theologians not to make an agreement. Moreover, the Saxon district official, Eberhard von der Tann, was sent along to Marburg to look after the fulfillment of these instructions.[48]

It was in these prearranged settings that the Marburg Colloquy took place. Philip's strategy was consistent with his assessment of the situation. Since he had a firm belief that there were no essential differences among the parties, his intention was for the discussions to reveal the real basis of controversy. The theological discussions began as private discussions among the principal parties. The landgrave arranged for Luther to speak with Oecolampadius, while

---

[46]See ibid., 44-60; Reu, *Augsburg Confession*, 12-15; Köhler, *Zwingli und Luther* 2: 35-36, 42-48.

[47]Heinrich Bornkamm, *Luther in Mid-Career, 1521-1530*, ed. Karin Bornkamm, trans. E. Theodore Bachmann (Philadelphia: Fortress Press, 1983), 632; Schornbaum, *Politik Georg*, 75-76; Köhler, *Zwingli und Luther* 2: 46.

[48]Fabian, *Entstehung des Bundes*, 58-59.

Melanchthon conferred with Zwingli, to reveal the contestants to each other as flesh and blood figures instead of the monsters they seemed to be on the printed page. These discussions occurred on October 1, the day after the arrival of the Lutherans.

Large group discussions then commenced on Saturday, October 2. As further upland participants arrived, the large discussions continued on the following day. Sunday evening the Landgrave arranged for renewed private discussions like those of the first day. During these October 3 private talks, Luther made serious attempts at compromise on the nature of the presence of Christ in the Sacrament. He pronounced the formula that Christ's body and blood are present truly, substantively, and essentially, but not qualitatively or quantitatively.[49]

The colloquy was supposed to last for eight days, but was shortened by the appearance of the *virus encephalitus*, or the English Sweats, in Marburg just prior to the meeting.[50] Because of shortened time, Philip again called for private discussions to work out a practical compromise on the morning of October 4. Moreover, he specifically called upon Luther to draft an agreement.[51] Luther's draft in turn was hammered into the Fifteen Articles on that Monday. Thus arose the only tangible result of the theological discussions at the time.

At the large group discussions between twenty-five and forty people participated. Besides the well-known individuals participating, a number of Hessian theologians and the princes, Duke Ulrich of Württemberg and Count Wilhelm of Fürstenberg, were present.[52] These were not public meetings, although Zwingli had requested such a forum. Danger from the English Sweats is undoubtedly the best explanation of why Philip closed the meetings to the public. It was the explanation offered by one of the participants.[53]

Philip participated in the discussions through private consultations and the maneuvering noted above. From several sources it is known that the Hessian leader was personally involved in the theological give-and-take. For example, the Wittenberg theologians presented a paper to the politician in which they attempted to prove to him that the Psalms backed their position.[54] In a revealing anecdote, Luther himself described how Philip circulated among the theologians, making suggestions about the issues being discussed.[55]

---

[49]See Sasse, *This is My Body*, 266-67. Bainton, "Luther and the Via Media," 396-97, argued that Luther was not intransigent, admitted errors, and proposed the formula of concord.

[50]*WA* 30, 3: 93 n. 2.

[51]*CR* 1: 1099-1102, nr. 1637; *WA* 30, 3: 94.

[52]Köhler, *Zwingli und Luther* 2: 65.

[53]Gerhard May, ed. *Das Marburger Religionsgespräch* (Gütersloh: Mohn, 1970), 51 n. 284. Contrast this explanation to Sasse, *This Is My Body*, 219-220, who claims that Philip shortened the meeting because Luther demanded it.

[54]*CR* 1: 1099-1102, nr. 637. This is told by Melanchthon in a report to the elector.

[55]*WA: Tischreden* 4: 625-30, nr. 5038.

In a letter to his wife at the end of the colloquy (October 4), Luther wrote, "He [Philip] did his best to make us united, hoping that even though we disagreed, yet we should hold each other as members of Christ. He worked hard for it. . . ."[56]

The landgrave really did achieve a great deal with the colloquy. He showed that, under the proper circumstances, one could elicit compromise from the leading theologians in the Sacramentarian controversy, particularly from Luther. This in turn lent credence to Philip's assertion that the controversy was a result of misunderstanding. By bringing the altercating theologians together, and especially through the use of private consultations, Philip succeeded in alleviating much of the atmosphere of hostility and malevolence that had beset intra-Protestant relations prior to the colloquy. Nasty reproaches of "anabaptist fanaticism" versus "papism" were not heard, nor did the sides a quarrel as much after the colloquy.[57]

This achievement of greater understanding and tolerance was nothing short of miraculous in the face of the original aversion of Wittenberg toward the Zwinglians and the idea of colloquy. This negativism was symbolized in Luther's early statement at the colloquy to the effect that the two parties were of a different spirit. And, again, in his first meeting with Martin Bucer he told the Strasbourg preacher, "You are a rogue . . . you are of the devil."[58]

Contrary to his initial intransigence, Luther proved to be open to compromise at the colloquy. He did propose a formula for compromise and showed some willingness to accept intercommunion without complete agreement when Philip suggested it. Melanchthon objected to this move, however.[59] It was not Luther, but Melanchthon and the Saxon counsellor, von der Tann, who prevented the achievement of brotherhood among Protestants at Marburg.

Another important result of the colloquy was that Martin Bucer became acquainted with Philip and was willing in the years ahead to work in the landgrave's cause. Bucer became convinced by the proceedings (or perhaps in private discussions with Philip) that the two sides were essentially in agreement and that it was a problem of words, as Philip believed, although concessions would need to be made.[60] After talking to both sides at Marburg and following the colloquy, the Strasbourg reformer wrote to Duke Ernst of Lüneburg in November 1530 that he was convinced "this whole strife stands more in words than in the fundamentals of the thing."[61]

---

[56]*Luther's Correspondence* 2: 496-97, nr. 85l.

[57]Köhler, *Zwingli und Luther*, 131-33.

[58]Hastings Eells, *Martin Bucer*, reprint of 1931 edition (New York: Russell & Russell, 1977), 93.

[59]Bainton, "Luther and the Via Media," 391.

[60]Eells, *Bucer*, 93-97.

[61]*Zwinglis Werke* 11: 236-47, nr. 1134.

Bucer is well known in the 1530s as the champion of reconciliation between the Upper German towns and the Lutheran princes and towns (but excluding the Swiss). His efforts led to the Württemberg and Wittenberg Concords. He also became the chief servant in the cause of religious harmony in Hesse. It was Philip, however, who first prepared the way for the Wittenberg Concord by arranging a meeting between Melanchthon and Bucer at Kassel.

Melanchthon was not totally unaffected by the colloquy either. His comment following the event, in which he tried to account for the agreement on fourteen articles and disagreement on the fifteenth, is revealing. He wrote, "But we find they [the Zwinglians] are not sufficiently informed about our doctrines . . . although they were able to repeat the words."[62] In other words, although he added other explanations, Melanchthon admitted that the differences were matters of misunderstanding, at least in part, as Philip believed.

It must also be admitted that progress was made toward a strictly theological agreement. The Marburg Articles, or the Fifteen Articles, represent a compromise, an agreement in the strictest sense. The theologians achieved concord on fourteen articles and agreed that they could not agree on the nature of Christ's presence in the Lord's Supper at the present time, but that they would not continue the strife publicly.[63] It is also important to note that Luther's formula for understanding the Presence, developed at Philip's insistence, was to be the basis for the later concords.

Finally, there were political achievements at Marburg. While the theological discussions were going on, and for several days prior to them (commencing on September 27), the Hessians consulted with political representatives from Strasbourg, Zurich, and Basel who had been sent along with the theologians. Clearly Philip intended to begin arranging a pan-Protestant alliance that ignored national sensitivities regardless of the immediate outcome of the theological discussions.[64] The result of the political discussions was the Marburg Sketch of an Alliance agreed upon by Hesse and the three towns.

The Marburg Sketch, like the Fifteen Articles, was to have later importance. Some parts of the document were incorporated verbatim in the protective alliance of November 1530 among these parties.[65] The Sketch also was the foundation of the Schmalkaldic treaty of 1531, although by that time Zwingli

---

[62]*CR* 1: 1099-1102, nr. 637; *Luther's Correspondence* 2: 500, nr. 853.

[63]The Marburg Articles were an agreement, a concord, a compromise, as Köhler states, *Zwingli und Luther* 2: 127. Sasse's wonderment, *This Is My Body*, 276-78, that Zwingli could agree on articles dealing with original sin, Word of God, grace, baptism, confession, and infant baptism is beside the point.

[64]See Sasse, *This Is My Body*, 215-18; Köhler, *Zwingli und Luther* 2: 63; Fabian, *Entstehung des Bundes*, 58, 211.

[65]Fabian, *Entstehung des Bundes*, 211-13.

was dead and Zurich defeated. Indeed, the constitution of the League, composed in 1535, took elements from it.[66]

Thus the Marburg Colloquy, by nearly gaining recognition of pan-Protestant brotherhood, nearly succeeded in winning Luther's blessings for Philip's pan-Protestant alliance. At the same time the proto-alliance did lay the basis for the Schmalkaldic League and its constitution. The League included the Upland Germans, whom the Wittenberg theologians had once thought to be Zwinglian, and it subsequently negotiated with non-German states against the emperor.

[66]Ibid., 214-16.

Harold Grimm, retirement dinner, 1972,
The Ohio State University.
Also pictured: Harry Coles and Thelma Grimm

"Perilous Events and Troublesome Disturbances" The Role of Controversy in the Tradition of Luther to Lutheran Orthodoxy

Robert Kolb
Concordia College, Saint Paul

THE OFT-REPEATED QUESTION, How 'Luther-an' was Lutheran Orthodoxy? raises a number of subsidiary questions, among them, How and in what spirit was Luther conveyed to the Lutheran Orthodoxy which came into existence some thirty years after his death? The third of the sixteenth-century lying between Luther's death in 1546 and the composition of the Formula of Concord in 1577 was filled with controversy, disputes not only pitting Lutherans against those outside Luther's following but disputes among Lutherans themselves. This essay focuses on the role assumed by Luther's image and ideas as it examines relationships between the polemical use of Luther during the controversies and the doctrinal expression of orthodox Lutheranism in the Formula of Concord, the document which officially resolved the intra-Lutheran controversies of that period.

The Formula presumed that Martin Luther had played a special role in the renewed revelation of the gospel of Jesus Christ:

> By the special grace and mercy of the Almighty, the teaching concerning the chief articles of our Christian faith (which had been hideously obscured by human doctrines and ordinances under the papacy) was once more clearly set forth on the basis of the Word of God and purified by Dr. Luther, of blessed and holy memory, and the popish errors, abuses, and idolatry were condemned.[1]

Luther's status as an extraordinary instrument of God's proclamation of His Word to his people became amply confirmed among Lutherans by 1577. He himself had insisted that Scripture alone could set forth and evaluate all the teaching of the church; yet his followers viewed him as a "living voice of the gospel," and one of particular authority because of his God-given role in ending "the dark night of error" under the medieval papacy.[2] The standard for orthodox Christian teaching ultimately set by the authors of the Formula of

---

[1] *Die Bekenntnisschriften der evangelisch-lutherischen Kirche*, 6th ed. (Göttingen: Vandenhoeck & Ruprecht, 1967), 829-30; *The Book of Concord*, ed. Theodore G. Tappert (Philadelphia: Fortress Press, 1959), 504.

[2] Robert Kolb, *Heroes, History, and the Holy: Saints and Martyrs in the Faith of the German Lutheran Late Reformation* (forthcoming), chap. 4, "Saint Martin of Wittenberg: Martin Luther in the View of His Students."

Concord lay exclusively in the "prophetic and apostolic writings of the Old and New Testaments, the pure and clear fountain of Israel." Also, theological writings by Luther's students of all genres during the period of controversy rest on copious citations from the Scriptures. But the formulators also left no doubt, as they listed documents to serve as guides for understanding the Scriptures—including the ecumenical creeds, Melanchthon's Augsburg Confession and Apology, and Luther's catechisms and Schmalkald Articles— that the Biblical message was to be understood as "the pure doctrine of the Word of God as Dr. Luther of blessed memory had explained it."[3]

The prefatory statement to the "Solid Declaration" of the Formula of Concord continued by noting that Luther's exposition of the gospel had met strong opposition:

> The opponents, however, regarded this pious reformation as a new doctrine and as wholly contrary to the Word of God and Christian institutions, attacked it violently (although unwarrantedly), and raised no end of slanders and insinuations against it.[4]

The opposition which Luther's presentation of God's Word encountered from papal foes was repeated, the preface to the Formula of Concord noted, by the gainsaying and misinterpretation of Luther's message among his own students and followers, even before but especially after his death, for they could not agree on precisely how to proclaim and defend his message:

> Very perilous events and troublesome disturbances took place in our beloved German fatherland shortly after the Christian death of that enlightened and pious person, Dr. Martin Luther, and . . . in this anguished situation and amid the disruption of well-ordered government the foe of mankind bestirred himself to scatter his seed of false doctrine and discord and to bring about destructive and scandalous division in churches and schools so that he might thereby adulterate the pure doctrine of God's Word, sever the bond of Christian charity and agreement, and in this way hold back and perceptibly impede the course of the holy Gospel.[5]

These conflicts profoundly affected the process by which Luther's theology was conveyed to succeeding generations. The Wittenberg gospel was

---

[3] *Bekenntnisschriften*, 834; Tappert, 503-504.
[4] *Bekenntnisschriften*, 830; Tappert, 502.
[5] *Bekenntnisschriften*, 4; Tappert, 3-14. For an overview of these controversies and an introduction to bibliography on them see Robert Kolb, "Historical Background of the Formula of Concord," in *A Contemporary Look at the Formula of Concord*, ed. Robert D. Preus and Wilbert H. Rosin (Saint Louis: Concordia Publishing House, 1978), 12-87, and *idem*, "Dynamics of Party Conflict in the Saxon Late Reformation: Gnesio-Lutherans vs. Philippists," *The Journal of Modern History* 49 (1977): D1289-1305.

passed to the Lutherans of the Age of Orthodoxy through the refining fire of polemics burning in the formulations of controversial writers who defended Luther's teaching during the disputes and smoldering in the relationship of these disputes to issues in the Late Reformation period.

The formation of Orthodoxy out of Reformation involves refining the ideas of its charismatic leadership. To be sure, Martin Luther played a decisive role in determining the teaching of theological faculties in Lutheran lands throughout the Orthodox period, into the eighteenth century and beyond, in the wake of the nineteenth century confessional revival. But other factors also influenced the formulations of the students whom he trained. The staying power of the remnants of the old, medieval system of thought should never be underestimated. Furthermore, the role of Philip Melanchthon in shaping both the method and the content of Lutheran Orthodoxy has been recognized and detailed, just as it is increasingly recognized that Calvinist Orthodoxy depended not only on John Calvin but also on Theodore Beza, Peter Martyr Vermigli, Jerome Zanchi, and Heinrich Bullinger.[6] In addition to Melanchthon, a number of Luther's colleagues and students also made significant contributions to the life and thought of Lutheran churches in the early modern period. Nonetheless, the figure of Martin Luther loomed over these churches in the subsequent centuries even more than Calvin's did over Calvinist Orthodoxy. Thus the situation in which Luther's students proclaimed the Word of God during the thirty years following his death is critical in determining the view of Luther's person and the use of his teachings among his spiritual descendants.

Luther's disciples digested their heritage in the midst of controversy during the years following his death. As they forged new expressions of the gospel they had received at his feet, they turned to Luther as a model for the practice of theology, as an authority figure, and as a source of good argument.

Martin Luther provided a model for the practice of theology to his students that projected the profile of the controversial theologian. Martin Luther provided an authority who could be cited against one's foes. Recognized at first as an authority in disputes with other Lutherans because he had been their common teacher, Luther increasingly came to be viewed as that special prophet or instrument of the Lord who had exercised authority beyond that of other non-biblical teachers. Martin Luther provided an outline for arguments used to support scriptural interpretations of his students in his own comments on topics under dispute in the Late Reformation period.

[6]The problem of the relationship of Melanchthon to Lutheran Orthodoxy has been handled with varying degrees of skill, but studies demonstrating Melanchthon's influence on his students in all the parties of the Late Reformation exist; see, among more recent elaborations of the point, Peter Barton, *Um Luthers Erbe, Studien und Texte zur Spätreformation. Tilemann Heshusis (1527-1559)* (Witten: Luther-Verlag, 1972), 7-18; on the development of Christology and of the definition of real presence, see Theodor Mahlmann, *Das neue Dogma der lutherischen Christologie, Problem und Geschichte seiner Begründung* (Gütersloh: Verlagshaus Gerd Mohn, 1969).

Luther as Model

His students had seen the model in action at Wittenberg in the 1530s and 1540s. From their professor they had absorbed not only an understanding of how to read the Scriptures and how to define specific articles of faith or doctrinal topics anew, in opposition to those elements of the medieval dogmatic tradition which Luther rejected. They had also acquired an understanding of theological method. Within months of Luther's death the Schmalkald War broke out, and the defeat of the leading Lutheran princes of the German Empire in that war thrust upon Luther's disciples a situation in which they would have been forced to develop a controversial theology even if earlier events had not predisposed them to polemics. The intentions of Emperor Charles V were quite clear: He was determined to enforce the Edict of Worms of 1521 and thus eradicate Lutheran teaching from his lands. He began that process by promulgating his *Formula for Reformation*, called the Augsburg Interim, in 1548. Luther's followers had to determine a way to oppose that threat effectively or surrender their faith; they could not do otherwise.

As Luther's students many of them had had a propensity to fight bred into their theological beings. To be sure, some also followed their mentor and wrote biblical commentaries, devotional tracts, catechisms, and other types of theological literature, but the predominant genre of the Lutheran Late Reformation was the polemical tract. Luther had learned that mode of the theological process himself as a faithful student of the Schoolmen. All the intellectual pursuits of the late Medieval period presumed that learning took place best in an adversary exchange. Added to this form of learning came the endless disputes between Nominalists and Realists; among Thomists, Scotists, and Occamists of varying positions; and then between humanists and scholastics. All this shaped a mind like Luther's to seek truth in the arena of intellectual tournament.

Luther experienced the tournament in more than academic fashion when he ventured into the public theological ring. There the attacks came quickly and viciously from his foes within the church. E. Gordon Rupp has observed that "Luther has never received sufficient credit for the books he never wrote."[7] The violence of Luther's own fierce polemics still hardly matched the attacks upon him. From the bull of excommunication and the declaration of outlawry in 1521, Luther was placed on a certain kind of defensive; his aggressive response betrays the seriousness with which he took both this conflict over truth and the situation imposed upon him. John W. O'Malley has further pointed out that this existential "discontinuity" extends backward in Luther's biography from his breaks with the hierarchy of the church and the leadership of the state in 1521 to his own break with his family's path for his career and to his gradual break with his monastic and scholastic past. O'Malley also notes

---

[7]*Luther's Progress to the Diet of Worms* (New York: Harper & Row, 1974), 71.

[8]John W. O'Malley, "Erasmus and Luther, Continuity and Discontinuity as Key to Their Conflict," *The Sixteenth Century Journal* 5, 2 (1974): 47-65.

the elements of "discontinuity" in Luther's theology, in the dialectic of law and gospel, for instance, or in his remnant ecclesiology.[8]

In sum, the disciples who ventured into the world beyond Wittenberg and beyond Luther's lifetime had been trained by a charismatic teacher who modeled for them a process for the discipline of theology which melded friendly disputation and fierce polemic. It was inevitable that the Orthodoxy shaped by Luther's students would rest upon the foundations of a *sic et non* approach. Perhaps it could be argued that, at least within Lutheranism, disputes could have been settled in a more irenic fashion than they were. That did not happen. In the view of Luther's students, the direct attack seemed best in defending God's Word against error's assaults. This polemical attitude was heightened by a sense of betrayal when those errors were seen to arise from within the Wittenberg movement, from the pens of former student colleagues.

Luther as Authority and Source of Argument

Indeed, at the beginning of the period, some in the Wittenberg movement thought it prudent to attempt another kind of response to the aggressive advance of the Roman Catholic party in the wake of the Schmalkald War. Faced with the challenge of the Augsburg Interim and entangled in an extremely complicated political situation, Luther's colleagues in Wittenberg chose the route of compromise rather than confrontation. Melanchthon and his associates at the university were recruited by their new prince, Charles V's Lutheran ally, Maurice of Saxony, to save the prince's shaky alliance with the emperor, on which he was certain retention of his lands and titles depended. The scholars were to do so by formulating another document, dubbed the Leipzig Interim by its opponents. The compromise Leipzig Interim rested on the presupposition that concessions in adiaphora were permissible in order to preserve the church from another northern campaign by the imperial armies, a campaign which could well result in the suppression of the Lutheran gospel altogether.[9] In defending this proposition and the document which elaborated its application, the Wittenbergers appealed to Luther's authority, arguing that he, too, had urged caution and compromise so that the gospel might not offend others, particularly at the time of the Wittenberg iconoclasm in 1522.[10] This case demonstrates very clearly how Melanchthon and his colleagues chose material from Luther which would support them and justify their actions in the particular, difficult situation in which they found themselves.

[9]The most complete description of these developments in English is found in Luther D. Peterson, "The Philippist Theologians and the Interims of 1548: Soteriological, Ecclesiastical, and Liturgical Compromises and Controversies within German Lutheranism," (Ph.D. diss., University of Wisconsin, 1974).

[10]*Grüntlicher vnd Warhafftiger Bericht der vorigen vnd jetzigen, fur vnd nach dem Kriege ergangen Handlungen, von den Adiaphoris oder Mitteldingen. Sampt eine Christlichen Kurtzen verantwortung* (Leipzig: Bapst, 1550).

The text of the Leipzig Interim was determined by the perception of its authors: It reflects what they believed could be re-expressed or compromised in their proclamation and practice in order to gain peace and safety without losing the faith. In reply, their foes had to deal with the issues and expressions incorporated specifically in the document. Thus, the events of 1546-1548 gave Lutherans an agenda for dispute, and the disputes became the arena in which Luther's disciples exercised their minds in the decades immediately following their master's death.

The Wittenberg faculty had had some practice at citing Luther as an authority, and even at developing an argument on the basis of his own published words, a few years earlier under then elector of Saxony, John Frederick, whom Charles V displaced and imprisoned at the end of Saxony's unsuccessful resistance to the imperial forces in the Schmalkald War. In the extensive propaganda campaign developed by the Wittenberg intellectual establishment in behalf of armed Lutheran resistance to the emperor, Luther had been cited copiously in behalf of the right of the lesser magistrate to resist the "notorious injuries" of the Habsburg emperor.[11] Even before that, Luther's colleagues had valued the authority of his words so highly that they had launched an edition of his works.[12] It was not as if they were turning to Luther for authoritative support in time of crisis for the first time.

Citation of Luther drew a storm of protest from others among Luther's students, however. They believed that compromise was wrong in such a time in which confession was called for against the coercive might of the papacy: There could be no indifferent matters on which to compromise. This group, later called the Gnesio-Lutherans, had already been attacking the Augsburg Intrerim. Their tracts did not hold up Luther as an authority; rather, they based their critiques of the imperial formula on biblical arguments.[13] Dependence solely upon biblical arguments appeared also in many of the host of tracts generated against the Leipzig Interim, often supported by practical, common-sense arguments why compromise would not serve the cause of the gospel.

However, the use of Luther's authority and a counter-argument from his writings occupied some of the critiques of the Leipzig Interim. Soon after the promulgation of the Leipzig Interim, Joachim Westphal, a pastor in Hamburg, collected a number of citations form Luther's writings which demonstrated the error of consorting with the Roman Antichrist. His catalog of

[11]Otto Waldeck, "Die Publizistik des Schmalkaldischen Krieges," *Archiv für Reformationsgeschichte* 7 (1909/1910): 1-55, 8 (1910/1911): 44-133.

[12]Eike Wolgast, *Die Wittenberger Luther-Ausgabe, Zur Überlieferungsgeschichte der Werke Luthers im 16. Jahrhundert*, Archiv für Geschichte des Buchwesen 11, 1-2 (Frankfurt am Main: Buchhändler-Vereinigung, 1970).

[13]This is the case even in the attacks on the Augsburg Interim by some of Luther's most loyal disciples; e. g. Caspar Aquila, *Wider den spoettischen Luegner vnd vnuerschempten verleumbder M. Isslebium Agricolam, Noetige verantwortung, vnd Ernstliche warnung, Wider das Interim, Apologia* (n.p., 1548), or Nikolaus von Amsdorf, *Antwort, Glaub vnd Bekentniss auff das schoene und liebliche Interim* (Magdeburg: Lotther, 1548).

condemnation with the words of Luther authoritatively rebutted the underlying principle of the Interim, that is, the appropriateness of compromise in adiaphora.[14] Two years later Westphal published a narrative analysis of "adiaphorism" in which he met the arguments of Melanchthon and his colleagues more directly. He pointed out that Luther's attitude toward adiaphora in 1522, when it was a matter of offending tender consciences, could not be compared with compromise on adiaphora when the compromise would betray and deny the central teachings of the Christian faith. Such, he believed, was the case with the Leipzig Interim. He recalled Luther's comments on Galatians in which he firmly stated that he would not yield a hair's breadth to the world when it attacked him. He cited Luther's opposition to imperial edicts which opposed God's Word as an indication of what Luther's attitude would be if he were alive at that time. Westphal further challenged the sincerity of the "Adiaphorists" in their allegiance to Luther. Their document, he wrote, dismissed Luther's authority by disposing of his form for public worship, substituting in its stead the regressive liturgy which they had fashioned as a compromise with Rome. Opponents accused Westphal and his associates of idolizing Luther and not allowing any departure from anything he had done; the Hamburg pastor replied that he did not want to reject Luther for the sake of the "Beast of the Babylonian Whore," as the Leipzig Interim had done in trying to compromise with the papacy.[15]

Matthias Flacius Illyricus, in his critique of the "Adiaphorists," followed somewhat the pattern Westphal set. Flacius reissued Luther's letters to theologians at the diet of Augsburg of 1530; these contained warnings against compromise with the Roman Belial. This use of Luther's authority presented his argument, but that argument was nearly twenty years old and needed to be set in context. Flacius did this in a preface which briefly led the reader into the proper frame of mind to understand the point Flacius wanted Luther to make for the situation in 1549.[16] At the same time, Flacius was composing other tracts arguing the case against the Leipzig Interim in his own words, on the basis of biblical and practical arguments. In some of these he used Luther as his authority and on occasion cited specific Luther passages to bolster his argument, but did not use extensive quotations from his mentor to develop and extend the argument. In fact, Flacius cited Melanchthon's *Loci communes*, Augsburg Confession and Apology, and preface to the report of the ecumenical negotiations at Regensburg in 1541, alongside his citation of Luther, to

---

[14]*Sententia reverendi viri D. M. Luth. Sanctae memoriae de Adiaphoris ex scriptis illius collecta* (Magdeburg: Lotther, 1549), also in German, *Des Ehrwiridigen vnd thewren Mans Doct. Marti. Luthers seliger gedechtnis meinumg von den Mitteldingen* (Magdeburg: Lotther, 1550).

[15]*Verlegung des Gruendlichen Berichts der Adiaphoristen zu diesen boesen zeiten* (n.p., 1551), lvs. Dij^r, Biij^v-C^r, Bij, Ciij^v [Ciiij]^v, Miij^v.

[16]*Etliche Brieffe, des Ehrwirdigen Herrn D. Martini Luthers seliger gedechtnis, an die Theologos auff den Reichstag zu Augsburg geschrieben, Anno M.D.XXX. Von der vereinigung Christi vnd Belials, Auss welchen man viel neutzlicher lehr in gegenwertiger gefahr der Kirchen nemen kan . . .* (Magdeburg: Roedinger, 1549).

prove that the Adiaphorists had betrayed their common Wittenberg heritage. This suggests that Luther was an authority not because he possessed a special prophetic role, though that increasingly was the view of many Lutherans, but because Flacius believed he could demonstrate Philippist disloyalty to the common heritage in treating their master's views lightly.[17] An interesting sidelight in Flacius' tracts against the Leipzig Interim is his subtle use of Luther to lend authority to himself as one who had heard the master. He mentioned Luther's last sermon in Wittenberg, urging that his readers follow Luther's advice in it to pray to overcome the devil, as if to remind the readers that the tract which they were reading came from an ear-witness to the Doctor's own words.[18]

The focus of controversy over the Leipzig Interim shifted quickly from relationships with the papacy, that is, the issue of adiaphora, to the proposition of the Interim that good works are necessary for salvation, a proposition defended by Melanchthon's colleague, Georg Major. This controversy was carried on in its initial stages in 1552 without significant recourse to Luther. An exception can be found in one tract, by Flacius, in which he quoted Luther briefly in the midst of his biblically based argument against Major's expression.[19] Then in 1553 Flacius and his colleague in Magdeburg, Nikolaus Gallus, published memoranda from four churches on Major's proposition. In their preface they cited Luther's rejection of a phrase similar to Major's in an earlier discussion in Wittenberg in the mid-1530s. They used an historical incident alive in the memories of Wittenberg alumni to support their rejection of the necessity of good works for salvation by appealing to their teacher's rejection of the same idea.[20] Still, at this point it is difficult to ascertain with certainty what kind of authority Luther had: Was it the authority of a revered professor or that of a prophetic instrument of God? It seems yet to have been the former.

However, a different tone appeared in the same year when Luther was cited by the ministerium of the county of Mansfeld as it acted on a case of

[17]*Eine schrifft widder ein recht epicurisch buch, darin die Leiptzische Interim verteidiget wird sich zu hueten fuer der verfelschern der waren Religion . . .* (n.p., 1549), lvs. B^v-Bij^r, [Biij]^v, D; *Widder den ausszug des Leiptzschen Interims, oder das Kleine Interim* (Magdeburg: Roedinger, 1549), lvs. Aij^r, B, Biij^v-[Biiij]^r; *Gruendliche verlegung aller Sophisterey, so Juncker Isleb, D. Interim, Morus, Pfeffinger, D. Geitz in seinem gründlichem bericht vnd jhre gesellen, die andere Adiaphoristen, das Leipsische Interim zu beschoenen gebrauchen* (n.p., n.d.), *passim.* Flacius' friend, Nikolaus von Amsdorf, somewhat reversed the pattern, issuing first a narrative analysis, *Das Doctor Martinus kein Adiaphorist gewesen ist, und Das D. Pfeffinger und das buch on namen ihm gewalt und unrecht thut* (Magdeburg: Roedinger, 1550), and then a brief collection of quotations from Luther against "adiaphorism," *Etliche sprüche aus Doctoris Martini Lutheri schriften, Darinne er, als ein Adiaphorist sich mit dem Bapst hat vergleichen wollen* (n.p., 1551).

[18]*Eine schrifft . . . widder ein recht epicurish buch,* lf. [Diiij]^r.

[19]*Wider den Euangelisten des heiligen Chorrocks D. Geitz Maior* (Basel [Magdeburg], 1552), lf. C^v.

[20]*Sententia ministrorvm Christi in Ecclesia Lubecensi, Hamburgensi, Luneburgensi & Magdeburgensi, de corruptelis doctrinae iustificatinis, quibus D. Georg. Maior adserit . . .* (Magdeburg: Lotther, 1553).

"Majorism" in its own midst, the case of Stephen Agricola, a supporter of Major. (Major himself had been appointed to be a superintendent in the county but had returned to Wittenberg at the end of 1552 after encountering opposition among the pastors of Mansfeld and, more importantly, from one of the counts of Mansfeld.) In their first statement on the proposition that good works are necessary to salvation, the ministers appealed to Luther's authority as that of "our dear master and preceptor, a true instrument of God." As instrument of God, Luther had rejected precisely the position Major was advancing with his thesis regarding the necessity of good works.[21] This initial memorandum argued against that position almost exclusively on the basis of biblical material, but a second memorandum, issued the same year, cited Luther at some length to bolster the case against Agricola and Major, quoting Luther's commentary on Galatians and *On Christian Liberty*.[22] Luther's authority was cited not as God's instrument but as proof that the opponents' claim to Luther as a patron of their proposition was false. Nonetheless, the earlier tract demonstrates a shifting attitude toward Luther as an authority, from his role as the Mansfelders' teacher toward his special status in God's arrangement for the proclamation of the divine Word.

Cyriakus Spangenberg, pastor in Eisleben, may well have been responsible for placing Luther in this status, although he is but one of a number of signatories. Within a decade, he demonstrated in a series of sermons why Luther should be regarded as a contemporary Paul, Elijah, or John, a prophet, a confessor, the angel destined to bring God's special message for the End Time to the earth.[23] Ernst Koch has shown that out of this ministerium also came a generation later a number of men who composed florilegia of Luther's wisdom on various topics because they regarded him as a special, latter-day prophet of the Lord.[24]

To be sure, this estimate of Luther as a prophet was not held only in Mansfeld at this time, nor did this view originate with the Mansfelders. As Mark U. Edwards, Jr. has pointed out in detail, Luther himself came to regard his role as closely akin to that of the Biblical prophets and apostles.[25] And others besides the Mansfelders were beginning to recognize that kind of authority in his writings. For example, under the name of a pastor of Magdeburg, Albert

[21]*Bedencken das diese Proposition oder Lere nicht nuetz, not, noch war sey, vnnd one ergernis in der Kirchen nicht moege geleret werden. Das gute werck zur seligkeit noetig sind. Vnd vnmueglich sey, one gute werck selig werden* (Magdeburg: Lotther, 1553), lvs.]Aiiij]ᵛ, [Diiij]⁴.

[22]*Der Prediger in der Herrschafft Mansfelt antwort, auff Stephani Agricole . . . aussgegangene schlussreden vnd schmerschrifften, die newen lere in vnsern Kirchen, Das gute werck zur seligkeit noetig sein, belangende* (Magdeburg: Lotther, 1553), lvs. Bᵛ-Bijᵛ.

[23]Spangenberg's sermons were drawn together into *Theander Lutherus* (Ursel, 1589); see Wolfgang Herrmann, "Die Lutherpredigten des Cyriakus Spangenbergs," *Mansfelder Blätter* 39 (1934/35): 7-95, and Kolb, *Heroes, History, and the Holy*, ch. 4.

[24]Ernst Koch, "Lutherflorilegien zwischen 1550 und 1600," seminar paper at the Sixth International Congress on Luther Research, Erfurt, German Democratic Republic, August 14-20, 1983.

[25]Mark U. Edwards, Jr.., *Luther and the False Brethren* (Stanford: Stanford University Press, 1975), esp. ch. 5, "The Mature Paradigm."

Christian, a tract appeared which called Luther "the Elijah of our time" and which reprinted Luther's disputation on law and grace of 1537 as a means of countering Majorism.[26] And four years later Nikolaus von Amsdorf added a new element to the dispute over the necessity of good works by recalling in print that Luther had often said, particularly early in his career when Amsdorf was still at his side in Wittenberg, that good works are detrimental to salvation. Amsdorf not only developed this position on the basis of a citation of Luther from the Galatians commentary but also claimed that it was the opinion of "Saints Paul and Luther," setting the two expositors of God's Word alongside each other, if not as equals at least as authorities above the common authority of Christian preachers.[27]

While the Wittenbergers of the Gnesio-Lutheran and Philippist parties were battling each other over the definition of Luther's doctrine on a range of issues, they both made common cause against the doctrine of justification taught by Andreas Osiander, reformer in Nuremberg, who emigrated to Prussia at the time of the Augsburg Interim. (Theodor Mahlmann has shown that neither group of Wittenberg disciples fully recapitulated Luther's Christology in their critiques of Osiander, but both groups took offense at Osiander's definition of the sinner's justification as the indwelling of the divine nature of Christ.[28]) Here not an ecclesiastical-political document, such as the Leipzig Interim, but rather an alien strain of medieval thought which had influenced Osiander's earliest thinking, the cabbalistic speculations of Hebraic Renaissance humanism, set the agenda for the discussion of justificatin through faith.

From the Philippist stronghold in Leipzig Bernhard Ziegler published two sermons of Luther to demonstrate that Osiander was wrong, and from the city of Frankfurt an der Oder came a collection of three of the Doctor's sermons to counter Osiander's view. They may have been edited by the Gnesio-Lutheran professor there, Andreas Musculus; the editor noted in the title of this collection that Luther had prophesied that something ungodly like Osiander would come upon the church. The Osiandrian controversy provided the occasion for Musculus to issue a catena of statements of Luther's "on the inseparable unity of the two natures of our Lord Jesus Christ, God's and

---

[26]*Dispvtatio reverendi patris D. Martini Lutheri, de operibus legis & gratiae. . .* (Magdeburg: Lotther, 1553), lf. Aij[v]. A decade later the attacks on Majorism continued, and in his *Erinnerung: Von der Newen Busse D. Georg Maiors. Repetition Widerholung vnd endliche erklerung der bekentniss D. G. Maiors genant* (Lübeck: Kroeger, 1568), Johann Wigand repeatedly evaluated Major's teaching by the standard of Luther's.

[27]*Das die Propositio (Gute werck sind zur Seligkeit schedlich) ein rechte ware Christliche Propositio sey durch die heiligen Paulum vnd Lutherum gelert vnd gepediget* (Magdeburg, 1559); see Robert Kolb, "'Good Works are Detrimental to Salvation,': Amsdorf's Use of Luther's Words in Controversy," *Renaissance et Réforme/Renaissance and Reformation*, n.s. 4 (1980): 136-51.

[28]Mahlmann, 93-124.

Mary's Son, in one person . . . against the Nestorian and Eutychian misunderstandings and errors which have recently arisen."[29] Flacius published several biblically based blasts at Osiander, but he could on occasion intertwine with the scriptural argument an argument from Luther, or at least spend considerable time correcting a misimpression of Luther's teaching which Osiander had set forth.[30] Osiander's opponents in Prussia also used "Saint Luther" to refuse Osiander's understanding of justification; Joachim Mörlin led his readers through an "antilogia" which displayed a series of differences between Luther and Osiander through citation from their works, and there was no doubt as to who was correct.[31]

The Osiandrian controversy confirms that in the early 1550s the appeal to Luther's authority, at least as a preceptor, was a widespread theological device among the Wittenbergers of both parties. It also demonstrates that Luther's students, as they voiced Luther's views, preferred to cite the Scriptures rather than their prophetic preceptor to support his viewpoint, as they understood it, while they were presenting it and defending it.

These controversies continued at the same time that another series of disputes over the real presence of Christ's body and blood in the Lord's Supper began warming up. These disputes were intitiated by Joachim Westphal's attack on a growing Calvinist menace which he perceived advancing unchecked in the early 1550s. It might seem strange that in a conflict with Calvinists Luther could serve as an authority, and indeed Westphal and his compatriots in the Hansa cities of northwestern Germany who joined him in this fray seldom featured Luther prominently. But they did review the controversy over the real presence within the Protestant camp, and in so doing they had to lay out Luther's position. Westphal could ascribe to Luther a special authority be-

---

[29]Ziegler edited *Zwo Predigten des Ehrwirdigen Herren Doctoris Martini Lutheri . . .* (Leipzig: Hantzsch, 1551); Musculus may be the editor of *Drei Sermon D. Martini Lutheri, darin man spueren kan wie ein herlicher Prophetischer Geist in dem manne gewesen ist, das er das, was itzt vngoetlich, vom Andrea Osiandro geleret wird . . . gesehen hat* (Frankfurt an der Oder: Eichorn, 1552). Musculus, *Von der vnzertrenlichen voreynigung in einer Person beider naturn vnsers Herrn Jesu Christi Gottes vnd Marien Son, Docto. Martini Lutheri bekentnis, Glaub, vnd Leer aus seinen buechern zusamengetragen wieder den neulichen erregten Nestorischen vnd Eutilchischen misvorstandt vnd jrthum* (Frankfurt an der Oder: Eichorn, 1553).

[30]*Wider die newe ketzerey der Dikaeusisten, vom spruch Christi Joan. am XVI. Der heilig Geist wird die Welt straffen vmb die Gerechtigkeit, das ich zu Vater gehe* (Magdeburg: Roedinger, 1552?), lvs. Aij[r], [Biij][r]-Biij[r], Cij[r]-Ciij[v]; *Verlegung des Bekentnis Osiandri von der Rechtfertigung der armen suender durch die wesentliche Gerechtigkeit der Hohen Maiester Gottes allein* (Magdeburg: Roedinger, 1552), lvs. [aviij][r]-b[r], biij[r]-biiij[r], Aij[r], Jiiij[v]-Oiij[v].

[31]Mörlin's *Historia Welcher gestalt sich die Osiandrische schwermerey im lande zu Preusen erhaben, vnd wie dieselbige verhandelt ist* (n.p., 1554), lvs. Fij[v]-Gij[v]; Mörlin and his colleagues, Georg von Venediger and Peter Hegemon cited "der heilige Luther," lf. Fij[v] in their *Von der Rechtfertigung des glaubens: gründlicher warhafftiger bericht, aus Gottes Wort, etlicher Theologen zu Kuenigsberg jn Preussen. Wider die newe verfurische vnd Antichristische Lehr Andreae Osiandri . . .* (Königsberg, 1552), and they developed an extensive argument against Osiander's use of Luther in his own behalf on the basis of Luther texts, lvs. Mij[r]-O[r].

cause he had begun the struggle against papist error.[32] He and others, such as the Hamburg pastor Johann Timann, could quote Luther, along with Melanchthon, Brenz, and others, in defense of their view; but in these tracts Luther does not assume a larger authority based on a special calling as an instrument of God.[33] Among the north Germans, including the early Chemnitz, Mahlman finds that only an obscure colleague of Westphal's in Hamburg, Johann Bötker, successfully captured and reproduced Luther's full understanding of the real presence.[34]

The south German Swabian party made more use of the Christological element of Luther's view, although its representatives elaborated it with their own peculiar emphases. From Tübingen came a republication of Luther's dicta on the real presence as early as 1560, perhaps in the wake of the confession written for the duchy of Württemberg the previous year.[35] In the succeeding decade Johann Brenz and Jacob Andreae defended this view against Reformed theologians in Switzerland and the Palatinate, both in dialogues and in printed works. In a treatise on the personal union of Christ's two natures Brenz not only cited Luther in his own argument but also added 35 pages of quotations from Luther as "testimonia" to support his position.[36] His younger colleague, Andreae, used the "superior" arguments of Luther in developing his own treatment of the Lord's Supper and backed up his approach with appeals to Luther's authority in tracts on the person of Christ.[37] Even face to face with the Reformed theologians of the Palatinate in colloquy at Maulbronn in 1564, the Swabian representatives could appeal to Luther although that appeal was not an intrinsic part of their argument.[38]

[32]*Aduersus cuiusdam Sacramentarii falsam criminationem, iusta defensio* (Frankfurt am Main: Braubach, 1555), 1-13, cf. 52, where Luther is called "most wise in discerning the spirits and exposing the deceit of false prophets," a characteristic which enabled him to reject the sacramentarian errors of Zwingli, Carlstadt, et al.

[33]E.g., Timann's *Farrago sententiarum consentiarum in vera et catholica doctrina, de Coena Domini . . .* (Frankfurt am Main: Braubach, 1555), 66-70, 168-70, 225-26, where Luther is cited in the same vein in which Melanchthon, Brenz, Bugenhagen, and others are.

[34]Mahlmann, 38-40, 44-48, 83-92. Bötker's work was entitled *Von des Hern Christi Hochwirdigen Abendmal Kurtzer und einfeltiger Bericht . . .* (Hamburg: Wickradt, 1557).

[35]*Verzeichnus etlicher fürnemer Spruch, ausser den Buechern Doctor. Martini Lutheri seelig, darinnen der recht Verstandt, von der Gegenwuertigkeit des waren Leibs vnd Bluetz Christi in dem Heiligen Abentmal, auch von der Himmelfart Christi, vnd seinem sitzen zue der rechten Gottes des Allmaechtigen Vaters, erklaert wurdt* (Tübingen: Morhart, 1560).

[36]*De personali vnione dvarvm natvrarvm in Christo, et ascensu Christi in Coelum, ac sessione eius ad dexteram Dei Patris* (Frankfurt am Main: Braubach, 1563), 32, 52-86.

[37]*Simplex, ac dilucida expositio sententiae de coena Domini . . .* (Frankfurt am Main: Braubach, 1561), 23, cf. 27-38, 42, for Andreae's use of Luther in argument. Luther appears simply as an authority (of uncertain role) in other Andreae tracts, e.g. *Hundert vnnd siben schlussreden, von der maiestet des Menschen Christi, vnd seiner warhafftigen . . . gegenwertigkeit im heiligen nachtmal* (Ulm: Gruppenbach, 1564), 2, or in *Brevis et modesta apologia captivm dispvtationis, de maiestate hominis Christi, deque vera & substantiali praesentia corporis & sanguinis Christi in eucharistia* (Tübingen: Morhart, 1564), 2-8, 53-54, 74-75.

[38]*Epitome Colloquij . . . de Maiestate hominis Christi, deque vera eius in Eucharistia praesentia, Maulbrunnae instituti* (Frankfurt am Main: Braubach, 1564), e.g., 80.

Among the many facets of controversy over the Lord's Supper in which Lutherans of this period were involved, the most significant for its ecclesiastical-political consequences was the so-called "crypto-Calvinist" controversy in electoral Saxony, which initiated the actual composition of the Formula of Concord. In the final stages of this controversy both the purged Saxon ministerium and its Gnesio-Lutheran critics used Luther in defense of their positions.[39] Martin Chemitz, one of the chief authors of the Formula, also had treated both the real presence and the two natures of Christ in print during the 1570s. In his works, Luther's views are cited alongside those of a variety of ancient fathers of the church and are apparently ranked along with them as valuable expositions of the scriptural truth.[40]

Luther was treasured as a special expositor of biblical truth above all by members of the Gnesio-Lutheran party, and it is no wonder that one particular controversy within that party became in large part a controversy over the proper interpretation of Luther's understanding of original sin. Matthias Flacius had argued in a formal disputation with the Philippist theologian, Viktorin Strigel, that the essence of the human creature after the fall is formally original sin and had defended his position with plenteous support from Luther's writings.[41] Flacius' bitterest opposition over this view came from his own fellow Gnesio-Lutherans; in the dispute between the "Flacianists" and their opponents, Luther was quoted and interpreted at great length by both sides—and frequently alluded to as God's third Elijah or chosen instrument.[42]

[39]*Kurtz Bekentniss und Artickel vom heiligen Abendmal des Leibs und Bluts Christi . . . Übergeben und gehandelt in juengstem Landtag zu Torgaw . . .* (Wittenberg: Lufft, 1574), lvs. Biiij^v-Cij^v states the Saxon theologians' firm commitment to both Luther and Melanchthon; lvs. E^r-Eij^r appeal to Luther's authority and position in support of the confession made in the document. Johann Wigand criticized this document, using Luther as a standard in *Christliche Erinnerung von der Bekentnis der Theologin in Meissen vom Abendmal . . . (Königsberg: Daubman, 1574),* esp. fols. 2v-3v, 5v-74.

[40]See occasional references to Luther and his positions throughout *Fvndamenta sanae doctrinae, de vera et svbstantiali praesentia, exhibitione & sumptione corporis & sanguinis Domini in coena . . .* (1570; Jena: Richtzenhain, 1590), and *De duabus naturis in Christo* (Leipzig: Rhamba, 1578). Both these works have been translated in English by J. A. O. Preus, as *The Lord's Supper* (Saint Louis: Concordia, 1979) and *The Two Natures in Christ* (Saint Louis: Concordia, 1971).

[41]*Disputatio de originali peccato et libero arbitrio, inter Matthiam Flacium Illyricum & Victorinum Strigelium . . .* (Eisleben, 1561), e.g., 17, 26, 32, 39, 41, 44-46, 54, 67, 69, 75, etc. The best analysis of Flacius' position is that of Hans Kropatscheck, "Das Problem theologischer Anthropologie auf dem Weimarer Gespräch von 1560 zwischen Matthias Flacius Illyricus und Viktorin Strigel," (licentiate dissertation, University of Göttingen, 1943). For an overview of the dispute, see Wilhelm Preger, *Matthias Flacius Illyricus und seine Zeit,* 2 vols. (Erlangen: Blaesing, 1859-1861) 2: 31-412. The struggle of Flacius' disciples against the Formula of Concord is described in Robert Kolb, "The Flacian Rejection of the Concordia: Prophetic Style and Action in the German Late Reformation," *Archiv für Reformationsgeschichte* 73 (1982): 196-217.

[42]E.g., Flacius' *Warhafftige und bestendige meinung und zeugnis, Von der Erbsuende und dem freien willen Des . . . D. Martin Luthers* (Jena: Rebart, 1560), and his *Etliche klare vnd treffliche Zeugnussen D. Martini Luthers von dem boesen Wesen . . . des irdischen todten Adams . . .* (n.p., 1574).

In this period of controversy Gnesio-Lutherans in particular recognized a need for new confessional statements, sometimes devising them as a means of reconciling differences, sometimes forging in them a new polemical instrument. Generally, these confessions anchored their statements of the faith in earlier Lutheran confessional documents, including the Augsburg Confession and its Apology and the Schmalkald Articles; but several of them added to these documents the "writings of Luther," presumably the entire corpus of Luther's "mature publications."[43] In addition to identifying so formally Luther's significance for defining public teaching, these confessions often appealed to Luther as an authority, with and without explicit mention of his special role in God's economy of speaking his Word to his people. Exceptions to this use of Luther can be found in two confessions composed at the edges of the German Empire. In Austria the confession of 1566 omitted any mention of Luther in identifying its standpoint within the biblical and catholic faith for the dominant Roman party of the Habsburg homelands. Flacius, Spangenberg, and others composed a confession in Antwerp in 1567; conflict there with both Roman Catholics and Calvinists may explain the limitation of Luther references to two rather incidental contexts: These confessors felt compelled to defend "Luther and our churches" on the subject of images, against inconoclastic and Calvinist critique. They also referred to Luther and Joachim Westphal in a review of the sacramentarian controversy while mentioning some of their Reformed opponents as well: a Lasco, Zwingli, Oecolampadius, and Carlstadt. Furthermore, in their final subscription, the Antwerp pastors recognized the "teachings of the Last Elijah, Dr. Luther," as a guide for the interpretation of the Scriptures.[44]

At the geographic heart of Lutheranism, Saxon Lutherans had no compunctions about appeals to Luther in their confessions. The first of these, which the Gnesio-Lutherans composed after the adiaphoristic crisis had

Flacius' foes replied, e.g., Tilemann Hesshus, *Klare und helle Zeugnissen Doctoris Martini Luther. Das Die Erbsuende nicht sey das wesen des Menschen* . . . (Jena, 1572), and Andreas Schoppe, *D. Martini Lutheri Sprueche vnd Zeugnis Das Die Erbsuende nicht sey das Wesen des Menschen* . . . (Jena: Richtzenhan, 1572). The dispute continued into the 1580s, with Flacius' supporters still citing Luther in defense of their position, e.g. Christoph Irenaeus, *Christliche Lere und Bericht, aus Gottes Wort und Schrifften D: Mart: Lutheri. Vom Bilde Gottes* . . . (Oberursel: Henricus, 1585).

[43]E.g., *Erklerung aus Gottes wort und kurtzer bericht der Herren Theologen . . . auf dem Tag zu Lueneburg im Julio des 61. Jars gehalten* . . . (Regensburg: Geissler, 1562), lf [Biij]^r; this confession appeals to Luther and the Augsburg Confession against synergism, lf. Dij^r. The *Confessionschrift. Etlicher Predicanten in den Herrschafften Graitz, Geraw, Schonburg* . . . (Eisleben, 1567), pledges faithfulness to the three ecumenical creeds, the unaltered Augsburg Confession and its Apology, the Schmalkald Articles, earlier Gnesio-Lutheran confessional documents, and the writings of Luther, described as God's instrument of salvation and the German prophet. See also the *Confessio ministrorum Jesu Christi, in ecclesia Antwerpiensi, quae Augustanae Confesioni adsentitur* (n.p., 1567), lf. Bij, for a similar commitment.

[44]*Confessio. Christliche Bekentnis des Glaubens, etlicher Euangelischen Prediger in Oster-Reich* (Eisleben: Gaubisch, 1567), and the Antwerp *Confessio*, lvs. E^r, [Fvij]^r, and [Mvij]^v.

passed, was the ducal-Saxon *Book of Confutation* of 1559. It contained numerous appeals to Luther's authority against Schwenckfeld, the Anabaptists, the sacramentarians, Osiander, adiaphorists, and others; but the positions of Luther are not quoted to bolster or elaborate the fundamentally biblical argument of the confession.[45] Although the Mansfeld ministerium cited Luther only rarely in a 1560 confessional critique of the errors of the day, in 1564 an updated address to certain opponents labeled Luther "the elect vessel of God," who offered a standard for the interpretation of the Bible and a model for polemical critique of false teachers. Frequent and very extensive quotations from Luther fill this document. Less frequent and extensive but nonetheless significant in providing both authority and argument are citations of Luther in the confession of the Gnesio-Lutheran ministerium of Reuss Schoenburg, issued two years later.[46]

Gnesio-Lutherans from ducal Saxony and Philippists from electoral Saxony met in dialogue in the autumn of 1568 and the spring of 1569 in the town of Altenburg to try to resolve their differences. The net result of their meeting was in fact deeper division, but the protocols of the colloquy, and exchanges of polemical correction which followed publication of the protocols, do demonstrate increasing reverence for Luther and increasing use of his authority for shaping arguments in the debates of the period. The protocols reveal that the electoral Saxon delegation as well as the ducal Saxon theologians were willing to accept "the writings of Luther" along with "God's Word in the Old and New Testaments, the true Augsburg Confession and the Apology, the Schmalkald Articles," as the standards by which doctrine was to be evaluated. Both sides also regarded Luther as a "precious instrument" whom God raised up to proclaim his word in a special way. The two sides disagreed on whether Melanchthon's theology was in basic agreement with that of Luther, and the Gnesio-Lutherans seem to have appealed to Luther more often than their Philippist counterparts. But both recognized and made use of Luther's authority and his arguments.[47] In the wake of the colloquy, the ducal Saxons, through the theological faculty an Jena where most of them taught, also issued brief summaries of their positions, one on free will and another on

[45]*Illustrissimi . . . solida & ex Verbo Dei sumpta Confutatio & condemnati praecipuoum Corruptelarum Sectarum & errorum. . .* (Jena: Rebart, 1559), e.g., 3, 17, 19, 20, 33, 38-39, 50-53. Mahlmann notes, 23-28, that the *Book of Confutation* may appeal to Luther's authority but that it develops a different basis of defending its doctrine of the Lord's Supper than Luther had, in the area of Christology.

[46]*Bekendtnis der Prediger in der Graffschafft Mansfelt, . . . Wider alle Secten, Rotten, vnd falsche Leren . . .* (Eisleben: Gaubisch, 1560), e.g., fols. 11v-11r, 236r-237v, 241r, 252v-254v, 279v-280r. *Confessio et sententia ministrorum verbi in comitatu Mansfeldensi, de dogmatis . . .* (Eisleben: Gaubisch, 1565), fols. 1r, 2v, 6r-v and passim. *Confessionschrift,* lvs. Cr-cij^r, Fiiij^r, Giiij, Niiij^r, aiij^r, biij, c, f, fiij, fiiij, hiiij, l, liij^v-liiij^r, and in other places.

[47]*Colloquium zu Altenburgk in Meissen, Vom Artickel der Rechtfertigung vor Gott* (Jena, 1569), fols. 1v-12v, 66v-68v; cf. uses of Luther on fols. 23v-24v, 50v-51r, passim. The Wittenbergers also issued their own report, *Gantze vnd Vnuerfelschte Acta und handlung des Colloquij zwischen den Churfuerstlichen und Fuerstlichen zu Sachsen etc. Theologen . . . Zu Aldenburgk . . .* (Wittenberg: Lufft, 1570), which confirms frequent citation of Luther.

justification and good works. In both, Luther's views were given in detail to support Biblical arguments demonstrating the authors' position.[48] Theologians from Wittenberg and Leipzig, in electoral Saxony, then challenged the judgments of the Jena faculty, accusing "the Flacians" of trying to undermine Luther in an underhanded, concealed way. They in turn used Luther as their polemical standard, along with the Augsburg Confession and the Apology, to oppose the Gnesio-Lutheran position and support their accusations.[49] The Jena faculty replied, again with copious citation of Luther.[50]

While Luther's authority and arguments were used to support and sustain polemicists' positions in works on specific issues, others were gathering citations from Luther into encyclopedic commonplace books of their mentor's theology. Johann Corvinus culled more than a thousand quarto pages of selective quotation for his readers, introduced with observations on the need for a commonplace collection of Luther's thoughts on the chief articles of the faith. His prophetic voice against error still needed to be heard, and his thought could better serve if organized topically, Corvinus reasoned. His list of topics followed somewhat the order of the Augsburg Confession but reflected concerns of the parish pastor wishing to console terrified consciences more than concerns of the polemicist of the period. Even so, polemics against the Gnesio-Lutherans' foes were present throughout the work.[51]

Timotheus Kirchner and Andreas Musculus prepared similar collections prior to publication of the Book of Concord. Musculus' topics were indeed dictated by the polemical battles in which he was involved: sin, free will, law, repentance, justification, good works, and the sacraments.[52] Similar works appeared later in the century, containing quotations from Luther alone and with others.[53] All of these works regarded Luther as worthy of hearing because God

---

[48]*Bekentnis von der Rechtfertigung fuer Gott. und Von guten Wercken* (Jena: Roedinger, 1569), e.g., lvs. D^v-D2^v, where Luther is called "father and preceptor" and is coupled with the apostle, "Saints Paul and Luther," [D4]v, E2r-F2v; *Bekentnis vom freien Willen. So im Colloquio zu Altenburg hat sollen vorbracht werden* . . . (Jena, 1570), e.g., lvs. Aiij^r, Gij^v, H^r-J^v.

[49]*Endlicher Bericht vnd Erklerung der Theologen beider Vniuersiteten Leipzig vnd Wittemberg . . . belangend die Lere . . .* (Wittenberg: Lufft, 1570), lf. Bij^v; cf. lvs. [Biij]^r, Ffiij^v-[Ffiiij]^r, [Ggiiij]^r-Jjiij^r, Nnij^r-Nniiij^r, Ppij^r-Ppiiij^r, Qqiiij, Rriiij^r-[Ssiiij]^r. See also the Wittenberg/Leipzig critique, *Warhafftiger bericht und kurtze Warnung . . . Von Den newlich zu Jhena im Druck ausgangenen Acten des Colloquii, so zu Aldenburg in Meissen gehalten* (Wittenberg: Seitz, 1570), lvs. [Biiij]^r, C-Ciiij^v, F^r.

[50]*Bericht Vom Colloquio zu Altenburgk. Auff den endlichen Bericht etc.* (Jena, 1570), lvs. Cij^v-Ciiij^v, Diiij^v, Eiij^r-Eiiij^v, F^r, Kiij^r-Liij^r.

[51]*Loci commvnes Doct: Mart: Lutheri totius Doctrinae Christianae. Das ist, Heubtartickel Vnsers Christlichen Glaubens vnd rechtschaffner Lere* . . . (Ursel: Henricus, 1564), lvs. A2r-A3r.

[52]Kirchener's *Thesavrvs: explicationvm omnivm articvlorvm ac capitvm catholicae orthodoxae, verae ac piae doctrinae Christianae, quae hac aetati controversa sunt, ex . . . D. Martini Lutheri . . . operibus . . .* (Frankfurt am Main: Rhebart & Feierabendt, 1566), of nearly 900 pages, had different quotations than his *Deutsche Thesavrvs, Des . . . Mans Gottes D. Mart: Luthers . . .* (Frankfurt am Main: Schmid & Feierabendt, 1568). Musculus, *Compendivm doctrinae Christianae collectvm, S. Scriptura, Ex S. Ecclesiae Patribus, S. Luthero* (Frankfurt an der Oder: Eichorn, 1573).

[53]E.g., *Loci communes D. Martini Lvtheri Viri Dei et Prophetae Germanici . . .* (Magdeburg: Kirchner, 1594).

had chosen him to be the prophet of the German nation, a special instrument of the proclamation of the divine Word.

That was the opinion of Martin Chemnitz, Jakob Andreae, and their colleagues who were charged with the task of formulating a confession which might produce concord among the disputing Lutherans in 1574. It is difficult to ascertain exactly how influential the Formula of Concord was itself in determining the teachings of the Lutheran Orthodox theologians of succeeding generations.[54] Nonetheless, the attitude toward Martin Luther embodied in the Formula paralleled the attitude developed in other kinds of literature of the period[55] and that view of Luther's significance and authority served the Orthodox teachers of the early modern period as they continued to operate within the categories set by the controversies which the Formula resolved.

The "Solid Declaration" of the Formula, as seen above, ascribes a special role to Luther in the economy of the proclamation of God's Word, and it uses him both as an authoritative standard by which doctrine can be judged and as a source for good judgment in defense of its doctrinal definitions. Over the question of whether to cite any contemporary theologians in their document of harmony, some urged that a number of contemporary teachers be used to support and demonstrate their position and mentioned the names of Melanchthon and Brenz in particular. Others thought that no contemporary leaders of the church should be cited. The formulators decided in the end to turn to Luther alone as an authority from their own time.[56]

The near-apostolic authority which contemporary Lutherans gave to their prophetic leader should be understood within the context of Luther's own concept of the "living voice of the gospel." He taught that God had selected human language as a special vehicle of divine, saving power when it expressed the message of forgiveness through Jesus Christ in the mouths of those who proclaimed, pronounced absolution, and administered baptism and the Lord's Supper. A "real presence" of the power of God reposes in the human language which conveys the gospel. Not just anyone who made the voice of the gospel come alive received recognition as such an authority, but the concept permitted a person from the contemporary era to be recognized as such an authority. Luther's critical role in what his students viewed as the restoration and revival of God's Word in their time lifted him above others who brought the "living voice of the gospel" to their contemporaries and bestowed upon him this special authority.[57]

[54]See Robert D. Preus, "The Influence of the Formula of Concord on the Later Lutheran Orthodoxy," in Lewis W. Spitz, ed. *Discord, Dialog, and Concord: Studies in the Lutheran Reformation's Formula of Concord* (Philadelphia: Fortress, 1977), 86-101.

[55]See Chapter 4 of Kolb, *Heroes, History, and the Holy.*

[56]Ernst Koch, "Striving for the Union of Lutheran Churches: the Church-Historical Background of the Work Done of the Formula of Concord at Magdeburg," *The Sixteenth Century Journal*, 8, 4 (1977): 117.

[57]On Luther's concept of the "living voice of the gospel," see Gerhard Ebeling, *Luther, an Introduction to his Thought*, trans. R. A. Wilson (Philadelphia: Fortress Press, 1970), 119-20 and Paul Althaus, *The Theology of Martin Luther*, trans. Robert C. Schultz (Philadelphia: Fortress Press, 1966), 35-42.

Reference is made to Luther in each of the twelve articles of the Formula except the last, on "other factions and sects which never accepted the Augsburg Confession." The very brief ninth article, on Christ's descent into hell, mentions Luther but once; however, that reference is the heart of the article: The formulators urged readers to find the answer to the question of Christ's descent into hell in a sermon of Luther's.[58] Luther is mentioned most often and quoted at greatest length in articles seven and eight, on the Lord's Supper and Christology respectively. They deal with the topics most pressing in the minds of the formulators, who were under the employ of elector August of Saxony. Since the elector had suffered recently the discovery that a number of his key advisors were maneuvering to move his church in a direction roughly akin to Calvinism, the Formula of Concord was in part designed to insure that such a move could not be made in his lands. Some had used Melanchthon's alteration of the tenth article of the Augsburg Confession as a legal defense for a more spiritualistic view of the real presence, and the formulators argued that Luther:

> . . . is rightly to be regarded as the most eminent teacher of the churches which adhere to the Augsburg Confession and as the person whose entire doctrine in sum and content was comprehended in the articles of the aforementioned Augsburg Confession and delivered to Emperor Charles V; therefore, the true meaning and intention of the Augsburg Confession cannot be derived more correctly or better from any other source than from Dr. Luther's doctrinal and polemical writings.[59]

In the article on the Lord's Supper the formulators referred to Luther seventeen times, in several cases in long quotations from his catechisms, the Schmalkald Articles, the Wittenberg Concord, and from his two confessions of the Lord's Supper, the Great Confession of 1528 and the Last Confession of 1544. Article eight, on the person of Christ, contains eleven appeals to Luther's authority, in shorter or longer form, including four extensive quotations from the Great Confession, *On the Councils and the Church*, and *On the Last Words of David*.[60]

These two articles are the longest in the Formula. Proportionately, Luther is mentioned and quoted about as frequently in the first two articles, on original sin (nine times) against Flacius' definition and on the free will (eleven times), and even more frequently per page in articles four and five, on good works and on law and gospel (five times each). Luther provided less authority

---

[58]*Bekenntnisschriften*, 1049-53, Tappert, 610.
[59]*Bekenntnisschriften*, 984-85, Tappert, 576 (para. 41).
[60]*Bekenntnisschriften*, 970-1049, Tappert, 568-610 (VII, paras. 10, 13-16, 17, 19, 20, 29, 32, 33, 38, 40, 58, 77, 78, 87, 91, 93-103; VIII, paras. 2, 18, 21, 26, 28, 38, 42-43, 44, 80-84, 85, 86).

and argument proportionately on the subjects of justification (five references), the third use of the law (one reference), adiaphora (one reference), and election (only one reference, a surprise in view of the significance of Luther's *De servo arbitrio*).[61]

The controversies which the formulators were charged to resolve played a major role in determining the ways in which this generation of Lutheran theologians thought about and categorized the heritage which Luther and his colleagues had bestowed upon them—though certainly the topical treatments of Christian doctrine by Melanchthon and others provided a major component of the framework by and in which these students organized their understanding of the Biblical message. The burning questions which lighted the path for their exploration and application of Luther's stimulating proclamation of the gospel came from the controversies of the Late Reformation period.

The Controversies and the Subsequent Understanding of Luther

We take for granted that most elements of our understanding of Luther and his career must have been as obviously important to his contemporaries as they are to us. In general that is true also of our picture of the polemical Luther. His earliest biographers could hardly avoid his battles against the papacy and no less his disputes with various brands of sacramentarians. But it is not true in every case. For example, the first two long studies of Luther's life, found in Ludwig Rabus' martyrology and Johann Mathesius' homilies, did not accord Luther's encounter with Erasmus any significance.[62] The controversy over the freedom of the will, or synergism, in the 1550s and 1560s substantially altered that chapter of Luther biography.[63]

Furthermore, one may indulge a bit of speculation to wonder whether some of the themes which twentieth-century scholars have "rediscovered" in Luther were "forgotten" during the early modern period and into the nineteenth century simply because they were not highlighted by the controversies of the third-century following Luther's death. Baptism, fundamental to the

---

[61]*Bekenntnisschriften* I (Paras. 6, 8, 33, 38, 52, 53, 61, 62); II (paras. 20, 23, 33, 34, 36, 40, 41, 43, 44, 89); III (paras. 6, 21, 29, 41, 67); IV (paras. 10, 25, 26, 27, 28); V (paras. 12-13, 14, 17, 22); VI (para. 9); X (paras. 19, 20, 24); XI (para. 33). A handy guide to the Formula's citations of Luther in English is provided by Karl W. Rutz, *Martin Luther and the Confessions: A Guide* (Saint Paul: private printing, 1980).

[62]Rabus, *Der Heyligen ausserwoehlten Gottes Zeugen, Bekennern vnd Martyrern . . . Historien* IV (Strassburg: Emmel, 1556): clr, where Rabus, in dealing with the year 1525, mentioned that Erasmus might have ghost-written the attack on Luther by King Henry VIII of England, to which Luther replied in 1526, but he all but overlooked their dispute on the bondage of the will. Mathesius, *Historien Von des Ehrwiridigen Gott Seligen thewren Manns Gottes, Doctoris Martini Luthers anfang, lehr, leben, vnd sterben . . .* (1566; Nuremberg: Gerlach/Berg, 1580), recorded Erasmus' early approval of Luther and his refusal to attack Luther, fols. 8 and 19; and later he noted Luther's disapproval of Erasmus, fol. 112r, cf. 69v, without mention of the *De servo arbitrio*.

[63]E.g., in Spangenberg's homiletic treatment of Luther's significance, *Die Fuenffte Predigt, Von dem Apostelampt des trefflichen Mannes, D. Martin. Lvthers. . . .* (n.p., 1565), lf. Aiijr.

way in which Luther thought of the Christian life, receded in importance in comparison to the Lord's Supper during the Orthodox period, even though both sacraments were equally vital for Luther. Conversely, baptism was not as prominently a controverted article of faith as the Lord's Supper in the formative period. The prominence of the Lord's Supper in both Orthodox thought and Orthodox piety is due *in part* to the fact that Lutheran preaching did not prove able to alter the relative importance each sacrament had held in the theology and life of the late Middle Ages. But the Lord's Supper retained a larger place in the *loci* of Orthodoxy also because neither Calvinists nor crypto-Calvinists challenged in public disputes the sacrament of baptism to the same extent that they and their Lutheran opponents had made the real presence of Christ's body and blood in the Lord's Supper an issue in the paper wars between them earlier. The teaching of the Anabaptists did remain an item on the Lutherans' polemical agenda, indeed, but the radicals exercised no significant ecclesiastical or political power. Therefore, they had a slighter impact on the Lutheran consciousness than the "sacramentarians" of Zurich and Geneva. Thus, one vital element of Luther's conception of the Christian life, baptism, lost in the dogmatics and piety of the Orthodox period much of that vitality and significance which it had in Luther's writings.

Even the "proper distinction of law and gospel," which was debated in one minor controversy in the 1550s,[64] was not drawn neatly, as it might have been, into the larger discussion of soteriology, which was categorized under the topics "justification" and "good works." Thus the conceptual framework of "law and gospel" did not gain the same prominence in Lutheran Orthodoxy as did the "doctrine of justification by grace through faith alone." Similarly, Luther's conceptual framework of the "two governments" and his "theology of the cross" did not figure as such in any of the controversies which engaged Luther's disciples, even though some of them used the principles involved in both. The result was that the concepts and categories of these principles did not play a prominent role in the articulation of Lutheran Orthodox thought. It is arguable that law and gospel, two governments, and theology of the cross are all elements belonging not to the categories of topic or commonplace, or even article of faith or doctrine, but rather to the presuppositional or conceptual framework of Luther's thought. That is why they were not easily grasped by the minds of Melanchthon's students trained to formulate truth in the prior categories. Whether the argument is valid or not, the fact remains that those topics which constituted the heart of Luther's faith as understood in the Orthodox era were largely those which were disputed in the period leading to the Formula of Concord.

[64]In this controversy Flacius defended his position, that upheld by the Formula of Concord article VI, with a reprinting of support almost entirely form Luther, *Das die Buss, Rewe oder erkenntnis des Zorns und der Suenden, eigentlich allein aus dem Gesetz: Und widerumb die vergebung der Suenden, oder Gnade, allein aus dem Euangelio zu predigen sey . . .* (Jena: Rebart, 1559).

By structuring their recapitulation of Luther's thought in categories determined largely by controversy—and to a certain extent, also by the earlier medieval dogmatic categories—his late sixteenth century and early seventeenth century successors did narrow and focus the light which shone from Luther's beacon into the early modern period. Some suggest that Luther's students were better able to render a reliable estimate of what was significant in his thought than are modern scholars, and that therefore our contemporary constructs of Luther's mind must be viewed with suspicion when they uncover "forgotten" concerns of Luther. Such caution is well-taken. We must also acknowledge that scholars today are not necessarily any more immune to the influence of personal agendas and special pleadings and prejudices than the Wittenberg alumni were. But those students of Luther's had studied under and been influenced by others as well. Furthermore, and more important for the argument of this essay, the disciples of Wittenberg lived in an age of crisis which threatened the very existence of their faith. Thus they were compelled to think of Luther and to reproduce his thought in terms imposed upon them by their controversial situation. The disputes in which they were engaged did dictate the terms in which they were able to think through what they had heard Luther say. At least some modern students of Luther come to the task of interpreting Luther in a more dispassionate mindset.

Among the various aspects of which we must take notice in studying the influence of Luther upon the theology of Lutheran Orthodoxy, the controversies of the Late Reformation period loom large. Luther profoundly affected the way in which his students met the challenges of that period, with a polemical style which he had modeled, and with appeals to his authority and the use of his argument. Inevitably, those controversies which he thus helped shape also shaped subsequent perceptions of him and his theology.

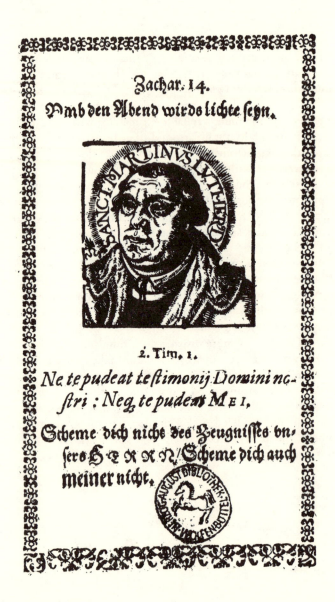

Zachar. 14.
Vmb den Abend wirds lichte seyn.

2. Tim. 1.
Ne te pudeat testimonij Domini no-
stri : Neq, te pudeat MEI.

Scheme dich nicht des Zeugnisses vnsers HERRN/ Scheme dich auch
meiner nicht.

Illustration 1 of Nischan article. Orthodox Lutheran portrayal of the Wittenberg reformer that shows "Saint Martin Luther, Doctor" with both the sign of divine inspiration and the nimbus of sainthood. The caption below the picture reads, "Do not be ashamed then of testifying to our Lord, nor of me his prisoner (2 Tim. 1:8)." (From Valerius Herberger, *Gloria Lutheri & Evangelicorum. Dess seligen Herrn D. Lutheri vnd aller Evangelischen Hertzen Ehrenkrone. Gründlicher / klarer / augenscheinlicher beweis / dass der Engel mit dem ewigen Evangelio / Apoc. 14. eine tröstliche weissagung sey / von dem tewren Mann D. Martino Luthero, vnd seiner Evangelischen Lehre* [Leipzig, 1609]. Courtesy of the Herzog August Bibliothek, Wolfenbüttel)

Reformation or Deformation?
Lutheran and Reformed Views
of Martin Luther in
Brandenburg's "Second Reformation"

Bodo Nischan
East Carolina University

IN LATE SIXTEENTH-CENTURY GERMANY, the followers of the Swiss reformers and many Philippists charged that another reformation was needed to continue and complete the work of Martin Luther.[1] In Brandenburg supporters of the "second reformation" were reacting partly to the conservatism of the Mark's earlier Lutheran reformation—specifically to the trappings of Catholic devotional and liturgical practices which had been retained—and partly to the rigidity of the Formula of Concord, which seemed to jeopardize the very evangelical freedom for which Luther had fought.[2] Their goal was to purify the late Reformation Lutheran church in order to preserve what they esteemed as its early Reformation evangelical heritage. Both proponents and opponents of the "second reformation" defended their positions by appealing to the authority of Martin Luther. A comparison of these views will reveal not only divergent attitudes toward the Wittenberg reformer, but will also show how members of the two major German Protestant churches assessed the Reformation roughly at the time of its first centennial. This essay will focus on the controversy surrounding the official adoption of Calvinism by Elector John Sigismund of Brandenburg and his court in 1613. The general emphasis will be on the Reformed *Lutherbild*, a topic which has thus far been virtually ignored by scholars.

An earlier version of this essay was presented at the Quincentennial Celebration of Luther's Birth in St. Louis on June 3, 1983.

[1] On the concept of the "second reformation" see Jürgen Moltmann, *Christoph Pezel (1539-1604) und der Calvinismus in Bremen* (Bremen: Einkehr, 1958); Thomas Klein, *Der Kampf um die Zweite Reformation in Kursachsen 1586-91* (Cologne and Graz: Böhlau, 1962); Franz Lau, "Die zweite Reformation in Kursachsen. Neue Forschungen zum sogenannten sächsischen Kryptocalvinismus," in *Verantwortung, Untersuchungen über Fragen aus Theologie und Geschichte. Zum 60. Geburtstag von Landesbischof D. Gottfried Noth*, ed. by Ev.-Luth. Landeskirchenamt Sachsen (Berlin: Evangelische Verlagsanstalt, 1964), 137-64; and Gerhard Zschäbitz, "Zur Problematik der sogenannten 'Zweiten Reformation,'" *Wissenschaftliche Zeitschrift der Karl-Marx-Universität Leipzig, Gesellschafts- und Sprachwissenschaftliche Reihe* 14, 3 (1965): 505-509; and Heinz Schilling, *Konfessionskonflikt und Staatsbildung* (Gütersloh: Gerd Mohn, 1981).

[2] See Bodo Nischan, "The Second Reformation in Brandenburg: Aims and Goals," *The Sixteenth Century Journal* 14 (1983): 173-87.

The origins of the Reformed attitude toward Martin Luther can be traced back to John Calvin.[3] Luther and Calvin never met; however, the Frenchman's enthusiasm for the German reformer and his identification with their common Protestant cause are well known. The mutual respect that the two men shared for each other survived even the sacramental controversies of the 1530s and 1540s. Yet for all his devotion to Luther, Calvin never treated the German reformer's ideas as though they were final and definitive, which was precisely what many contemporary Lutherans seemed to be doing.[4]

The prototype for this Lutheran view of the Wittenberg reformer can be traced back to the early days of the Reformation.[5] Depictions of the reformer in the evangelical propaganda literature of the early 1520s "reveal a desire to place Luther within the framework of divine history, and to single him out as a chosen tool of the divine plan."[6] During the theological controversies of the post-Interim period his followers tended to absolutize his teachings even further. They called him a prophet and compared him with other divinely inspired figures from the Old and New Testaments.[7] For instance, Andrew Musculus, a theology professor at the University of Frankfurt who helped draft the Formula of Concord, described Luther as "the German apostle and prophet."[8] Others called him the "last Elijah" or compared the reformer to the angel in the Book of Revelation who heralds the end of the world.[9] Such apoc-

---

[3]On Calvin's attitude toward Martin Luther, see Alexandre Ganoczy, *Le jeune Calvin* (Wiesbaden: F. Steiner, 1966), esp. 67-72 and 139-50; B. A. Gerrish, "John Calvin on Luther," in *Interpreters of Luther,* ed. Jaroslav Pelikan (Philadelphia: Fortress Press, 1968), 67-96; Rudolf von Thadden,"Calvin und der Fortgang der Reformation im Reich," *Historische Zeitschrift* 208 (1969): 1-23; Charles Boyer, *Calvin et Luther. Accords et différences* (Rome: Università gregoriana, 1973); and W. Nijenhuis, "Der ökumenische Calvin: Calvin, Luther, und das Luthertum," *Nederlands Theologisch Tijdschrift* 24 (1980): 191-212.

[4]For details, see Georg Hoffmann, "Die Beurteilung und Einschätzung Luthers in der altlutherischen Theologie," *Zeitschrift für systematische Theologie* 16 (1939): 505-515; Horst Stephan, *Luther in den Wandlungen seiner Kirche,* 2d ed. (Berlin: Töpelmann, 1951); Ernst Walter Zeeden, *Martin Luther und die Reformation im Urteil des deutschen Luthertums,* 2 vols. (Freiburg: Herder, 1950-52); Heinrich Bornkamm, *Luther im Spiegel der deutschen Geistesgeschichte,* 2nd ed. (Göttingen: Vandenhoeck & Ruprecht, 1970); and Hans-Jürgen Schönstädt, *Antichrist, Weltheilsgeschehen und Gottes Werkzeug. Römische Kirche, Reformation und Luther im Spiegel des Reformationsjubiläums 1617* (Wiesbaden: Steiner, 1978).

[5]Bernhard Lohse, *Martin Luther. Eine Einführung in sein Leben und Werk* (Berlin: Evangelische Verlagsanstalt, 1983), 230: "Generell sei vorweg bemerkt, dass die Prototypen zahlreicher späterer Lutherbilder schon in den ersten Jahren der Reformation begegnen." [sic]

[6]Robert W. Scribner, *For the Sake of Simple Folk. Popular Propaganda for the German Reformation* (Cambridge: Cambridge University Press, 1981), 19. See also the illustrations and accompanying texts in the excellent exhibition catalogues that were published at the occasion of the quincentennial of Martin Luther's birth: Heimo Reinitzer, *Biblia deutsch. Luthers Bibelübersetzung und ihre Tradition* (Wolfenbüttel: Herzog-August Bibliothek, 1983), 13-56; and *Martin Luther und die Reformation in Deutschland. Ausstellung zum 500. Geburtstag Martin Luthers Veranstaltet vom Germanischen Nationalmuseum Nürnberg in Zusammenarbeit mit dem Verein für Reformationsgeschichte* (Frankfurt a. M.: Insel, 1983), 219-54.

[7]For details, see Hans Preuss, *Martin Luther: Der Prophet* (Gütersloh: Bertelsmann, 1933).   [8]Ibid., 240.   [9]Ibid., 49-54; cf. Rev. 14:6 ff.

alyptic and eschatological language was particularly popular with Matthias Flacius and his gnesio-Lutheran circle.[10]

"God's word and Luther's doctrine will never pass," proclaimed the inscription on a memorial coin issued by Elector Joachim II of Brandenburg in 1564.[11] The electorate's new church order of 1572, prepared by Musculus and George Cölestin, instructed preachers and teachers in the Mark to follow "the writings and books of the blessed Doctor Martin Luther, because through God's providence he restored the unadulterated pure doctrine."[12] Luther, the Formula of Concord concluded, was "a highly enlightened man . . . in the Spirit."[13] The reformer's teachings thus had been elevated to the status of finished dogma and the Wittenberg reformation absolutized to the point that no further development seemed possible or even desirable.

For all his devotion to the Wittenberger, Calvin could never accept that elevated position assigned by some to Luther. He feared that some of Luther's adherents had made their master's opinions the touchstone of all dogmatic truth, thereby repudiating, in effect, Luther's own fundamental principle that the Word of God must always stand above the teachings of man.[14] For Calvin, Luther was not a "last Elijah" or an oracle, but a pathfinder in whose footsteps he followed and whose trail had to be pushed further.[15] Calvin saw the reformation as "plainly a continuing reformation . . . as defined by 'progress' (*profectus*) and 'movement' (*promoveri*). Yet it is still movement from a fixed point, at which stands the extraordinary figure of Martin Luther, God's chosen pioneer."[16] Calvin thus interpreted Luther and the early Reformation historically, in a relativistic evolutionary manner.[17] Most Lutherans, by contrast,

---

[10]Günter Moldaenke, *Schriftverstandnis und Schriftdeutung im Zeitalter der Reformation: Matthais Flacius Illyricus* (Stuttgart: Kohlhammer, 1936), gegenwartigen Lage der Calvinforschung" in Peter Manns, ed. *Zur Lage der Lutherforschung heute* (Wiesbaden: Steiner, 1982), 70: "So darf Calvin als ein kreativer Lutheraner an gesehen werden."

[11]"Gottes Wort und Luthers Lehr wird vergehen nimmermehr," Zeeden, *Luther im Urteil* 2: 69.

[12]"Vorrede zur Kirchenordnung von 1572," in Wolfgang Gericke, *Glaubenszeugnisse und Konfessionspolitik der Brandenburgischen Herrscher bis zur Preussischen Union, 1540 bis 1815* (Bielefeld: Luther Verlag, 1977), 116 f.

[13]Formula of Concord, Solid Declaration, Article VII, 28, in Theodor Tappert, ed., *The Book of Concord* (Philadelphia: Fortress Press, 1959), 574. In the original Latin version Luther is called a "singularibus et excellentissimis spiritus sancti donis illuminatus heros," *Die Bekenntnisschriften der evangelisch-lutherischen Kirche* (Göttingen: Vandenhoeck & Ruprecht, 1959), 981.   [14]Stephan, *Luther Wandlungen*, 21 f.

[15]"In hoc cursu adhuc hodie pergimus," *Ioannis Calvini, Opera quae supersunt omnia*, vol. 6, vol. 34 of *Corpus Reformatorum* (Brunswick: Heinsius, 1867), 437.

[16]Gerrish, "Calvin on Luther," 84. Note also the conclusion of Alexandre Ganoczy, "Zur gegenwärtigen Lage der Calvinforschung," in Peter Manns, ed., *Zur Lage der Lutherforschung heute* (Wiesbaden: Steiner, 1982), 70: "So darf Calvin als ein kreativer Lutheraner angesehen werden."   [17]See also Zeeden, *Luther im Urteil* 1: 104 f.

treated history as the maidservant of theology (*ancilla theologiae*);[18] they viewed Luther in theological and therefore increasingly dogmatic and absolutistic terms.

There were, however, important exceptions to this pattern. Significantly, Philip Melanchthon and his disciples approached the past, much like the Calvinists, from a more humanistic perspective.[19] The result was an understanding of Luther and the early Reformation which resembled the Swiss view. Not surprisingly, many Philippists eventually ended up either in the Reformed camp themselves, or they at least helped prepare the way for a Calvinist or "second reformation." The influence of the *Praeceptor Germaniae* on the study of the past generally, and the Reformation specifically, was particularly evident at the University of Heidelberg in the late sixteenth century.[20]

When Elector Frederick III of the Palatinate converted to Calvinism in 1560, he insisted that he had remained loyal to Luther's evangelical faith and "conformable with the confession of Augusta and apologie thereof."[21] He thought that Martin Luther "had done great things for the church of Christ;" only Luther's followers had perverted the message. "You have turned the blessed Dr. Luther into the third Elijah and by such excesses have muddled the necessary distinction which needs to be maintained between the prophets, apostles, and other teachers and preachers. . . . Luther could and did err just like other human beings."[22] Similarly Zacharius Ursinus, the renowned Reformed theologian at the University of Heidelberg, rejected much of the contemporary Luther glorification.[23] Like other Palatinate Reformed, Ursinus insisted that he stood in the tradition of the Lutheran Augsburg Confession— "properly understood," to be sure. He too viewed Luther as a great teacher and excellent servant of God, but denied that he was a prophet or the third Elijah.[24] Luther was human and did make mistakes. His weaknesses and the limitations of his theology, Ursinus insisted, became particularly evident in the

[18]Hans-Jürgen Schönstadt, "Das Reformationsjubiläum 1617," *Zeitschrift für Kirchengeschichte* 93 (1982): 44.

[19]On Melanchthon's view of history and his influence on sixteenth century historiography, see Emil C. Scherer, *Geschichte und Kirchengeschichte an den deutschen Universitaten* (Freiburg: Herder, 1927), 29-51; Walter Nigg, *Die Kirchengeschichtsschreibung. Grundzüge ihrer historischen Entwicklung* (Munich: Beck, 1934), 45-48; and Moltmann, *Christoph Pezel*, 74 ff.

[20]See Gustav A. Benrath, *Reformierte Kirchengeschichtsschreibung an der Universität Heidelberg im 16. und 17. Jahrhundert* (Speyer: Zechner, 1963), 1-16.

[21]John Casimir's preface to [Frederick III], *A Christian Confession of . . . Friedrich of that name the third, Count Palatine by ye Rhein* (London, 1577).

[22]August Kluckhohn, ed., *Briefe Friedrichs des Frommen, Kurfürsten der Pfalz*, 2 vols. (Brunswick: Schwetschke, 1868-72) 1: 558 f. See also August Kluckhohn, *Friedrich der Fromme, Kurfürst von der Pfalz, der Schützer der reformirten Kirche, 1559-1576* (Nördlingen: Beck, 1879), 108-10.

[23]See [Zacharius Ursinus], *Christliche Erinnerung. Vom Concordibuch . . . der Theologen und Kirchendiener in der Furstlichen Pfaltz bey Rhein* (Neustadt a. d. H., 1581), 322-401.

[24]Ibid., 325, 330.

eucharistic controversies with the Swiss reformers.[25] Other Palatinate theologians concurred, most notably David Pareus, the well-known Reformed irenicist, Quirinus Reuter, and Abraham Scultetus, who spent most of 1614 in Berlin helping Elector John Sigismund establish a Reformed church.[26] The Luther picture that emanated from Heidelberg, the intellectual center of German Calvinism in the late sixteenth century, thus basically agreed with Calvin's. Luther was interpreted historically, not dogmatically; his teachings were relativized, not absolutized. While acknowledging their great indebtedness to the Wittenberg reformer, the Heidelbergers insisted that they also needed to move beyond Luther.[27] Like Calvin they viewed Luther and the early Reformation in historical evolutionary terms. "In the Palatinate" summarized Scultetus, "the Reformation began with Elector Frederick II; . . . Elector Frederick III brought it to its laudable conclusion."[28] "Luther may have been the first one to attack the pope publicly, but he was not the only one . . . for there were also other pious and learned men in Switzerland and Upper Germany . . . who preached God's pure Word."[29]

This ambivalent attitude toward Martin Luther in the German Reformed tradition reached its fullest expression in the early seventeenth century at the court of Elector John Sigismund of Brandenburg, who in 1613 announced his conversion to Calvinism. Unlike Frederick of the Palatinate and the dozen or so other minor German princes in the empire who had opted for Calvinism, the Hohenzollern decided not to impose his new faith on his subjects who had been Lutheran since the days of Joachim II in the early sixteenth century. John Sigismund decreed instead that the two churches were to coexist in peace and harmony in his domains.[30] At the same time, however, the elector hoped that

---

[25]Ibid., 354-363.

[26]See Benrath, *Reformierte Kirchengeschichtsschreibung*, 14-37. On the Palatinate's role in Brandenburg's Second Reformation, see Karl Pahncke, "Abraham Scultetus in Berlin," *Forschungen zur Brandenburgischen und Preussischen Geschichte* 23 (1910): 357-75; and Bodo Nischan, "The Palatinate and Brandenburg's 'Second Reformation,'" in *Controversy and Conciliation*, ed. Derk Visser (Pittsburgh: PickwickPress, forthcoming).

[27]Benrath finds that these Palatinate theologians subscribed to a "'Fortschrittstheorie' nach der die reformierte Kirche die vollkommener gereinigte und wahrhaft orthodoxe Kirche ist," *Reformierte Kirchengeschichtsschreibung*, 36.

[28]Abraham Schultetus, *Newjahrspredigt. Das ist: Historischer Bericht, wie wunderbarlich Gott der Herr die verschiedene hundert Jahr seine Kirche reformiert, regiert, und biss dahero erhalten* (Heidelberg, 1617), 270.

[29]Abraham Scultetus, *Historischer Bericht Wie die Kirchenreformation in Teutschland vor hundert Jahren angangen* (Heidelberg, 1618), 7. Note also Scultetus' observation in his *Newjahrspredigt*, 272: "Ebenmässigerweise hat Gott zu unserer Zeit neben und nach Luthero, Melanchthone, Zwinglio, Oecolampadio, viel herrlicher männer erweckt/ welche die grewel des Bapstthumbs *je lenger je mehr* geoffenbaret / und die Biblische schrifften *je lenger je besser* erkläret haben" [italics mine].

[30]"Verordnung, dass allenthalben gute Bescheidenheit und Moderation von denen Geistlichen auff den Cantzeln und sonsten, Ergernüss, Verwirrung der Gewissen und Benachtheilung der Kirche zu verhüten, gebrauchet und geführet werden solle; sub dato

his public conversion to Calvinism would signal the beginning of a "second reformation" in Brandenburg in which the work begun by Martin Luther would be continued and completed.

The group which actually supported the elector and shared his religious sentiments, though, was small. It included mostly members of his family and government in Berlin, a few nobles such as the Dohnas and Knesebecks, and a number of professionals—lawyers, teachers, physicians, and several professors at the University of Frankfurt on the Oder.[31] Among this group of supporters must also be counted Philippists such as Christoph Pelargus, the Mark's Lutheran superintendent,[32] and the elector's court preachers, Solomon Finck, Charles Sachse, Martin Füssel, Abraham Scultetus in 1614, and, somewhat later, John Bergius.[33] Regardless of their particular motives, all seemed convinced that their reformation was simply a continuation of the earlier Lutheran reformation. Indeed, in a country whose population remained almost solidly Lutheran, and where the estates and a majority of the clergy supported the Formula of Concord, it would have been foolhardy for the elector and his supporters not to emphasize the continuity of their faith with that of Martin Luther.

There can be little doubt that most of the new reformers actually regarded themselves as Luther's true heirs. "Luther is dead and his holy doctrine has died with him, even though his name continues to be invoked," observed Moritz Neudorff, a Reformed preacher from the Uckermark, in 1612.[34] "Today's so-called Lutherans have deserted Luther's teachings . . . and the Augsburg Confession."[35] The authors of the Lutheran Formula of Concord

Cöln an der Spree den 24. Februar 1614," in Christian Otto Mylius, ed., *Corpus Constitutionum Marchicarum*, 11 vols. (Berlin & Halle, 1737), vol. 1, pt. 1, no. 12; recently reprinted in Gericke, *Glaubenszeugnisse* 44, 132-36; English translation in C. A. Macartney, ed., *The Habsburg and Hohenzollern Dynasties* (New York: Harper Paperback, 1970), 223-27.

[31]See Daniel H. Hering, *Historische Nachricht von dem ersten Anfang der Evangelisch-Reformirten Kirche in Brandenburg und Preussen* (Halle, 1778); and Ernst Opgenoorth, "Die Reformierten in Brandenburg-Preussen, Minderheit und Elite?" *Zeitschrift für historische Forschung* 8 (1981): 439-59.

[32]See Valentin Ernst Löscher, *Ausführliche Historia Motuum zwischen den Evangelisch-Lutherischen und Reformirten*, 3 vols. (Frankfurt and Leipzig, 1722-1724), 3: 216-23, 271; and Conrad Schlüsselburg, *Christliche / Gründtliche / Bestendige Erklärung / und nothwendige Antwort / Auff die Calvinische Schmähekarten und Lästerschrifft . . . D. Christophori Pelargi* (Rostock, 1615).

[33]See Johann C. Müller and Georg G. Küster, *Altes und Neues Berlin* (Berlin, [1737]), *passim*; Rudolf von Thadden, *Die Brandenburgisch-Preussischen Hofprediger im 17. und 18. Jahrhundert* (Berlin: Walter de Gruyter, 1959), *passim*; and Bodo Nischan, "John Bergius: Irenicism and the Beginning of Official Religious Toleration in Brandenburg-Prussia," *Church History* 51 (1982): 389-404.

[34]See Mortiz Neudorff, *Wahre Brüderschaft Lutheri* (Hanau, 1618).

[35]Moritz Neudorff, *Lutherus Orthodoxus* (Frankfurt, 1615), 23.

were denounced as "Formulists" and "New" or "Fake-Lutherans" (*Schein-lutheraner*). They were not Luther's true disciples but constituted a new generation of spiritualists who tyrannized men's souls and threatened true Christian freedom.[36] "The Reformed," as one defender of the events of 1613 put it, "hold much more rigidly and firmly to Luther's doctrine than those false Lutherans who invoke the reformer's name but actually have departed from his basic teachings."[37]

This effort to out-lutheranize the Lutherans was evident not only in the many apologetic tracts that John Sigismund's reformation produced; it also was the underlying theme in the confession of faith that the elector published in 1614. The *Confessio Sigismundi* termed the introduction of Calvinism into Brandenburg not a new reformation but simply a continuation and completion of the earlier Lutheran reformation. The words of scripture, the original creeds, the Augsburg Confession—of 1540, to be sure—and Luther himself repeatedly were cited as authorities. Calvin and Zwingli, though, were never mentioned even when their teachings were espoused.[38] Similarly, Martin Füssel, the former superintendent from Zerbst in Anhalt who was one of the new Reformed preachers at the Berlin court, defended the elector's religious innovations on the basis of Luther's *Small Catechism* without ever mentioning once the names of any of the Swiss reformers.[39] Brandenburg's new confession of faith, insisted Solomon Finck, stood firmly in the Lutheran tradition. He too defended his thesis with an abundance of quotations from Luther's writings, but never mentioned the names of Zwingli, Calvin, or even Melanchthon.[40] "You Lutherans may quarrel with our teachings," argued Abraham Scultetus, "but you cannot shoot a single arrow at us that would not first also pierce the heart of Dr. Luther."[41] "If Luther were still alive today, he himself would approve what was done in Berlin," noted another writer. He thought that "once all honorable Lutherans in Berlin understood Luther's true

[36]Mortiz Neudorff, *Examen Examinis Reinecciani* (n.p., 1613), esp. 10 and 13.

[37]Job Friedrich, *Ein gar kurtzer Bericht von dem heutigen Religionsstreit und ärgerlichem Gezänck der Praedicanten* (Frankfurt/O., 1616).

[38]The confession is found in Heinrich Heppe, ed., *Die Bekenntnisschriften der reformierten Kirchen Deutschlands* (Eberfeld: Friderichs, 1860), 284-94; and Gericke, *Glaubenszeugnisse* 44, 122-31. See also Philip Schaff, ed. *The Creeds of Christendom, with a History and Critical Notes*, 3 vols. (New York & London: Harper, 1919) 1: 554-58.

[39]Martin Füssel, *Confessio Oder Kurtz Glaubens-Bekenntnuss / Erholet und aussgeführt auss des Hocherleuchten Mannes Gottes D. Martini Lutheri Kleinen Catechismo, und andern seinen geistreichen Schrifften* (Frankfurt/O, 1615).

[40]Solomon Finck, *Sacrament Spiegel / Darinnen zusehen / wie die alten Schmeissvögel / nach der Apostelzeit / das Sacrament des Abendmals/ mit Aberglauben und Menschentandt besudelt* [Berlin, 1614].

[41]Abraham Scultetus [Peter Frey, pseud.], *Ein Christlich und ernst Gespräch/ Von den zween ersten Artickeln . . . Gehalten Im Freyen Felde/ zwischen Berlin/ und Brandenburgk/ am ende des Monats Maij dieses 1614 Jahrs* (Berlin, 1614), 49.

opinions about the ceremonies [which the Reformed had abolished] they will stop . . . criticizing us."[42]

The Reformed argued that they were preserving Luther's true heritage; they also claimed to complete the work which he had begun. In this context, the meaning of the term "second reformation" becomes particularly evident. The Reformed, while appealing to Luther, insisted that his teachings had to be judged as he had judged the old church's teachings: on the basis of scripture and the Word of God. He had always reminded his followers that they are "not Luther's but Christ's disciples."[43] He had urged his supporters to call themselves Christians, not Lutherans.[44] The reformer's words and actions therefore were never to be canonized to the point where they became a rigid dogmatic system. However, the Reformed charged, this was precisely what had happened in contemporary Lutheranism. The "Formulists" had forgotten what the Reformation was all about; they "pay greater respect to Luther's writings than to God's infallible Word."[45] Margrave John George, the elector's brother, noted that Lutherans who oppose John Sigismund's actions ought to take a lesson from the reformer himself and realize "that an opinion cannot be defended by shouting 'church, church' or 'custom, custom.'"[46] They should "recognize that not all the faithful immediately achieved perfection" when the reformation started; further changes therefore were necessary.[47] Solomon Finck noted that Luther had made some concessions in liturgical matters to old believers, but had expected additional reforms later.[48] Elector John Sigismund thought that Luther had done much to set the gospel free, but "still had remained deeply stuck in the darkness of the papacy . . . and therefore had not been able to extricate himself completely from all human teachings."[49] What was true for Luther applied equally to the *Augustana* and other Lutheran confessions. "The Word of God must judge and explain the Augsburg Confession, not the Augsburg Confession the Word of God. Otherwise one might find things in it that could perhaps be understood in a good papal manner," feared Martin Füssel.[50]

[42]Paul Kihnstock, *Newe Zeitung von Berlin* (Pfirt, 1614).

[43]Finck, *Sacrament Spiegel*, 81.

[44]Lazarus Theodorus, *Synopsis doctrinae Lutheranae et Calvinianae* (Frankfurt/O, 1615), 5 f.; and Abraham Scultetus [Theoph. Mosanus, pseud.], *Vialia, Das ist/ Ein Christlich unnd freundlich Reyz-Gespräch* (Hanau, 1618), 20.

[45]Kihnstock, *Newe Zeitung.*

[46]"Margrave John George to Simon Gedicke, Cölln/Spree, 8 September 1613," Niedersächsische Staats- und Universitätsbibliothek, Göttingen, Federal Republic of Germany, Cod. MS. hist. 189. I: fol. 94. Hereafter cited as UB Göttingen.

[47]UB Göttingen, Cod. MS. hist. 189. I: fol. 74.

[48]Finck, *Sacrament Spiegel*, 81.

[49]"Erklerung die Religion betreffendt/ an die versamblete Landstende zu Berlin, 6 April 1614," UB Göttingen,Cod. MS. hist. 189. I: fol. 47.

[50]Martin Füssel, *Ceremoniae Christianae* (Frankfurt/O, 1616), 92.

What Elector John Sigismund and other Calvinists particulary objected to was Luther's doctrine of the real presence in the Lord's Supper, specifically its later definition in the Formula of Concord.[51] They spoke derogatorily of the Lutheran dogma of "ubiquity." Scultetus called it a "crude and clumsy" doctrine,[52] John Sigismund a "false, divisive, and highly controversial teaching."[53] "No matter how much they try to cover and beautify it, the teaching of ubiquity is a completely novel doctrine, not found in God's Word and completely unknown in the old church," wrote Margrave John George in 1613.[54] "It opens the doors and gates to old heresies," maintained Martin Füssel.[55] Ubiquity was like a poison that destroyed the gospel message.[56] It was a first step toward Catholic transubstantiation and amounted to a return to "magical consecration" and the "papal mass."[57] "All of which proved," Agricola felt, "that the Lutheran church and religion itself needed another reformation"[58]—a reformation, Scultetus added, in which "the leftover papal dung is to be swept completely out of Christ's stable."[59] The result of this reformation, the Reformed claimed, would be a "fully reformed Evangelical church" or a "reformed Lutheran church."[60]

The attitude of Brandenburg's Reformed toward Martin Luther was clearly ambivalent—a fact which should hardly surprise, for no matter how much they might protest in public, at bottom they were Calvinists. In their approach to Luther they were following essentially the interpretative tradition of John Calvin and the Palatinate Reformed. While insisting on the one hand that they were preserving Luther's heritage, they also maintained that the German reformer had not gone far enough. They were convinced that his followers, with their Formula of Concord, not only had betrayed Luther's heritage but actually had taken it in the wrong direction. Another reformation

[51]On the sacramental controversy in Brandenburg, see Bodo Nischan, "The 'Fractio Panis': A Reformed Communion Practice in Late Reformation Germany," *Church History* 53 (1984), 17-29.

[52]Scultetus, *Christlich . . . Gespräch*, 16.

[53]UB Göttingen, Cod. MS. hist. 189. I: fol. 43.

[54]UB Göttingen, Cod. MS. hist. 189. I: fol. 88.

[55]Martin Füssel, *Brutum Fulmen, Excommunicationis Apologiae Fusselianae* (Berlin, 1617), 39.

[56]Johannes Bergius, *Das die Wort Christi noch veste stehen* (Berlin, 1624), 204-38.

[57]Ibid., and Kihnstock, *Newe Zeitung*.

[58]Adam Christian Agricola, *Widerlegung der Schlussreden D. Lucae Backmeisters, Superint. zu Güstrow* (n.p., n.d.), 166.

[59]Abraham Scultetus' Introduction to the "Confession of Germany's Reformed Churches," reprinted in Brandenburg under the title *Auff sonderbahrem Befehl und Anordnung Des Durchlauchtigsten Hochgebornen Fürsten und Herrn / Herrn Johannis Sigismunds / Marggraffen zu Brandenburg / . . . Glaubensbekenntnus der reformirten Evangelischen Kirchen in Deutschland* (Frankfurt/O, 1614).

[60]UB Göttingen, Cod. MS. hist. 189. I: fols. 96, 108.

therefore was needed which, while preserving the best of Luther, completed what he had left undone.

How did the Lutherans react to all of this? As can be expected, they denied both the claims made by the Reformed to continuity with the Lutheran tradition and the need for another reformation. John Behm of Königsberg noted that the Reformed "constantly invoke Luther's name and writings, but do him injustice before God and the world by cutting up and disfiguring his writings and imposing either a foreign meaning or maliciously and surreptiously omitting what does not serve their cause."[61] "They have put on Luther's coat . . . cunningly and deceitfully," thought Adam Praetorius.[62] Philipp Arnoldi of Tilsit referred to the Reformed as "creeping sneaks, sycophants, and soupeaters . . . who have arrogated to themselves the Augsburg Confession and who appeal to the writings of the blessed Dr. Luther, as if their own opinions agreed with this confession and Luther's faith."[63]

Arnoldi was especially critical of the author of the *Confessio Sigismundi*, Martin Füssel. He called him an "arch-Calvinist" and accused him of "shamefully misusing and falsely interpreting Luther's writings."[64] Berlin's new reformers "are trying to turn him [Luther] into a Calvinist even though the whole world knows with what divine fervor the holy man Luther fought against this sacramentarian abomination," wrote Hoe von Hoenegg, the Saxon court chaplain.[65] Leonard Hutter, another Saxon theologian and leading Lutheran polemicist, seconded Hoenegg's point: "The Berlin propagandists unabashedly appeal to Luther's authority and writings, but with the greatest insincerity. I therefore intend to show to the Christian reader . . . with what treachery Calvinists work and how they mislead people by perverting and distorting Dr. Luther's words."[66] And Hutter spent the remaining two years of his life writing against the Berlin reformation and defending Luther's authority.[67] In the process he produced a number of widely read pamphlets that earned him the title *malleus Calvinistarum*.[68]

[61]Johan Behm, *Gantz Trewhertzige Warnung / An alle und jede des Herzogthumbs Preussen Untersassen / Sich für der verdämlichen Zwinglianischen oder Calvinischen Sect zu hütten* (Königsberg, 1614), 17.

[62]Adam Praetorius, *Refutatio Pseudolutherani Martini Fusselii* (Königsberg, 1614).

[63]Philipp Arnoldi, *Confessio vera et Lutherena* (Königsberg, 1614).

[64]Ibid. Praetorius noted that "Fusselii Bekändnis nicht sey confessio fidei, sed perfidiae," *Refutatio*.

[65][Matthias] Hoe [von Hoenegg], *Wolgegründete / und zuförderist denen Evangelischen Christen in der Chur und Mark Brandenburg / zu nothwendiger nachrichtung/ verfertigte Verantwortung / Wider das zu Berlin newlich aussgeflogene Calvinische Lästergespräch* (Leipzig, 1614).

[66]Leonard Hutter, *Gründliche und nothwendige Antwort / Auff die ohne langsten / aussgesprengte / Berlinische newe Zeitungen* [Wittenberg, 1614].

[67]His most important work, the *Concordia concors de origine et progressu Formulae Concordiae* (Wittenberg, 1614), contained a chapter, "De Lutheri autoritate," 96 ff.

[68]*Allgemeine Deutsche Biographie*, s. v. "Hutter, Leonard."

The Lutherans were even more outraged about the Reformed claim that another reformation was needed. "We do not need the dark lanterns of the Calvinists to reach perfection,"[69] asserted Simon Gedicke, the elector's Lutheran court chaplain, only a few weeks before John Sigismund made his conversion public. The Reformed speak of the need for another reformation, complained Hoenegg, but by introducing the "Calvinist soul poison" actually have carried out a "dangerous deformation."[70] Leonard Hutter categorically rejected the Reformed argument that "in the [Lutheran] Church of the Brandenburg electorate horrible and crude papal superstitions remained . . . that needed to be swept out and discarded."[71] He thought that what the Reformed really wanted was not the "extermination of the papacy" but the "introduction of Calvinism."[72]

Lutherans thus felt that the "second reformation" was little more than a pretext for a "Calvinist reformation."[73] It was an excuse, Hutter thought, which had been dreamed up by "political court Calvinists, especially those in high positions of power who have free access to the princes."[74] Simon Gedicke, who was in Berlin in 1613 and could observe what was happening, concurred. He noted that before John Sigismund converted to the "alien church" his political advisers and "important gentlemen" from other countries introduced him to the Reformed faith.[75] They had given him Calvinist books and other material to read and had gradually weaned him away from the Lutheran church. The foreign advisers to whom Gedicke alluded included theologians from the Palatinate and Anhalt. Similarly Hoe von Hoenegg insisted that this "dangerous deformation had been started by a few people and agitators that had crept in[to]" the country from without.[76] The whole thing, thought Hutter, was reminiscent of what had happened earlier in the "principality of Anhalt . . . where at first they claimed to eliminate remaining papal superstitions . . . and ended up with Calvinism."[77]

[69]"Simon Gedicke to Margrave John George of Brandenburg, Berlin, 18 September 1613," UB Göttingen, Cod. MS. hist. 189. I: fol. 97.

[70]Hoe, *Wolgegründete . . . Verantwortung.*

[71]Leonard Hutter, *Calvinista Aulico-Politicus Alter. Das ist: Christlicher unnd Nothwendiger Bericht / von den fürnembsten Politischen Haupt Gründen / durch welche man / die verdampte Calvinisterey / in die Hochlöbl. Chur und Mark Brandenburg einzuführen / sich eben starck bemühet* (Wittenberg, 1614), 3.

[72]Ibid., 5.

[73]Ibid., Vorrede.

[74]Leonard Hutter, *Beständige und Gründliche Widerlegung Des Heillosen und verworrenen Gesprächs Harminii de Mosa, und Gregorii Brandenburgers* (Wittenberg, 1615), 38.

[75]UB Göttingen, Cod. MS. hist. 189. I: fol. 101.

[76]Hoe, *Wolgegründete . . . Verantwortung.*

[77]Hutter, *Calvinista Aulico-Politicus Alter,* 7 f.

Lutherans thus rejected Elector John Sigismund's reformation as a "deformation [of the faith] of the Augsburg Confession."[78] Brandenburg's Evangelical Church, they insisted, did not need another reformation. "Luther had faithfully and squarely accomplished just such [reformation]. No one has yet come nor will come who could improve on it. Hence we justly refer our listeners . . . to the teachings of the blessed Dr. Luther," concluded Leonard Hutter.[79]

This comparison of the Lutheran and Reformed reactions to the events of 1613 reveals rather divergent views of Luther and his Reformation. The *Lutherbild* of the Reformed—that is, supporters of John Sigismund's reformation, the origins of which can be traced back to sixteenth century Geneva and Heidelberg—was the product of an interpretative tradition which saw the Wittenberg reformation in historical, evolutionary terms. By contrast, the Lutheran view of the reformer—which also has roots that go back to the early years of the Reformation—stemmed from what was essentially a dogmatic interpretation that tended to absolutize both Luther and his reformation. What to the Reformed was simply another reformation that continued and corrected the Wittenberger's earlier reformation was to the Lutherans a deformation of the very things for which Luther had fought. While they agreed on the importance of the German reformer, whom both used as the starting point in their deliberations, the Lutherans and Reformed clearly could not agree on his authority.[80] The controversy surrounding John Sigismund's conversion, epitomized by the catchwords "reformation" or "deformation," suggests the extent of these disagreements and shows just how wide the gulf had grown which separated the heirs of Martin Luther and the Swiss reformers roughly at the time of the Reformation's first centennial.

[78]Ludowig Seltzer, *Warhaffter Lutherischer Gegenbericht* (Marburg, 1637).

[79]Hutter, *Widerlegung*, 46. Note also Bernhard Lohse's conclusion on "Das Lutherbild in der Zeit der Orthodoxie," in *Luther*, 232: "Dabei spielte seit dem Ausgang des 16. Jahrhunderts die Frage keine Rolle mehr, ob Luthers Reformation gleichsam noch durch eine 'zweite Reformation' vollendet werden müsse; mit dem Konkordienwerk von 1580 war dieses Problem 'amtlich' erledigt, auch wenn es noch manche Auseinandersetzungen um eine zweite Reformation geben sollte."

[80]This same disagreement also surfaced during the 1617 anniversary celebrations of the beginning of the Protestant Reformation. See the above-mentioned studies by Hans-Jürgen Schönstadt and Ruth Kastner, *Geistlicher Rauffhandel: Form und Funktion der illustrierten Flugblätter zum Reformationsjubliäum 1617 in ihrem historischen und publizistischen Kontext* (Frankfurt a.M. and Bern: Lang, 1982).

Illustration 2 of Nischan article. Catholic broadside ridiculing Protestant disunity by portraying the dissection of Martin Luther's corpse. Before the dissection table are gathered from left to right Nicolas Gallus, Matthew Flacius, Paul Eber, Peter Viret, and Huldrych Zwingli (swinging an ax used to amputate Luther's limbs). The "theological dissecters" behind the table are Erasmus Sarcerius on the left, Cyriacus Spangenberg, Jacob Andreae, Philip Melanchthon, John Calvin, and John Aurifaber. (Courtesy of the Herzog August Bibliothek, Wolfenbüttel)

Index

women, 57; restrictions on clergy concerning marriage matters, 68; roles, 14; Scribner, Robert, 19; Sixteenth Century Studies Conference, 2; social history, 5; surrender of Malmø, 59; third phase and earlier, 18; town composition, 20-21; views of concubines and children of priests, 63; and views of women, 76; Woltjer's phase, 17; women and divorce, 76-77; *see also* Grimm, Harold J.: schooling, social history; Woodcut; Writings and publications, Grimm

Reformation Era, 1500-1650, 4-5

"Reformation History and Social History: The Contribution of Harold J. Grimm": Bebb, Phillip N., 1

"Reformation or Deformation? Lutheran and Reformed Views of Martin Luther in Brandenburg's 'Second Reformation'": Nischan, Bodo, 203

Reformers, Protestant: religious culture, 90

Religion: Grimm, 5-6; oral presentation, Münster, 6; *Reformation Era, 1500-1600*, 4-5; *see also* Social needs

Religious culture: Bishops' War, 91, 98; common people, 89-91; Company of Pastors, 92; contradictions to Pappus' complaints, 95; elders, 95; failings of the people, 95; Marbach, Johann, 92; Pappus, Johann, 92; Pappus' complaints of villages, 95; Pappus reports difficulties, 95; Pappus' specific findings, 96, 99; Protestant reformers, 90; reconstituting history, 90-91; superstition, 89; understanding reports, 99; visitations, 93-94; visitation unclarity, 100

Rents: and churches, 25; Committee of Ten, 31; definition, rent, 24; definition, rent charges, 24; evangelical movement, 27-28; government orders, 25-16; insurrection, 23, 29; Martin Luther, 23-24, 33; Peasants' War, 23; reform defeats, 33; reforms, 32-33; secondary rent charges, 25; taxes, 33; urban revolt of 1525, 23; *see also* Ecclesiastical rent charges; Evangelical movement

Sachs, Hans, 127-129

Safley, Thomas Max: author, 35

Sartorius, Diethrich, 28

Schilling, Heinz: citizen movement in Münster, 18; phase analysis, 18

Scribner, Robert: Luther movement, Protestantism, and reformation, 19

Second Reformation: goal, 203; need for, 211

Self-sufficiency: *see* Divorce

Septembertestament, 114

Servants, household, 81

Sessions, Kyle C.: author, 123

Sigismund, John, 213; conversion to Calvinism, 207; Lutheran rejection of his reformation, 209, 213-14; supporters, 208

Sixteenth Century Studies Conference, 2

Social groups: *see* Social needs

Social history: definition, 11; recent research, 12

Social needs: education, 6; Lazarus Spengler and Nuremburg, 8-9; *Reformation Era, 1500-1650*, 9; religion and society, 8; "Social Forces in the German Reformation," 7; social groups, 6-8; *see also* Imperial cities; Writing and publications, Grimm

Sola Scriptura, 129

Solid Declaration, 197

Spengler, Lazarus: and Nuremberg, 8-9

Superstition: and ordinary people, 89; and popular religious culture, 89

Supplications: and responses, 85

"The Reformation, Purgatory, and Perpetual Rents in the Revolt of 1525 at Frankfurt am Main": Buck, Lawrence P., 23

Torgau League, 164

Totalitarianism: Martin Luther, 3

"Toward a Social History of Ideas in the German Reformation": Midelfort, H. C. Erik, 11

Urban revolt of 1525: rents, 23; Westerburg, Gerhard, 31

Visitations: Pappus, Johann, 93; Pappus' reports, 94

"Visitations and Popular Religious Culture: Further Reports from Strasbourg": Kitelon, James M., 89

Von Greyerz, Kaspar, 14

Waldis, Burckhard, 129

Waltersches Gesangbuchlein, 126

"We Must Have the Dear Ladies: Martin Luther and Women": Zophy, Jonathan, 141

Westerburg, Gerhard, 30

Westphal, Joachim: and adiaphora, 186; citations from Luther's writing, 186

Wettges, Wolfram: reformatory roles, 13-14

Wiesner, Merry E.: author, 79

Wild Man: illustration no. 3, 113; imagery, 112

The Authors

PHILLIP N. BEBB. Associate Professor of History at Ohio University; co-editor of *Occasional Papers of The American Society for Reformation Research* (1978) and author of articles on Germany, cities, and Reformation.

LAWRENCE P. BUCK. Academic Vice President and Provost at Widener University; co-editor of *The Social History of the Reformation* (1972), translator of *Monemvasia: The Town and its History* (1981), and author of articles on the Peasants' War.

RICHARD G. COLE. Professor of History at Luther College, Decorah, Iowa; author of numerous articles on printing, pamphlets, and the spread of the Reformation.

GRETHE JACOBSEN. Sometime Research Fellow in the Department of History at The University of Copenhagen; author of articles in English and Danish on guilds, women, and economic development in Denmark in the late Middle Ages.

SUSAN C. KARANT-NUNN. Professor of History at Portland State University; author of *Luther's Pastors: The Reformation in the Ernestine Countryside* (1979) and articles in English and German on economics, women, and the city of Zwickau.

JAMES M. KITTELSON. Associate Professor of History at The Ohio State University; co-editor of *Rebirth, Reform, and Resilience: Universities in Transition* (1984), author of *Wolfgang Capito* (1975), and articles on the Reformation.

ROBERT KOLB. Associate Professor of History and Chair of the Religion Department at Concordia College, St. Paul; author of *Andreae and the Formula of Concord* (1978), *Nikolaus von Amsdorf (1483-1565)* (1978), *Speaking the Gospel Today* (1984), and other works on the Reformation.

H. C. ERIK MIDELFORT. Associate Professor of History at the University of Virginia; co-editor and co-translator of *Imperial Cities and the Reformation* by Bernd Moeller (1972) and *The Revolution of 1525* by Peter Blickle (1981); author of *Witch Hunting in Southwestern Germany, 1562-1684* (1972) and articles on witchcraft and the occult.

BODO NISCHAN. Professor of History at East Carolina University; author of articles on the late Reformation in Germany in *Central European History, Church History, The Sixteenth Century Journal*, and other journals.

THOMAS M. SAFLEY. Assistant Professor of History at Wabash College; author of *Let No Man Put Asunder* (1984), and articles on family and marriage in Early Modern Europe.

KYLE C. SESSIONS. Associate Professor of History at Illinois State University; editor of *Reformation and Authority: The Meaning of the Peasants' Revolt* (1968), author of *Faces in the Peasants' Revolt* (1976) and articles on Reformation and music.

MERRY E. WIESNER. Assistant Professor of History at the University of Wisconsin, Milwaukee; author of *Working Women in Renaissance Germany* (1986), *Women in Sixteenth Century Germany, A Bibliography* (1983), and articles on womens' occupations in Early Modern Europe.

WILLIAM J. WRIGHT. Associate Professor of History at the University of Tennessee, Chattanooga; author of articles on Hesse, education, and poor relief in such journals as *Church History* and *The Journal of Modern History*.

JONATHAN W. ZOPHY. Associate Professor of History at Carthage College, Kenosha; co-editor of *The Social History of the Reformation* (1972), editor of *The Holy Roman Empire: A Dictionary Handbook* (1980), and author of articles on Germany and the Reformation.